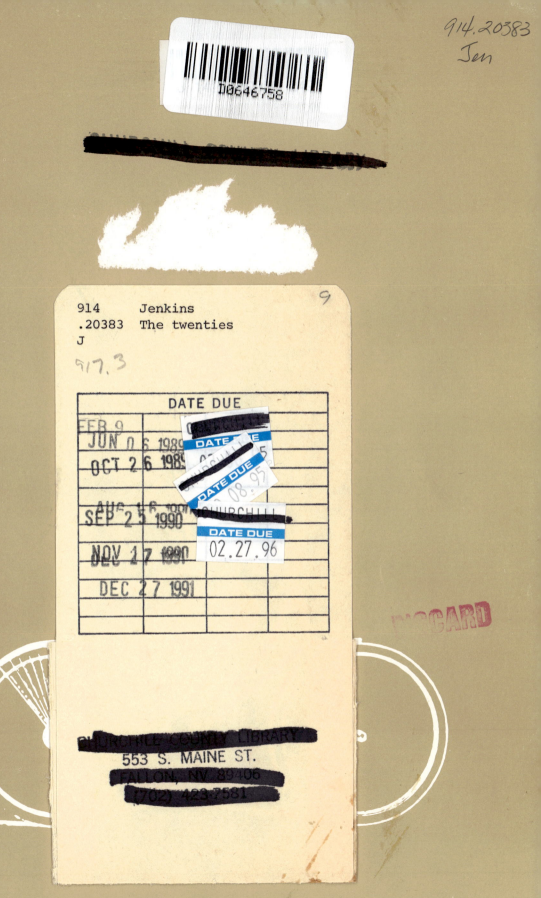

ALAN JENKINS

The **Twenties**

ALAN JENKINS

The Twenties

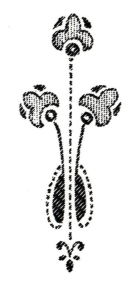

UNIVERSE BOOKS
New York

Published in the United States of America in 1974
by Universe Books
381 Park Avenue South, New York, NY 10016

© Alan Jenkins 1974

Library of Congress Catalog Card Number: 74–77360
ISBN: 0–87663–208–8

Designed and produced by George Rainbird Limited
Marble Arch House
44 Edgware Road,
London, W2 2EH, England

Picture research Mary Anne Norbury

Design Trevor Vincent

Indexer E. F. Peeler

The text was set and printed and the book was bound by
Jarrold and Sons Limited, Norwich, Norfolk, England.

The color plates and jacket were originated and printed by
Westerham Press Limited, Westerham, Kent, England.

Printed in Great Britain

CONTENTS

LIST OF COLOR PLATES

CHAPTER 1

Child's Eye View

I am thirteen. I am sitting with other children on the veranda (or *loggia* – that was the new estate agent's vogue word) of a prosperous provincial draper's house, set in the clearing of a pine wood, watching my elders playing tennis on a lawn fringed with rhododendrons. It is talkative tennis, with plenty of 'Oops!' and trilling laughter, of 'Yours, partner!' and 'Hard luck, old thing!'

Everyone is dressed in white; the women in opaque white stockings, the men in tight flannel trousers still known by their Edwardian name of 'white ducks'. I am wearing my long cricket trousers (they are an inch and a half too short) because you have to, when you are invited to tea in other people's gardens (just as you have to wear an Eton suit with stiff white collar for people's Christmas parties). It will be a beautiful tea with raspberries and cream and Scribbans's Dundee cake.

I am allowed to wind the mahogany gramophone. I play, over and over again, the vocal gems from *Show Boat*:

Why do I love you?
Why do you love me?

The innocent soprano of Edith Day filters through the trees. I change the record and in a moment my throat will tighten, for Paul Robeson's enormous bass will hit me in the solar plexus and my eyes will sting with tears when he gets to the words

Ah gits weary and sick of tryin'
Ah'm tired of livin'
And feared of dyin'

After tea the grown-ups light cigarettes – they have long-forgotten brand names like Army Club, Mitchell's Prize Crop, De Reszke, Ardath – and I go round asking for cigarette cards: 'Cries of London', 'Struggles for Existence', 'Famous Cricketers', 'College Crests'. Then the animal-skin rugs are rolled back in the sitting room, whose walls are hung with tapestry in the pseudo-Tutankhamen style, and the grown-ups dance. I am mortified. I do not like to see my parents doing the Charleston: grown-ups should not kick about in this undignified

Lunch at Eton, '4th June', 1921

1920 : A NEW DEPARTURE A "HIS MASTER'S VOICE" GRAMOPHONE WITH LUMIÈRE PLEATED PAPER DIAPHRAGM.

(below) **Paul Robeson and Edith Day in 'Show Boat'**

JOE CHATS TO MAGNOLIA AT THE SHOW-BOAT WINDOW : MR. PAUL ROBESON, THE COLOURED VOCALIST, AND MISS EDITH DAY.

way, it is as bad as when your mother comes to Sports Day in an unsuitable hat. My father doesn't really like it, and I am relieved when he slips back into a fox trot.

Or, I am seven. Miss Mackail, the new assistant teacher at the village school, is nineteen. She has the first bobbed hair I have ever seen, and the sun streaming through the window catches the gold in it as she plays the grand piano. It is the most exciting music I have ever heard: it is Grieg's 'Butterfly'. I know that Miss Mackail is pretty. I cannot know that she is about to run away with the headmistress's husband, but when she does (I visualize them literally *running*, hand in hand and panting hard) I hear, for the first time, the word 'divorce'.

Divorce is a Twenties word. I hear it again when I am ten. To our annual boarding house on the Kent coast comes Major Borthwick, thirty-eight, unmarried, just retired from the Indian Police (Britain had an Empire full of early-retiring soldiers

and policemen in those days). He uses not-quite-up-to-date catchphrases to amuse us kiddies, like 'abso-bally-lutely' and 'have a banorange'. He spends much time with Mrs Carthew, whose husband is away on business and comes home only at weekends. She plays the tinny upright piano while he sings. Together they sing:

I'll be loving you Always!
With a love that's true Always!

Bobbed hair – a feature of a Lux advertisement

They, too, Run Away together; panting, I am sure, like mad.

At the seaside there are always concert parties, sometimes in the open air, and a few still wear pierrot costumes. They have names like the Fol-de-Rols and the White Coons, the principal comedian is often fat, like Rex ('Tubby') Harold, and they keep alive in winter by 'doing Masonics'. There is always a military band playing Gilbert and Sullivan and 'Salut d'Amour', and if it is the Royal Artillery they turn suddenly into a string orchestra and play on the pier in the evening. There are still a few bathing machines on wheels. Hot sea baths are still recommended by doctors.

You go to the seaside by train, which smells acridly of gas. Even in a third-class compartment you can order a packed lunch. Children can be sent separately, 'care of the Guard'. When you get to the seaside station there are only one or two motor taxis, and you probably ride to your boarding house or lodgings in a cab known as a 'growler', which smells (in Richard Aldington's words) of 'horse-piss and oats'.

Gala Day at the new Thames resort at Hampton Court

'Old Regent Street', painted in 1924, by J. Kynnersley Kirby

Almost every house you visit has a piano, because in every middle-class family someone plays it (radio has not yet dominated the scene). Our piano is piled high with selections from wartime musical shows (*The Bing Boys, Arlette, Chu Chin Chow*), and soon they are joined by *Mercenary Mary, Rose Marie, Sunny*. The people next door have a pianola – not an authentic player piano, which can reproduce the individual renderings of Pachmann or Godowsky, but a pneumatic attachment, worked stiffly by pedals, so that playing it is like being on a treadmill. The people next door play, over and over, Liszt's *Hungarian Rhapsody*, the one that sounds like a barrel organ. They are too damn lazy to change the roll.

In our village there is no central heating, no electricity, and (until towards the end of the decade) there are very few telephones. We didn't know we needed them.

I saw the Twenties, between the ages of six and fifteen, from a semi-detached house in a village near Birmingham, England, on the edge of the South Staffordshire coalfield. Over the ridge of Barr Beacon lay the mines and the Black Country, another world than this.

To me, the Twenties were romantic, funny, sad, often heroic, strangely innocent, and always preferable to the guilty, frightened Thirties. The Thirties were dominated by the fear of war; in the Twenties war was unthinkable except between small troublemakers like Greece and Turkey. All those hopeful peace conferences in sunny places beside Swiss and Italian lakes; all that idealism we had pumped into us at school! And yet the Great War, as it was called, hung over everything. Ex-soldiers with the rank of captain and above tended to retain the title in civilian life; it helped them to sell more cars, or advertising, or whatever. Father's commanding officer used to rally the drooping spirits of trench warfare by saying gaily 'Let's go out and pot a few Huns before breakfast.' I tried to reconcile this idea with Father's old gas mask, Sam Browne belt and artillery field glasses mouldering away in an upstairs cupboard. The truth was too dreadful to tell – yet. At school we watched two shell-shocked masters have nervous breakdowns (it was called 'neurasthenia') and did not understand why. Not until the spate of war books from 1927 onwards did the wives and children of ex-soldiers have any idea. Those books from the circulating library had red labels and were hidden under cushions.

Scott Fitzgerald said the Jazz Age was due to America's 'unexpended energy' in the War. In Britain it was partly due to exhaustion. The British had no bull market to speak of, and our Depression began, not in the Thirties, but two years after the War ended. Our nostalgias are different. Our Twenties did not roar quite as America's did. And yet this was the decade in which the American way of life invaded Europe as never before – in films, songs, dancing, drinks, language, vitality.

I remember things like the front page of the London *Daily Mirror* (a paper we were not allowed to read) showing the police trying to find the knife with which Frederick Bywaters killed his mistress's husband, Percy Thompson, in 1922. Crystal sets. The Wembley Exhibition, 1924, of which only one image remains in my mind – the Prince of Wales modelled in Canadian butter. Armistice Days: every November 11th the school Cadet Corps paraded in the town square in drizzling rain led by our classics master, who pronouned Cenotaph 'Keenotaph', and sang those dreariest of all hymns, 'Fight the Good Fight' and 'O God our Help in Ages Past'. (You see how the War keeps coming back and back.)

The General Strike, climax of some 2,000 strikes (too young to wear a Fair Isle pullover and drive trains and trams, like certain older cousins, I had one consolation: to enable me to get to school, I had to be given a new bicycle). Pogo sticks. Mr Bottomley going to prison (at last) for the Victory Bonds swindle. Captain C.W.R. Knight and his film lectures on the Golden Eagle (whose name was Mr Ramshaw) at the Polytechnic in Regent Street, London. Douglas Fairbanks (Sr.) in *The Thief of Baghdad*. Maskelyne's magic show at St George's Hall, London, W. I am taken to my first musical comedy, *No, No, Nanette*: I embarrass everybody by shouting 'Why did that lady suddenly start singing?' (That lady is Binnie Hale.) A lantern lecturer comes to our village hall and speaks sibilantly about Tutankhamen's Tomb: he keeps repeating the words 'magnificent lapis lazuli'.

On Empire Day 1923, as the youngest boy in my new grammar school, I was allowed to release a gas balloon bearing a message of goodwill from the British Empire to the world. (It fell to earth, pre-

Edith Thompson

Frederick Bywaters

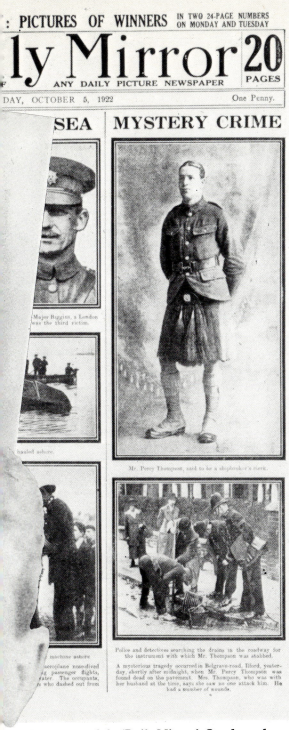

Major Biggins, a London was the third victim.

hauled ashore.

Mr. Percy Thompson, said to be a shipbroker's clerk.

machine ashore

aeroplane nose-dived g passenger flights, ater. The occupants, s who dashed out from

Police and detectives searching the drains in the roadway for the instrument with which Mr. Thompson was stabbed.

A mysterious tragedy occurred in Belgrave-road, Ilford, yesterday, shortly after midnight, when Mr. Percy Thompson was found dead on the pavement. Mrs. Thompson, who was with her husband at the time, says she saw no one attack him. He had a number of wounds.

Front page of the 'Daily Mirror', October 5th, 1922

dictably, because of the prevailing westerly wind, on a dike by the Zuyder Zee.) And there is a tune (much more a hit in America than here) which I can still hum:

> I've danced with a man
> Who's danced with a girl
> Who's danced with the Prince of Wales.

Suppose I had been a few years older, and had lived, not in the Midlands of England, but in the Middle West of America. What would I remember about the Twenties? Frederick Lewis Allen has answered the question for me. Allen pulled off that astonishing feat which only Malcolm Muggeridge (in *The Thirties*) has achieved on the British side of the Atlantic: he wrote the social history of a decade only a year after it was ended. Here are some of the things he listed:

Emil Coué. Mah-jongg. Auction bridge. Bananas. Crossword puzzles. Bathing beauty contests. J.J. Raskob. The Dayton Trial. Racketeers. Companionate marriage. The Teapot Dome scandal. Coral Gables. The *American Mercury*. Sacco and Vanzetti. Brokers' loan statistics. Michael Arlen. The Wall Street crash. 'True Confession' magazines. The Hall-Mills case. Radio stock. Speakeasies. Al Capone. Automatic traffic lights. Charles Lindbergh.

Some of these phenomena happened in Britain too, generally a few years later. Some of them the British never had at all. Some will reappear later in this book. A few, for the benefit of British readers, had better be explained at once. But first let us remember three things: the First World War had completely different impacts on Britain and on America; Britain never had a stock-market binge in which all classes gambled (as they do today on football pools), often with money they had not got; and – thank God – the British never had Prohibition, so that the word 'speakeasy' probably has to be explained to young Britons under thirty as an illicit drinking place such as flourished all over the United States during those weird thirteen years.

Auction bridge was what people used to play before Ely Culbertson promoted contract bridge. The first laws of contract bridge were drafted by the Knickerbocker Whist Club of New York in 1927, and a code for Britain was issued by the Portland Club two years later. Mah-jongg (topically alluded

Binnie Hale and Seymour Beard singing 'Tea for Two' in 'No, No, Nanette', Palace Theatre, 1925

to in Noël Coward's *The Vortex*, 1924) was adapted by Joseph P. Babcock, the Soochow representative of the Standard Oil Corp., from an ancient Chinese game; introduced to English-speaking clubs in Shanghai, and imported into America by a San Francisco lumber merchant named W. A. Hammond. In no time at all beautiful bamboo pieces were selling at anything up to $500 a set, and the English-speaking world was exclaiming Red Dragon, South Wind, *pung, chow* and *kong*.

Crossword puzzles had been appearing in the *New York World* Sunday supplement since 1913, but they became a craze only when young Richard Simon, who had just started a small publishing company, dropped by to see his aunt, who asked 'Why doesn't someone publish a whole book of crosswords?' Richard Simon did so, and advertised it thus: '1921 – Coué; 1922 – Mah Jongg; 1923 – Bananas; 1924 – The Crossword Puzzle Book!' Soon the Baltimore and Ohio Railroad was providing dictionaries on all main-line trains; everyone

was learning new long words like 'disestablishment' and very short ones like 'Ra' and 'gnu'; and the prosperity of Simon and Schuster was assured.

J.J. Raskob was the director of General Motors who switched from Republican to Democrat in order to chair the Democratic National Committee, and wrote articles saying that *everybody* could become rich by investing fifteen dollars a month in 'sound common stocks' and that it was patriotic to do so. The Dayton Trial in 1925 was of John Thomas Scopes, a biology teacher who had offended sundry Fundamentalists by teaching evolution, and found himself being prosecuted by William Jennings Bryan and defended (in mauve braces) by Clarence Darrow. Teapot Dome was a naval oil reserve in Wyoming which, in the strange atmosphere of the Harding administration, somehow got leased to one Harry F. Sinclair without competitive bidding. Coral Gables was a citrus grove near Miami that, under the guidance of George E. Merrick, suddenly became a residential city ('America's most beautiful suburb') in the Florida Boom of 1925 and after. The Hall-Mills murder – now why should Frederick Lewis Allen find anything peculiarly Twenties-ish about this never-quite-solved double killing, in New Jersey, of an Episcopal minister and his paramour who sang in the choir?

Perhaps because it was something which had never happened before, in a decade which knew, living always in the present, that it was full of things that had never happened before, and was determined, if not enough of them occurred, to *make* them occur.

A British counterpart to Frederick L. Allen – more muddled, far less observant – was Douglas Goldring, whose left-wing conscience was tortured by his own enjoyment of the corruption he saw all around him. The Twenties, he said, writing fifteen years after they ended, 'contained co-educationists, Morris-dancers, vegetarians, teetotallers, professors of economics, drug-takers, boozers, Socialists, gossip columnists, playwrights, Communists, Roman Catholic converts, painters and poets' all having 'an uninhibited fling. . . . They were years of "psychological compensation" for what preceded them. . . .

The writer looks back upon them as the happiest in his life.'

When asked to account for their behaviour, the people of the Twenties generally blamed the War. 'Here was a new generation,' cried young Scott Fitzgerald melodramatically in *This Side of Paradise*, 'grown up to find all Gods dead, all wars fought, all faiths in man shaken . . .' To their British and French brothers-in-arms, who had 2,250,000 dead and 6,000,000 wounded between them, after four solid years in the mud, the Yanks seemed to protest a little too much and too soon; yet each continent changed back into civilian clothes with the same intention. Swords were going to be ploughshares, so much so that as a child I was given, not toy soldiers, but a toy farm with cows instead of grenadiers, made by the same firm as the soldiers. There was never going to be, never could be, another war. What we had got instead was not exactly peace, and before long the press would label it Post-War Chaos; but it could be – feverishly, hysterically, innocently, cynically, hopefully or any other way – enjoyed.

Zelda and Scott Fitzgerald

CHAPTER 2

Let's Do It!

Do what? Practically anything you can get away with. Dance. Make love. Sing. Laugh. Make money. Lose money. Drink. Fly. Smash something. Spit on the carpet. At first it looks like a youth movement, but soon age is at it too.

At the Jungles Casino, Charleston, South Carolina, some time in 1913, a new dance step had been born. 'It was just a regulation cotillion step' said James P. Johnson, composer with Cecil Mack of the famous 'Charleston' and the man who taught Fats Waller about ragtime. 'One regular at the Casino, named Dan White, was the best dancer in the crowd and he introduced the Charleston step as we know it.'

Johnson wrote the music for a New York show, *Runnin' Wild*, whose coloured chorus demonstrated this step, and the Charleston tune preceded the dance to Britain.

In London the Charleston was introduced, in July 1925, to sixty teachers of ballroom dancing at a special tea dance organized by *The Dancing Times* at the Carnival Club, Dean Street, Soho, but it was considered 'vulgar' until the Prince of Wales learned it and performed it very skilfully. It required a curious mixture of loose limbs and discipline and, like tap dancing (another Twenties craze), was not easy for white people to do. Readers of Carl Van Vechten's *Nigger Heaven* will recall that Negro waiters could Charleston between restaurant tables while carrying several plates of soup.

The peculiar energizing syncopation of the Charleston may be defined musically as a dotted

James P. Johnson

(opposite above left) Dorothy Dickson and her first husband Carl Hyson demonstrate the formality of a dance in 1921
(opposite above right) Bee Jackson, once said to be the finest Charleston (solo) dancer in America
(opposite centre) Learning the Charleston

quarter note (crotchet) followed by an eighth note (quaver) tied to a half note (minim); and it took rather less than a year to overwhelm the whole of Britain.

Two of its nimblest professional exponents, born Winogradsky, travelled the world's vaudeville stages as 'the Delfont Brothers': they were eventually to become known as Sir Lew Grade and Bernard Delfont, twin emperors of British show business.

For the first few choruses you held your partner, and then, as new steps were added or invented,

you drifted apart and turned around and kicked out rather dangerously. It was, and is, very good for your health. The Bishop of Coventry liked it, and said so; but the Vicar of St Aidan's, Bristol, thought that 'Any lover of the beautiful will die rather than be associated with the Charleston. It is neurotic! It is rotten! It stinks! Phew, open the windows!'

Dancing, as a national obsession in Britain, can be traced back to the War years, when soldiers on leave could console their loneliness (in cities, at any rate) by finding an inexpensive *thé dansant* to go to.

The Black Bottom illustrated by Mr and Mrs Victor Silvester

All through the Twenties there was never much difficulty in finding somewhere to dance – or to learn to dance. In London you learnt from Santos Casani, who demonstrated the Charleston on top of a taxi driven through the West End: fox trot, one step, blues, Black Bottom (an ugly, foot-stamping dance which didn't last long), and – certainly for the duration of the Valentino swoon period – a revival of the tango. Or from young Victor Silvester, son of a Vicar of Wembley, who himself learnt to dance only because the Bishop of London held an annual ball at Lambeth Palace for the sons of the clergy, and who had won the World Professional Ballroom Championship of 1922.

In New York in 1925 appeared Arthur Murray, a protégé of Vernon Castle, who standardized five basic steps for the great mass of dancers who wished to acquire ('in a hurry') a social accomplishment. Some jobless ex-officers danced for a living: it was said that most of the chorus boys in one of Albert de Courville's revues at the London Hippodrome had either the M.C. or the D.S.O. Among the posher tea dances in London were those at the Savoy (5s. or $1), the Café de Paris and the Piccadilly Hotel (4s.); and if you could not afford these, there were always the Regent Palace and the Astoria Dance Hall (2s.), which however had the reputation of being pick-up places.

But this was only daytime dancing (and it was astonishing how many people could take time off to do it). It went on all night, too, at the night clubs which were mushrooming all over London and New York. In New York *all* drinking was illegal: in London it was illegal only between certain hours. The Twenties were not, in Britain, particularly drunken times; but it was assumed that if you wanted to dance you also wanted to drink.

At the beginning of the decade the respectable London place to take an unchaperoned girl – the Prince of Wales was a member, but was seldom seen there – was the Grafton Galleries. It had a Negro band, but closed at 2 a.m. You were supposed to dance with your gloves on. It wasn't quite a night club in the sense that Rector's was: here you got the authentic cellar atmosphere in the sleaziness of Tottenham Court Road. Silver Slipper, Manhattan, Uncle's, the Little, the Hambone, Cave of Harmony – the names are part of Twenties social history; and some of them were run by 'Ma' Meyrick.

The Hambone Club, December 1928

(above) The Cave of Harmony, Elsa Lanchester's night club in Seven Dials, London
(below) Mrs Kate 'Ma' Meyrick on her release from Holloway Prison, January 27th, 1930

OUR CARICATURIST DEPICTS SOME OF TH

The above picture shows the Fifty-Fifty in Wardour Street, which is organised by the Stage and Bohe

			JEAN CADELL	CARL BRISSON	JACK BUCHANAN	MALCOLM KEEN
ERNEST THESIGER		DELYSIA	AUSTIN MELFORD		FAY COMPTON JACK HULBERT	AUBREY SM
NOEL COWARD	IVOR NOVELLO	CONSTANCE COLLIER				SIDNEY
MICHAEL ARLEN					LEON QUARTERMAINE	MARGARET BANNERMA
TOM DOUGLAS			GERTRUDE LAWRENCE		DOROTHY DICKSON	

EMBERS OF A WELL-KNOWN NIGHT CLUB

...ined, and is one of the cheeriest places of its kind in London. The key to this picture is as follows :—

RALPH LYNN   LOTTIE VENNE
RRY KENDELL   BILLY MERSON   PHYLLIS MONKMAN   LESLIE HENSON
THER MISS O'KELLY   EDWARD BREON
        JUNE   ROY ROYSTON
        GEORGE GROSSMITH   BINNIE HALE

GWEN FARRAR   HOLMAN CLARK
JACK HOBBS   OWEN NARES
        SEYMOUR HICKS   BEATRICE LILLIE
GERALD DU MAURIER   HERBERT MUNDIN
JOSEPH COYNE   GLADYS COOPER

21

This extraordinary woman, who made enough money to send two sons to Harrow and four daughters to Roedean but died leaving only £58, became a folk heroine of the West End. She did it because she had to. The daughter of an Irish doctor, she married a medical student who left her with a large house, Sylvan Hall, Brighton, to look after – and six children. After experimenting with a tea-dance club in Leicester Square, and Brett's Club in Charing Cross Road – learning the trade, as it were – Mrs Kate Meyrick began in earnest with the Cecil Club in 1921, better known as 'the 43'. Barbara Cartland describes her as 'a wispy little woman who always had holes in her stockings', and calculates that she bought champagne at 12s. 6d. ($2·50) a bottle, and sold it at 30s. in licensing hours and £2 after hours. Her well-educated daughters acted as hostesses or 'dance instructresses' and two of them married peers.

By 1924 she had several more clubs, and was often in trouble with the police. Her defence was usually that the clubs were necessary for people who 'required early breakfast'. Asked by the judge at one of her trials what time breakfast began, she replied 'Ten p.m.'.

Britain had, at this time, the most unpopular Home Secretary in her history, Sir William Joynson-Hicks ('Jix' to the cartoonists), who seemed determined to stamp out everything that gave anyone any pleasure. He disliked foreigners, especially if they were coloured; he disliked sex of all kinds, and drinking of most kinds; above all, he hated night clubs, and was prepared to use the police as a kind of private army to suppress them. In doing so, he caused the police to become more unpopular than they had been in living memory: they made fearful mistakes, pouncing upon perfectly respectable people in public places for suspected 'immorality', such as poor Miss Savidge, who became notorious for having dared to talk to Sir Leo Money in Hyde Park.

'The 43' had a distinguished clientèle: it wasn't one of the Prince of Wales's favourite haunts, but other Royalty was to be seen there, and the King of Roumania, like Steve Donoghue the jockey or Tallulah Bankhead the actress, would have been no more than amused to have his name taken in a police raid. But that was the funny thing: of the innumerable night clubs that sprang up between 1924 and 1928 (sixty-five of them were prosecuted for selling drinks after hours, and many of them opened up again in the next house under another name the night after they had been closed down), 'The 43' alone went unraided for four whole years. Why?

One day Scotland Yard received an anonymous letter suggesting that they might like to ask themselves how Sergeant Goddard, the most active officer in Jix's vice squad, whose pay was £6 15s. a week, could afford a house in Streatham, a sizable car, and two safe deposit accounts containing £12,000? The money had come from 'Ma' Meyrick and a man called Ribuffi, who ran Uncle's in Albemarle Street. 'Ma' Meyrick and Mr Ribuffi got fifteen months' hard labour, and Sergeant Goddard got eighteen months' hard labour and was fined £2,000. 'Ma' Meyrick inspired *Punch*'s A. P. Herbert, a lawyer and lifelong hater of licensing laws, to write:

Come all you birds
And sing a roundelay,
For Mrs Meyrick's
Out of Holloway . . .

Ambrose and his orchestra
on the cover of 'When Day Is Done', 1924

Had I been lucky enough to be of night-club age in the London of the Twenties, I would have gone to 'Ma' Meyrick's for kicks: but for the bliss of soft lights and sweet music and the knowledge that I had reached the inner core of Society I would always have chosen the Embassy. It was at the Piccadilly end of Bond Street. Everything I know about it is from hearsay. How Luigi, the proprietor, would toss you double or quits for the price of your dinner. How all the women wore chiffon and diamond bracelets. A one-legged man sold you gardenias as you went in, along a sort of tunnel. I have it on the authority of Barbara Cartland that the ladies' loo was superb, presided over by one of those motherly souls in black whose breed is still to be found, fifty years later, at the Savoy Hotel and Claridges, with needle and thread and aspirins and bicarbonate, for emergencies.

The Embassy – it eventually had Bert Ambrose's Band – was basically a restaurant with a small square of dance floor for cheek-to-cheek dancing. If you took a new partner there, all London knew it. Over by the wall was the Prince of Wales's sofa table: he always came on Thursday nights (and when he wasn't here, he was at Ciro's), and you could tell *when* he was about to arrive because his equerry Major 'Fruity' Metcalfe was there first. Would the 'little man' bring Mrs Dudley Ward, or would it be Thelma, Lady Furness, Gloria Vanderbilt's sister?

Poulsen, the Danish head waiter, eventually left to open the Café de Paris, which had more room for Charlestoning, and where there was always a cabaret. The décor, for some macabre reason, was meant to be a replica of the Palm Court of the *Lusitania*, and among its dance hostesses were Estelle Thompson, who would one day be known as Merle Oberon, and Nora Turner, who became Lady Docker.

These dancing years made it almost impossible for any restaurant or hotel in London to flourish without providing a band and a floor show. Lyons's Corner House, in Coventry Street, had an orchestra on each floor: musicians have never had it so good. (For serious eating, you went to small French or Italian family restaurants in Soho, where you could get a six-course meal for as little as half-a-crown – 50 cents.) The Midnight Follies at the Hotel Metropole, said to cost £1,000 a week, were supplied by an

Thelma, Lady Furness

impresario named Sir Francis Towle, who was also a director of such hotels as Gleneagles in Scotland, where his nephew Henry Hall ran a small band. The Princes Restaurant had *four* bands and an ebony dance floor. The Florida had a glass floor lit from beneath, which could have a strange effect on a dress of very thin material. At the Piccadilly Hotel, where Jack Hylton's band played for some years, dinner, dance and floor show (wine extra) cost a guinea. Charles B. Cochran was in charge of the

An advertisement for Jack Hylton, 1927

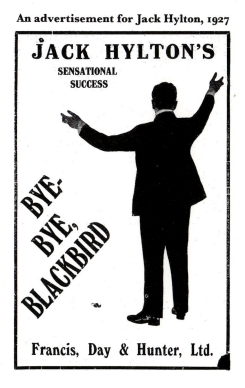

floor show at the Trocadero, opposite the stage door of the London Pavilion, in Shaftesbury Avenue, and filled it with rather highbrow turns such as Grock, the Swiss clown, Alice Delysia singing faintly naughty songs, and a ballet. The Queen's Hotel in Leicester Square boasted a 'ladies' Russian orchestra', balalaikas and boots and all.

'Jix' and his American counterparts had cause to be worried about the young. These matters could only be hinted at in the press, where Dame Madge Kendal, a distinguished elderly actress, was always criticizing the Modern Girl. The Modern Girl's sexual behaviour was not referred to in so many words, but the implication was there. Promiscuity, thought at first to be mainly restricted to the upper classes, led by Nancy Cunard and the *Green Hat* set, was already down to tennis-club level.

Could it all be blamed on 'post-war chaos'? During the war women had done men's jobs, earned their own money, and (following upon the New Woman of H. G. Wells and the last years of Edward VII's reign) begun to claim the right to give their bodies to men of their choice; and the short leaves and sudden partings of wartime ('a subaltern's expectation of life is three weeks') had made it a privilege, not a sacrifice.

'Petting parties' (going to what lengths is not clear) had been a feature of American youth culture since about 1916. "I've kissed dozens of men" said the girl in *This Side of Paradise*. "I suppose I'll kiss dozens more." This was in 1919, and was a commentary on the fact that, five years before, a kiss might have constituted an engagement. Did she really enjoy kissing dozens of men, or was it a gesture of defiance against "the older generation who ruined our world for us"? And what did Scott Fitzgerald precisely *mean* by kissing?

In Zenith, George F. Babbitt had heard gossip about girls of his daughter's age parking their corsets at dances, and in sophomore circles it was generally held that "men won't dance with you if you're wearing a corset." Men, in fact, were for the first time in history putting their ungloved right hands on the bare skin of a girl in a backless dress as they danced. The next stage was cheek-to-cheek dancing.

Women not only wore lipstick but put it on in public. They now smoked as well as drank in public. Dancing, it was declared from pulpits, was "synco-

pated embracing", automobiles were "brothels on wheels". Hell! there was this guy Freud, not that one had actually read him, but didn't he say you should obey your libido? And if you felt better for swearing, and sprinkling your conversation with words like 'lousy' and 'damn', why not?

There was much talk of 'companionate marriage', which simply meant that you lived with and 'were faithful to' one partner in an experimental way, probably with the ultimate intention of getting married anyway; and a certain Judge Lindsay in 1927 tried to get it legalized. There was a good deal of amateur prostitution, softened by words like "gold digger" and "sugar daddy" (what were the heroines of Anita Loos's *Gentlemen Prefer Blondes* doing but just that?).

Maybe it was true that one girl in ten carried a contraceptive in her vanity case, as it was certainly true (for America) that by 1928 there was one divorce for every six marriages, if only because 'it's much more exciting to be a divorcée than an old maid.' But the sexual *mores* of the Twenties found a

Anita Loos photographed by Cecil Beaton

The programme front of *Jig-Saw!*, Albert de Courvilles' tenth London Hippodrome revue, June 1920

(overleaf) 'The Models' Day Out, Taggs Island', 1920, by Sir Alfred Munnings. Taggs Island, near Hampton Court Palace, was a popular 'place to go' during the Twenties since it was the home of Fred Karno's *Karsino*. It was never a financial success and led to his bankruptcy in the 1930s

'The Dancing Girls' Paradise', 1921, by H. M. Bateman

sturdy champion in the late Sir Maurice Bowra, Warden of Wadham College, Oxford, who in 1967 delivered a remarkable foundation oration to London University on this very subject. The Twenties, he said, gave men and women a great new vision of each other:

> I am sure this is the thing the young value most – that they know their own personalities, which are too serious to be badgered and pushed about by a lot of silly rules they do not agree with . . . There the Twenties laid the foundations, and we ought all to be grateful to them.

Those contraceptives in vanity cases and wallets, the first reliable ones ever available, were not so easy to come by: only back-street pharmacies sold them, and they were kept out of sight and never advertised. Life for young lovers and married couples was difficult and uncomfortable, unless you could afford a strange gynaecologist named Norman Haire, who fitted intra-uterine rings. But help was on the way. In America there was Mrs Margaret Sanger; in Britain, Dr Marie Stopes, wife of Humphrey Verdon-Roe of the aviation firm.

Mrs Sanger actually coined the expression 'birth control', in her magazine *The Woman Rebel* in 1914. Her first clinic, opened in Brooklyn in 1916, had been raided by police and closed, and she had served thirty days in jail for 'obscenity'. Undaunted, she organized the first American birth control conference in 1921, and went on to found, and be first president of, the American Birth Control League. Two years later she was allowed to open, in New York, America's first permanent birth control clinic, eventually known as the Margaret Sanger Research Bureau. Her work was not made easier by the different attitudes of different States: as late as 1927 there was 'A Bill for the Prevention of the Sale of Condoms in the State of North Carolina'.

Encouraged by the success, or at least the non-prosecution, of the Malthusian League which had established a clinic for good mothers in South London, Dr Stopes (she was a Doctor of Science, not of Medicine, and her subject was palaeobotany) hired the Queen's Hall, in London, for her first public meeting in 1922, which was followed by others. Dr Stopes had to endure more ridicule than persecution: it was noted that she was addressing *mixed* audiences (the word *mixed* in the Twenties, as in *mixed bathing*, carried a slight implication of misconduct), and her

message, which she believed came from God, fell gratefully upon the ears of people who could no longer afford large families, and of girls who believed the current rumour that 'since the War there are 2,000,000 surplus women.'

Of course the Roman Catholics were upset; but it was Jix-minded Protestants who were nastiest to Dr Stopes. She was 'a rich madwoman', some said; and when she started her clinic she was compelled to bring a libel action against a journalist who accused her of making money out of the sale of contraceptives. All she was saying, in her books *Mother England* and *Married Love*, was that contraception was better than abortion. I do not know how far her books penetrated the United States, but in 1929 the American Civil Liberties Union forced the customs to admit a copy of *Married Love*, in a law case memorably entitled 'U.S. v. Married Love'.

Among Dr Stopes's critics was a Mr W. N. Willis, who wrote *Wedded Love or Married Misery*. The nub of his argument was 'At a time when Britain needs every ounce of good, solid British flesh and bone . . . we are confronted by diatribes on how *not* to provide sons to carry on our traditions.' And *Punch* published a famous cartoon with a wealth of social implication: it showed a childless young couple lovingly bathing their Baby Austin Seven car.

The Bright Young People (or Things) do not seem to have been unduly worried about birth control. They became a label for *all* the young in Britain who did anything unusual at all, but we know the names of the hard core, the foundation members. No doubt they had their counterpart in New York, but some young Americans came over to London to be bright. For a piece of real Twenties nostalgia, hear Daphne Fielding, formerly Marchioness of Bath, and born Daphne Vivian:

'That American trio, Bob Coe, Ben Kitteredge and Eugene Reynal, set the new fashion of cocktails. One sip of a White Lady now evokes David Plunket-Greene bent over a piano playing 'Harlem Blues', or Mark Ogilvie-Grant vociferously imitating Clara Butt singing 'Land of Hope and Glory' . . .' (A White Lady is $\frac{1}{4}$ lemon juice, $\frac{1}{4}$ Cointreau, $\frac{1}{2}$ dry gin: shake well and strain into cocktail glass.) Simple pleasures, but wait: Indira, Maharanee of Cooch Behar, gave parties in Hill Street at which she served champagne with *crème de menthe*, while everyone, male and female, tried on saris. Brian Howard, described by Evelyn Waugh as 'mad, bad and dangerous to know', took a gang of B.Y.P.s to Wembley Fun Fair, where there were River Caves (similar to Tunnels of Love). They hired little boats and sailed through dark caverns which were decorated with scenes from Dante's *Inferno*; then they annoyed the attendants and everyone else by jumping out of their boats, taking off shoes and stockings and paddling as they played on ukuleles. (Is it perhaps needful to explain that the ukulele was a very simple form of four-stringed guitar, reputed to be Hawaiian, which anyone, having mastered three or four basic chords, could strum and sing to?)

This same little gang played 'follow my leader' through Selfridge's Oxford Street store, climbing all over the counters and generally disrupting business. (Shrewd Gordon Selfridge didn't complain: it was all publicity.) None of them seemed to have jobs, and if you were one of those radical thinkers, you might be forgiven for feeling that they ought all to have been guillotined. But Barbara Cartland does not think so: 'Quite frankly, I think that the Bright Young People brought a great deal of brightness to a world which was still sadly in need of it.' She was, of course, one of them.

On to Mrs James Corrigan's 'stunt' parties, *circa* 1927, when you generally had to arrive in fancy dress. Laura Corrigan, widow of an American steel millionaire, lived in a house in Grosvenor Square which, being famous for Malapropisms, she called her little *ventre-à-terre*. It was said that she

A little Charleston on deck, Norfolk Broads, 1926

The Jungman Sisters by Cecil Beaton

gave away jewellery and gold sock-suspenders to persuade people to come to her parties.

Parties, parties – 'masked parties, Savage parties, Greek parties, almost naked parties,' said Evelyn Waugh in *Vile Bodies*; river parties at Maidenhead, with dinner at Skindles Hotel. 'Baby' parties, with cocktails served in nursery mugs. A dance at St George's Baths in swimming costumes created a particular scandal: not only had it the familiar taint of mixed bathing but, since there was a Negro band, mixed bathing watched by *black* men.

Cecil Beaton, keeping his diary in 1928, tells us that the leader of the Bright Young People was the Hon. Loelia Ponsonby, daughter of the first Baron Sysonby, then Treasurer and Keeper of the Privy Purse. Loelia, 'of the raven's-wing shingle and magnolia complexion', was to become one of the Duchesses of Westminster. With 'Zita, Baby [Jungman] and others of the Guinness contingent', she 'organized "stunt" parties; paper chases, find-the-hidden-clues races, bogus impressionist exhibitions, and bizarre entertainments based on the fashion of the latest Diaghilev ballets'.

Loelia, now Lady Lindsay, is critical of some historians of the Twenties for confusing her with her cousin Elizabeth, daughter of the first Baron Ponsonby of Shulbrede. Elizabeth, who died in 1940, was, it seems, the begetter of some of the wilder escapades I have recorded. Loelia is credited with having invented the champagne bottle party, the first one being held at St James's Palace, where her father lived. Elizabeth is believed to have been the original of Agatha Runcible in *Vile Bodies*.

The bogus art exhibition was organized by Brian Howard, the witty, eccentric and eventually sad figure who had founded a 'set' at Oxford known as 'the Hearts', which included Evelyn Waugh, the reporter of all these activities. Howard painted abstract pictures, geometrical splodges with titles like 'Adoration of the Magi', and, posing as a German artist named 'Bruno Hat', exhibited them at the house of Mr and Mrs Bryan Guinness. It was all 'too, too amusing', and possibly also a little 'sick-making' (yes, the B.Y.P. actually talked like that).

The paper chases and treasure hunts involved anything up to fifty cars (there was apparently room in London then to do this sort of thing). There were also "scavenger" parties, rather like Boy Scout initiative tests, in which one had to bring back things like a spider in a matchbox, one of Prime Minister Baldwin's pipes, a lump of coal or a policeman's helmet. Clues were planted all over London – in the evening papers, or, on one occasion, at Buckingham Palace.

There were historical parties, Mozart parties, and a great deal of fancy dress: you were not supposed to betray any surprise if the Prince of Wales arrived as a Chinese coolie, or Winston Churchill as Nero. If you were in the Loelia set, you were often expected to 'do a turn', sing for your supper, bring some oysters or caviare or at least a bottle of wine. This soon degenerated, in less tasteful circles, into the bottle party, where it was not unknown for champagne, gin, stout and vermouth all to be poured into one punchbowl. 'Meanwhile,' Cecil Beaton continues, 'Mrs Beatrice Guinness had ordered breakfast foods and the Embassy Band for the King of Greece and Charlie Chaplin, while Mrs Brigit Guinness was planning an ambitious costume ball complete with a ballet on a raft . . .'

All this was happening in a very small set of extremely rich people in that part of the West End of London known as Mayfair. But the impact of the cocktail, America's most pervasive contribution to European culture before the age of Coca-Cola, was everywhere. If you could afford to drink spirits at all, you drank cocktails. I have heard it said that it was a way of concealing the rank flavour of American bathtub gin. Yet the word occurs in American folklore as early as 1809, meaning an alcoholic concoction of some kind.

Before the First World War, it seems, nobody ever offered drinks before dinner in Britain or America, with the possible exception of sherry, sherry and soda, sherry and bitters and (in the Oscar Wilde set) hock and seltzer. During the Twenties it was thought that you had to be fairly high to face your dinner at all (which in an era of Good Plain Cooks, and mistresses who had little idea how to train them, was perhaps understandable). By 1929 there were about 120 cocktail recipes in fairly common use. Of these, only about ten survive in Britain today, and it may be advisable to explain to anyone under thirty that a Manhattan is $\frac{2}{3}$ rye whiskey, $\frac{1}{3}$ Italian vermouth with a dash of bitters (stir well with cracked ice, strain into cocktail glasses, decorate with Maraschino cherry); a Sidecar is $\frac{1}{3}$ Cointreau triple-sec, $\frac{1}{3}$ brandy, $\frac{1}{3}$ lemon juice (shaken with *shaved* ice and strained into glasses).

A Bronx was originally $\frac{1}{3}$ orange juice, $\frac{2}{3}$ gin and a dash of both Italian and French vermouths; but it somehow became $\frac{1}{4}$ French vermouth, $\frac{1}{4}$ Italian, $\frac{1}{2}$ gin with orange peel and ice. It was invented by Johnny Solon, bartender at the Old Waldorf Bar, New York, and was named after the Bronx Zoo.

Notice the importance of the bartender: he had become a creative personality, an advertised feature of a hotel. One great symbol of the Twenties or Cocktail Age was the grinning barkeep, in white mess jacket, athletically operating his cocktail shaker, individually mixing a drink for each customer. It took a rather longer time that we should have patience for now, but it was an art. 'Harry makes the best Sidecar in Streatham' (or Flatbush or Glendale or wherever) was high praise and social one-upmanship; and people invented ever more new cocktails, keeping the recipes secret if they were successful. Eric Linklater's novel, *Poet's Pub* (1929), was about a number of characters chasing a runaway barman who had perfected a Blue Cocktail of unknown formula.

At home, the cocktail cabinet joined the phonograph and the radio as articles of furniture, though in America it was often concealed behind a swing-out bookshelf.

In vain did gourmets like Boulestin and André Simon protest. 'The cocktail is intended to be like unto a bugle call to meals' wrote Simon. 'One cocktail helps, two do not, and three harm the flow of gastric juices.' The gastric juices of the Anglo-Saxon, by 1930, would have dissolved marble chips, liberating, if I remember my school chemistry, pure hydrogen.

Henry Ford

Model A Ford

CHAPTER 3

Wheels and Wings

Gastric juices were being shaken, almost as cocktails were shaken, as never before in history, by transportation. What, if anything, do the following names mean to you? Pierce-Chalmers. Ajax. Auburn. Crane-Simplex. Dagmar. Doble. Stutz Bearcat. Scripps-Booth. They are all cars manufactured in America between 1920 and 1930. All over the United States were young engineers and bicycle manufacturers, some of them tinkering away in backyards, fired by the example of Henry Ford (Babbitt's 'poet of business') and convinced that there was a slice of trade for them too.

There was an infinite variety of design, in which 'styling' played little part as yet. One memorable feature of Twenties two-seaters was the dickey, known in America as a rumble-seat, which folded into what the British would now call the boot (or trunk in America) and could accommodate two extra passengers.

Some fell by the wayside; some were acquired by the big mass producers like Chrysler and General Motors. The Pierce-Arrow, a prestige job, was taken over by Studebaker, the Chalmers by Chrysler, the Ajax by Nash. There were three-wheelers, like the Martin Scootmobile, which claimed a top speed of 40 miles per hour and 75 miles per gallon. The Doble was a *steam* car, launched in 1923, which took about eighty seconds to warm up after the electric ignition switch lit the burner, and could go 1,500 miles on 24 gallons of water. It was elegant and it gave a three-year guarantee; but it cost $12,000. That steam-propulsion should have lasted so long in the land that coined the expression 'gas-garden'

may seem astonishing, but the petroleum industry had not yet girded its loins. The Doble Steam Motors Corporation, of Emeryville, California, managed to make only forty-five of their superb cars, and finally died in 1931.

There were no Ralph Naders around in the Twenties, and nobody bothered overmuch about safety. The highways were less crowded (although by the end of the decade there would be both one-way streets and traffic lights); four-wheel brakes were an optional extra; safety glass for windshields took some years to arrive. In 1927, the year in which his Model A replaced his Model T, Henry Ford himself had a car smash, and received an immediate cable from Reginald Delpech in England, who had acquired the rights of the French Benedictus process for making unsplinterable glass: 'Fit Triplex and be safe!' Not until 1929 was safety used as a selling point, when the 'Safety Stutz' was launched with one year's free insurance.

Ford, Chrysler, General Motors: by 1928 the three automobile empires were settling into shape. It was Walter P. Chrysler's 'wonder year': he had just taken over Dodge and now launched two new makes, the Plymouth Four in the lower price bracket and the De Soto Six a little higher up the market. Next year he would sell 98,000 cars.

Quite a number of American cars (other than Ford, who had had his own English factory in Manchester since 1911) came to Britain. We had the Buick Six tourer (the one launched in 1921 and priced at $1,795), enough to inspire a parody of a wartime song:

You made me shove *you –*
I wish I'd bought a Buick,
I wish I'd bought a Buick!

The Essex two-door sedan ($1,295 in 1922) also did well in Britain.

The impact of the automobile on American life – on the pattern of spending (workers wanted cars more than they wanted bathrooms), on social mobility, on the love life of the young, on the divorce rate, on crime (the getaway car and bullet-proof windows soon came to Chicago) – can be measured at least in figures. In 1919 there were 6,771,000 private cars in the United States; in 1929 there were 23,121,000. Among wealthier people, two-car families had already begun, and there were fathers who advised 'Give the boy a car of his own to teach him responsibility.' The boy was learning how much a car could increase his sex-appeal, for he could drive a girl to a weekend party or into the country for back-seat petting or worse. The rise in the British rate of car ownership was even higher – it rose from 186,801 in 1920 to 579,901 in 1925, and there was besides an astonishing outburst of motor-cycles – from 287,739 in 1920 to 571,552 in 1925. There were expensive A.J.S.s (every part hand-made) and Harley-Davidsons, and cheaper ex-Army Broughs, Royal Enfields and Triumphs. Many motorbikes were equipped with pillions for girl-friends, known as 'flapper brackets'.

'Down to the Sea in a Harley-Davidson Sidecar'

Over this scene brooded the heroic presence of Henry Ford. In England the war profiteer was a hated figure, especially if he wore the wrong clothes and dropped his aitches – *Punch*, in the early 1920s, had an almost weekly joke about him. But this man Ford had actually handed $29 million war profits back to the Government! Nobody in Britain (except Stanley Baldwin) ever did anything like that. Henry Ford wasn't like any other capitalist. There were stories of photo-snooping, of men fired for talking, of tormenting petty rules. He paid his workers well, forbade smoking, encouraged sobriety and thrift, but would have nothing to do with trade unions. He sold more and more Model-Ts by cutting prices again and again. He distrusted Wall Street and tried never to expand by borrowing. He held out obstinately against the conventional gearshift (on the Model-T you changed gear like a motorbike with a pedal, down-one up-three); against hydraulic brakes, more cylinders and any colour other than black. Yet electric starters had been available since 1912, so that George F. Babbitt, in Zenith, need no longer lie awake in the early morning listening to his neighbour cranking up (*snap-ah-ah, snap-ah-ah*).

Diet faddist, folkdance enthusiast, collector of early Americana, philanthropist, practical joker, endower of an anti-Semitic newspaper, and very nearly a Presidential candidate in 1924, Henry Ford had, in the fateful year of 1927, a surplus balance of nearly $700 million. In the hiatus between the end of the Model T and tooling up for Model A, Ford began losing out to Chevrolet in the cheap car market, and Chevrolet now meant General Motors. Chevs. might not be able to beat Ford's rock-bottom 1925 price of $260, but they could exceed his top speed of 45 miles per hour and they had a lever gearshift. To catch up, Ford launched the Model A with the biggest-ever ad-vertising campaign (full pages in 2,000 papers for five days). Temporarily, it seemed to crush all competition. Two years later came a station-wagon version.

Driving in the Twenties was haphazardly learned, but skilfully applied. You had to be able to judge revs. before you changed gear (the Cadillac La Salle was the first car to have synchromesh gears, in 1929). Everybody learnt to 'double-de-clutch'. Garages were not so common that you could risk being unable to do your own running repairs, and

American and British backyards were full of young men, on Saturday afternoons, 'taking down the big end' and doing their own decarbonizing. Driving lessons were taken from fathers and friends, and nobody had to pass any kind of test. Petrol was carried in cans on board. The first petrol station in Britain, set up by the Automobile Association, was at Aldermaston, Berkshire, in 1920. Wolverhampton, in 1927, was the first English city to have automatic traffic lights, though from 1925 hand-operated lights had been controlled by policemen at the junction of St James's Street and Piccadilly, London. Balloon tyres arrived around 1925, and the invention of pyroxylin finishes meant a whole new range of colours, even for Fords.

With radio shares, motors led the bull market on Wall Street until 1929. Thereafter there were fewer new cars, and the used car market began to boom instead.

London, England, 1921. Owen Nares, the matinée idol (there's a real Twenties expression for you), had just been fined £1 for driving a car at 29 miles per hour. The speed limit in Britain stayed officially at 20 miles per hour all through the decade, but everybody broke it. We had, it seems, a romantic rather than a practical attitude towards the automobile. Contemporary popular fiction is full of glamorous names like Hispano-Suiza, Bugatti and Isotta-Fraschini, hand-made with special bodywork, and the novels of Captain Mercer, better known as Dornford Yates, pursued the adventures of one Berry and his friends, gentlefolk of leisure who spent all their lives motoring through France in their Rolls-Royces, having small adventures on the way. This was, indeed, what every decent Englishman wanted to claim as his reward for war service. 'What I want to do when peace comes', wrote Harold Nicolson towards the war's end, 'is to motor in a two-seater through France and Spain. I have no wish at all to put on a stand-up collar and go to a reception at Londonderry House.'

There had been a car boom in 1919 which had slowed up considerably by 1920. The kind of car most people in Britain actually bought was small. (Among other things, there was a horse-power tax.) The Co-Operative Wholesale Society even tried to produce a 'people's car', but simply could not compete with Ford, Austin and Morris. Morris, however, was in low water, nervously price-cutting,

The Austin Seven prototype

at the beginning of the decade. By 1925 he was producing more than 55,000 cars a year – 40 per cent of all cars made in Britain: the famous bull-nose radiator was a symbol of the age. But it was Sir Herbert Austin, knighted for the guns and aircraft he had produced during the War, who produced at Longbridge, near Birmingham, the first satisfactory 'people's car' in 1922 – the Austin Seven was a *four-seater* and cost £165, £20 cheaper than the Model T.

The British car industry, like the American, spawned new makes before the big groups planned their own survival. In 1925, *Autocar* magazine advertised 230 of them, and Lambert & Butler ran two series of cigarette cards on them. As a schoolboy I could stand for hours on the sidewalk car-spotting. Hillman, Riley, Lea-Francis, Swift, Triumph, Bean – two of these still exist as brand names; but where are Clyno, Arrol-Johnston, Jowett (the first car to cross Africa), the three-wheeled Morgan, the chain-drive Trojan, with its engine under the seat and solid rubber tyres?

Despite the Isotta-Fraschinis, there was a general feeling that while American heavy cars were better you couldn't beat a British light car. William Morris flew the Union Jack above his Cowley works, and his slogan was 'Even if you don't buy a Morris, buy a car made in Britain.' In 1928 he launched his own 'people's car', the Morris Minor, at the then unbeatable price of £125–£135 (safety glass windshield £2 extra). This was a big difference from the 1923 price of £145 for a 13.9 horse-power Morris Oxford two-seater, and very serious competition for Austin.

35

(above) A luncheon party at Ascot with
'The Rolls' serving as partial sitting
accommodation, June 1921

Speed may have been discouraged on the roads,
which still bore a great deal of horse-drawn traffic
(the charabanc did not take over from the horse-
brake for Sunday school outings until the mid-
Twenties); but you could get it out of your system at
Brooklands Motor Course, which reopened in 1920.
And in 1927 Sir Henry Segrave managed to touch
203 miles per hour in a Sunbeam, at Daytona Beach,
Florida. Segrave went on to win the world speed
record in 1929 in his ice-cooled 1,000 horse-power
Golden Arrow, reaching 231 miles per hour at
Daytona Beach, Florida, but was killed next year.

Speed was not the main consideration in the five
days it took to cross the Atlantic. Or rather, there
was disagreement about it. Did you sail to and from
New York to get there quick, or for the ride, or to
meet interesting and influential people with whom

Sir Herbert Austin and his racing team, 1922

The famous speed track at Daytona Beach

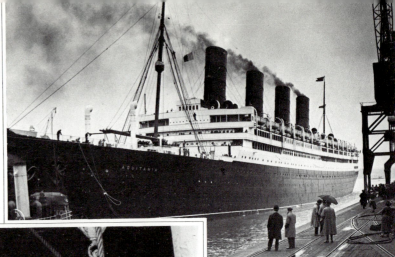

(right) 'Aquitania', September 1923

(below) A group sitting out
during a ball on board
the 'Berengaria', 1927

(below) A lady having a Turkish
bath, 'Berengaria', July 1923

you might transact a little leisurely business on the way? After the War, Cunard built five *Franconia* type ships of 20,000 tons with a speed of 17 knots. Hamburg-Amerika built four *Deutschland* type ships of 21,000 tons which did only 16 knots. Not until 1926 did the Compagnie Générale Transatlantique launch the *Ile de France* of 43,450 tons, which had the astonishing speed of 24 knots (I speak from experience – in the Second World War it was my troopship to Bombay); and two years later North German Lloyd hit back with the *Bremen* and the *Europa* (50,000 tons, 28 knots).

'How you travel is who you are' said Lucius Beebe, America's connoisseur of everything. 'Going Cunard', ran the slogan, 'is a state of grace.' 'The motion of the ship', the *Aquitania*'s first-class menu apologized, 'precludes carrying the older red wines.' That menu listed eighty-six dishes.

Aquitania, Mauretania, Berengaria – when shall we see their like again? All had been laid down before the War; all were still going strong. They were floating hotels, and everything possible was done to conceal the fact that you were at sea, which only became apparent when they rolled. The *Aquitania* had a Caroline smoking room, an Elizabethan grill room, a Louis XIV dining room, a Palladian lounge, an Egyptian swimming pool. On B deck, which like all other decks was reached by a battery of elevators, there were Reynolds, Gainsborough, Romney, Raeburn, Holbein, Vandyke and Velasquez suites. Over the 'parlours' and 'lounges' were glass domes – anything so that you should forget you were in a ship. Every room, in first and second class, was panelled in fine English woods (no doubt the actuaries had worked out the fire risk), and the furniture tended to be walnut, covered with *petit-point* tapestry.

The *Aquitania* accommodated 750 in first class, 600 in second, and up to 2,000 in third. The restaurant seated 700. It was reckoned that the ship's company provided three 'servers' for every passenger. Over all, Captain James Charles (afterwards Sir James and Commodore of the Cunard line) presided for ten years. He it was, Lucius Beebe tells us, who established the Grand Manner of the Captain's Table. For dinner you were expected to wear full evening dress, with decorations. 'Stewards rolled in carcasses of whole roasted oxen one night, and the next evening small herds of grilled antelope surrounded a hilltop of Strasbourg *foie-gras* surmounted

by peacock fans. Electrically-illuminated *pièces montées* representing the Battle of Waterloo and other patriotic moments made an appearance while the ship's orchestra played Elgar.'

It took four days and three nights to cross America from coast to coast. Motor coaches were already beginning to steal some of the trade, but one thing you could do on American railroads which you couldn't do even on the *Aquitania* was rent a private railroad car with gold-plated plumbing. I have never met anybody who did this, and all the accounts I have ever heard of trans-America rail journeys in the Twenties bemoan the fact that air-conditioning hadn't yet arrived. It was too hot in summer, too cold in winter, and seldom safe to open the windows. Tycoons had their 'drawing rooms', but most continent-crossers had to make do with crowded sleeping cars, sympathetically attended by Negro 'vergers' in white jackets. You took the *Century* from New York to Chicago. You changed trains at Chicago, taking a bus between stations. Then you took the *Chief* (or the *Super-Chief*) to the West Coast, and in the unlikely event that you wanted to work, you could hire the train stenographer. In spring and in the fall this great journey could be a rest cure. At any season, especially with show business characters on board, it could be a five-day blind. 'For three days', reports Cecil Beaton, travelling to Hollywood with Anita Loos and many other film folk just after talking pictures had arrived, 'we ate enormous tenderloin steaks. . . . At Las Vegas, John Emerson bought a bow and arrow from an Indian.' Old-timers thought it was at least better than an ox-wagon.

In Britain a strange thing had happened. In the flurry of amalgamations and streamlining of 123 different companies, second-class rail travel had been dropped, so that you went either first or third. No foreigner could ever understand this, any more than he could understand our neat little country station gardens, lovingly tended by stationmasters and porters to whom winning one of the national prizes for the best-kept gardens was at least as important as getting trains away on time. Yet third class differed from first class only in that first class had separate seats, arm-rests and antimacassars. In the south, we were electrifying like mad, all the way from London to Brighton, and most of the suburban lines (but not the south-east, which retained its old reputation for backwardness and discomfort). Result: you could commute from Wimbledon to Waterloo in fifteen minutes for 9d.

It was an age of glamour trains, with marketable names, such as the first Blue Train: 'Sleep your way from the City's fogs to the Riviera sunshine.' Britain's pride and joy were two famous trains – rivals – called the *Royal Scot* and the *Flying Scotsman*. The *Flying Scotsman* was born as a Gresley Pacific 4472 at Doncaster, Yorkshire. Built by the Great Northern Railway in 1922, and put into service on the London & North-Eastern the following year, this coal-burning pride of the steam age was displayed at the British Empire Exhibition, Wembley. In 1928, equipped with a walk-through tender to allow crew changes at high speed, it began non-stop journeys between London and Edinburgh covering 392¾ miles in 7 hours.

After an unsuccessful attempt to use it as a travelling shop window for British exports, it has now come home to operate peacefully on the Torbay Steam Railway in Devon. 'Somehow,' said an observer, 'she never seemed at home in America, where sleepers are called Pullmans, Pullmans are dining cars, chimneys are smoke stacks, footplates are cabs, regulators are throttles, and safety rules demand cattle guards, bells, searchlights and whistles loud enough to frighten the non-existent bison from the right of way.'

What, meantime, had happened to those Splendid Young Men in their Flying Machines who had done deeds of valour in the War? Nobody believed, for several years, that flying was, or could be, safe. Well, it wasn't; in 1921 the London-Brussels airmail crashed in the Channel, killing two; next year, two London-Paris planes collided over Beauvais (six killed); in 1923 a French liner fell near Folkestone (three dead) and the London-Manchester Air Express crashed at Ivinghoe (five dead); in 1929 Imperial Airways' *City of Ottawa* crashed in the Channel, killing seven. No, it was not safe, nor could it cover big enough distances yet. So unpleasant was the idea of flying to some people that on July 4th 1922 we find John Galsworthy writing a perfectly serious letter to *The Times* suggesting the banning of all aircraft 'for any purpose whatsoever'.

America had had a transcontinental airmail service since 1919, but the huge mileage between the coasts made her slow to develop commercial avia-

The Duchess of Bedford and Captain C. D. Barnard

tion. Britain, with her still strong Empire links, started Imperial Airways in 1924. Most parts of the Empire could be reached in a series of short hops. And since 1919 we had had daily scheduled flights from London to Paris (at 200 feet, flying time 165 minutes) for £20 return. Five of those pioneer pilots, Jerry Shaw, A. C. Campbell-Orde, A. S. Wilcockson, Walter Rogers and R. H. McIntosh, are alive today.

The scary novelty of flying made news every day. The *Daily Mail*, never slow to spot a publicity opportunity, with a plane piloted by Major J. C. Savage, wrote its name in sky-writing over Epsom Downs on Derby Day, 1922. Two years later the Savoy Orpheans Band broadcast from an aeroplane circling above Croydon Airport. In 1929 the Duchess of Bedford, aged sixty-two, who thought that flying was good for her deafness, learnt to pilot a plane and flew with Captain C. D. Barnard to Karachi and back in eight days.

You had to be the *first* to do something, or press and public soon forgot you. John Alcock and Arthur Brown flew non-stop across the Atlantic (Newfoundland to Ireland) in sixteen hours as early as 1919, and were knighted for it. In September 1922 James Doolittle flew across the United States (Jacksonville, Fla., to San Diego, Cal.) in a single day. He couldn't be knighted because he was an American. Alan Cobham was knighted because he flew to Australia and back, 28,000 miles, by seaplane in 1926. In May 1928 Lady Heath flew alone from the Cape to Croydon, and in June Lady Bailey flew to the Cape *and back*. They couldn't be knighted because they were Ladies. Amelia Earhart was the first woman to cross the Atlantic in 1928, from Newfoundland to Wales, but she did it as a passenger. Even so, it made almost as much front-page news as when, seven years later, she flew solo from Honolulu to Oakland in 18 hours 16 minutes.

Young Francis Chichester made the *second* solo flight from London to Sydney in 1929–30 (180½ hours). The first had been made by Bert Hinkler in 1928. Chichester followed this with the first solo crossing (two-thirds of the distance between Britain and America) of the Tasman Sea. Turning his *Gipsy Moth* into a seaplane, he invented a new system of navigation so that he could hop from New Zealand to Norfolk Island and so, via Lord Howe Island, to Australia. But *he* had to sail single-handed round the world, nearly forty years later, to get *his* knighthood.

We still believed in airships, too. The R.34 had successfully crossed the Atlantic both ways. The R.100 and R.101 were designed to open up a great Commonwealth air service. In 1929 Dr Hugo Eckener's *Graf Zeppelin* flew from New York to

Amelia Earhart after her Atlantic flight, 1928

Friedrichshaven in 55½ hours, and then completely circumnavigated the earth in 21 days 7 hours. It is difficult to realize, today, the shock of the R.101's crash in flames at Beauvais, France, in 1930, on the way to India, killing forty-eight of its fifty-four passengers. Among them were many of the top brass of British aviation, including the Director of Civil Aviation himself, Sir Sefton Brancker. Apart from his distinguished flying career, he was noted, in an

(left) R.101 at its mooring mast
(below) The wreckage of the crashed R.101

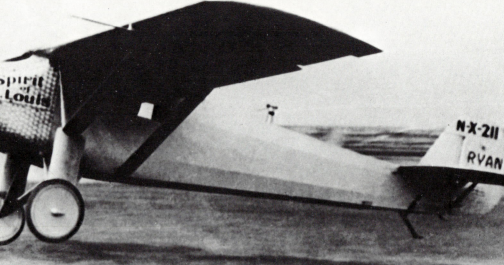

(above) Still from the newsreel
of Charles Lindbergh's take-off
in the 'Spirit of St Louis', May 20th, 1927
(right) Charles Lindbergh
after his successful flight

era of peculiar party tricks such as goldfish-swallowing, for eating his monocle, which he did with all the appearance of relish.

So the commercial airship died – because inflammable hydrogen had been preferred to inert helium. Here is the story of the R.101 radio operator, who survived: 'The fire was awful – awful. . . . It was just one mass of flame roaring like a furnace. My one ideas was to get out of the ship. I threw myself at the fabric cover and tried to break through, but could not. Then I sat down and found myself sitting on wet grass. . . . It was all over in a minute.'. . . .

We have strayed over the border into the 1930s, but with reason. What happened to the R.101 was violent and tragic, but the public imagination had been seized by another personality three years before, who seemed to be showing that the aeroplane, after all, was going to carry the future of long-distance flying. What flying needed was a hero, and in Charles A. Lindbergh a hero was found. He was twenty-five, and an all-American boy if ever there was one.

He was competing, for $25,000 put up by a New York hotel owner, against Commander Byrd, who had been to the North Pole. Lindy himself had the confidence of one who, only a week before, had set up a record by flying from San Diego to Long Island via St Louis in 21 hours 20 minutes. Now he was going to fly 3,600 miles non-stop from New York to Paris.

'Stunt merchant – flying fool – home-made plane,' pessimists said. If you ever saw the newsreel of his take-off at Roosevelt Field on May 20th 1927, you would have understood their fears. (It was one of the first newsreels with sound, and the publicity effect was quadrupled by the fact that you could actually hear his engine.) His plane was overloaded, he took off downwind in driving rain, he only just missed (by twenty feet) some trees and telephone wires. His silver monoplane had one engine and no radio. He had no map, no parachute. He had an inflatable raft, two pints of water and five sandwiches: he dared not eat any more for fear of falling asleep. He flew over Newfoundland but did not come down.

He wasn't going to come down in Ireland either.

'Flying fool . . .' At Yankee Stadium, where Sharkey was fighting Maloney, the referee asked 40,000 people to pray for him.

He had never flown over water before. The Atlantic was foggy and he had no blind-flying equipment. He went above the fog into freezing air: he had left the cabin window open so that he shouldn't fall asleep. He was flying by the Pole Star, and his compass. For some hours he couldn't account for the position of the moon – until he realized that he was flying with the rotation of the earth, which made the night shorter. When dawn came, he dropped to a few feet above the ocean. He had made it half way.

Lindbergh afterwards described a feeling of 'sleeping with my eyes open.' At twenty-one hours out from New York, he noticed that he had drunk half his water supply but couldn't remember doing it. Five hours later he saw a school of porpoises, and then a gull. Land must be near. Two hours after that he skimmed over some fishing boats, circled low so that he could see a man's face at a cabin window, and shouted to him 'Which way is Ireland?' The sailor either didn't hear him or couldn't speak English.

Fifty minutes later he sighted a rocky coastline. He pointed the *Spirit of St Louis* vaguely towards where he guessed Paris might be, but fog was gathering. He had crossed the Atlantic, but still had no idea where he was. But the world knew. In the Place de l'Opéra in Paris electric signs flashed the news. Streams of cars converged on le Bourget airfield and left their headlights on to guide him. The airfield beacon was switched on, rockets and star shells were fired, everybody who had any source of light flashed it like mad. At 10.20 p.m. he landed, after $33\frac{1}{2}$ hours in the air, and met a crowd of about 100,000 people. It was inevitable that he should ask 'Where am I?' Inevitable that they should reply 'Paris'. Asked how he felt, he said 'I've been to eternity and back. I know how the dead would feel to live again.'

CHAPTER 4

David and Family

If Lindbergh was the all-American boy, David was the all-British one. Aunts and Nannies taught us to recite all his names: Edward Albert Christian George Andrew Patrick David, covering all his Royal, English, Scottish, Irish and Welsh heritage.

No prince had ever been so thoroughly trained in the art of monarchy. Under H. P. Hansell, his tutor between the ages of eight and twenty, he had shown 'quick intelligence but little concentration'. Like many little boys, even in the Twenties, he had been made to wear a sailor suit with pockets sewn up so that he shouldn't put his hands in them. At Osborne, once his grandmother Victoria's summer residence in the Isle of Wight but after her death a preparatory naval college, and afterwards at the Royal Naval College, Dartmouth, he had chafed under the discipline and seamanship which is thought essential for any man, king or consort, who sits on or near the British throne. On his sixteenth birthday, June 23rd, 1910, he was created Prince of Wales, Earl of Chester, and Knight of the Garter, and a year later he was invested by his father, George V, in the solemn setting of Caernarvon Castle. On this occasion he addressed his Welsh subjects in their own language, the first time in centuries that any Prince of Wales had done so. He had also collected the Duchy of Cornwall, from which he derived a large portion of his income. Back to sea as midshipman in H.M.S. *Hindustan*; then five glorious months learning French in Paris before his first real experience of 'meeting the people', which became his overriding ambition and, for him, the most important mission of Royalty: then going up to Oxford. Here he was known, in the

Oxford slang of 1912, as the Pragga-Wagga. Twenty-one years later, buying my first pipe at Cooke's in the High, I was sold an ounce of 'the Prince of Wales's own mixture'.

No doubt Mr Hansell, who was still with him, screened his associates carefully, but for the first time in his life he was choosing his own friends, not all of them out of the topmost drawer. How else can we explain the story of a Socialist undergraduate who, having argued with His Royal Highness about the uselessness of the Monarchy, was rewarded – and forever reconciled – by David's roaring with laughter and singing *The Red Flag* to his own banjo accompaniment.

When war came, like every normal young man in Britain and America he was mad keen to go 'over the top' and grapple with his German cousins. 'I am not irreplaceable' he told Lord Kitchener heatedly. 'I have four younger brothers.' To which Kitchener replied 'If I were certain you would be shot, I do not know that I should be right to restrain you. What I cannot permit is the chance, which exists till we have a settled line, of your being taken prisoner.' He advised him to learn a bit more about soldiering and then perhaps he could go to France.

So David joined the 1st Battalion of the Grenadier Guards at Warley Barracks, Essex (Guards are supposed to be tall, but David was only 5ft 6in.), and some months later found himself A.D.C. to Sir John French at G.H.Q., St Omer. He seems to have accepted this post rather rebelliously, and his desire to fraternize with 'other ranks' was only partly satisfied by joining in games of football behind the

(opposite) Detail from 'Their Majesties' Return from Ascot', 1925, by Sir Alfred Munnings

Fashion plate from *Art Goût Beauté*,
Christmas 1923.
(left to right) Mikado by Dœuillet;
Caprice by Dœuillet;
Green velvet cape by Phillippe and Gaston;
Infidèle by Martial and Armand;
Royal blue mantle by Martial and Armand

lines. The year 1916 found him in Egypt; 1917 on the Italian front, where the first of a thousand marriage rumours started: the real reason he was there, tongues wagged, was so that he could become engaged to Princess Yolanda of Savoy, eldest daughter of the King of Italy. But in no time at all he was away to serve with the Australians, then the New Zealanders, and then with General Pershing at the United States headquarters at Coblenz.

He had, after all, 'met the people', and in the next few years his memory for faces had a magical effect. In the Carlton Grill in London he saw some rough, leather-skinned Australian soldiers whom the waiters would not serve. He went straight over and shook their hands. The Australians were obsequiously shown to a table. And in New York he met Patterson, the Australian tennis star, and was able to greet him with: 'Didn't I see you at Arras one cold winter's day when things were not quite so pleasant?'

All through the Twenties the Prince was travelling. He was 'the Empire's travelling salesman'; 'the best Ambassador we've got,' my headmaster used to tell us. It is difficult, fifty years later, to imagine the glamour of 'the Little Man'. He was sometimes wild; but people loved it. I am unable to check a story told to me by every Hungarian I have ever met who was in Budapest in those years, but it seems that the street outside his hotel had to be cleared because the Prince, after sampling Imperial Tokay, stood at his window joyfully letting fly with a shotgun. This was the young man of whom his father said 'After I am dead the boy will ruin himself in twelve months.'

The travelling had begun in 1919, to Newfoundland and Canada, where he pleased everybody by buying a ranch in Alberta; then on to the United States, where he paid a dutiful call on President Wilson and then got down to the serious business of enjoying himself. A New York magazine ran a competition for 'the best love letter to the Prince of Wales'. In Australia, where in 1920 he laid the foundation stone of the new federal capital Canberra, there were accusations of bad manners in that he danced only with pretty girls and neglected his hostesses. But in Sydney, where he arrived after a train accident in which he had shown remarkable coolness, calmly collecting his scattered papers before extricating himself, the Sydney *Sun* was all praise: 'Before the Prince landed, the popular idea

of princes was of something haughty and remote; but this smiling, appealingly youthful man smiled away the difference which Australians believed lay between Royalty and the common people.'

He returned to America in 1924, where he was seen in Oxford bags, in motor boats, dancing, playing polo. He seems, in particular, to have bewitched the staff of *Vanity Fair*, which said of him 'Who would suppose – on encountering this delicate physiognomy – that its owner was possessed of a fortitude and endurance unexampled in human history?' The magazine then produced some cheerfully libellous statistics: he had survived 2,754,911 snapshots, laid 7,003 cornerstones, fallen off his horse no fewer than 2,431 times, been proposed to by 4,187 young ladies, kissed 2,329 blondes, quaffed 19,218 quarts of champagne . . . 'Hats off to the indestructible Dancing Drinking Tumbling Kissing Walking Talking and Sleeping – but not Marrying – idol of the British Empire!'

Most Americans, mesmerized, seemed to regard him as the stuff of which twentieth-century Royalty should be made. Yet he had his critics, such as the leader-writer of a New York paper who wrote 'He managed, by his choice of friends and diversions, to provoke an exhibition of social climbing on the part of a few Americans which has added nothing to his prestige nor to the prestige of Royalty in general.'

David was always at home in America; but now, in 1921, they sent him to India. India didn't like the British very much at that time: two years before, General Dyer, trying to establish instant law and order, had opened fire on an unarmed mob, killing 379 people, and then decreed that all Indians using a street in the town where a woman missionary had been 'insulted' should crawl along it on all fours. Although he was boycotted at Lucknow and Allahabad, David managed to win back a little respect for the Raj; and when H.M.S. *Renown* docked at Bombay, he did a thing no prince or Englishman had ever done before: he saluted a crowd of Untouchables. Did it do any good? No matter – he did it.

Japan, Colombo, Singapore, Manila, Borneo, Cairo – how could the son of George V, of whom it was said that he 'didn't like abroad', travel so much? Of course, it was much more comfortable in a battleship than it would be today in a jet, especially with harum-scarum young Lord Louis Mount-

The wedding of Lord Louis Mountbatten and Miss Edwina Ashley, July 1922

batten as his personal aide-de-camp. In Delhi in 1922 Lord Louis had become engaged to Edwina Ashley, and the Prince of Wales was best man at their wedding at St Margaret's Westminster. But the Prince's attention to his health – running in Buckingham Palace grounds for an hour before breakfast, golf at Sandwich, squash at the Bath Club – was paying off.

In March 1925 he sailed, this time in H.M.S. *Repulse*, for West Africa, and then to South Africa, where he was greeted by 50,000 Basuto horsemen; and anon to South America. Only East Africa had

A typical formal wedding group of 1929

been omitted, and three years later, with his brother the Duke of Gloucester, he went on safari; and of the many thousands of hands he shook, one very frail one must have impressed him: that of Chuma, the last surviving servant of David Livingstone who had carried the explorer's body from Central Africa to the coast fifty years earlier.

Never before had a future king 'met the people' at such close quarters that students of Southampton University danced round him singing 'Here we go round the Prince of Wales.' When the Café de Paris was doing badly, the proprietor telephoned the Prince, begged him to be seen there; and lo! it became fashionable again. In any night club he was liable to take over the jazz drums, and I have heard high praise of his rimshots. He spoke with a very slight Cockney twang, which he was sometimes said to have learnt from his nurse Lala. That twang was heard by several million people when he became, in 1922, the first Royal to speak on the radio. Two years later his father's first broadcast was heard when he opened the Wembley Exhibition.

David was eventually forbidden to go steeple-chasing for fear he should break his neck. He always had time for ex-servicemen's organizations such as the British Legion and Toc H. He visited Mill Hill School and congratulated a science class on 'getting America' on their home-made radio set ('getting America' was the miracle aimed at by all radio amateurs in those days). He took advanced banjo lessons from Clifford Essex. His favourite tune was Noël Coward's 'A Room With a View'. Was he or was he not the lover of Florence Mills, the coloured star of *Blackbirds*? In his fashion, despite Lady Furness and others, he was faithful for seventeen years to Mrs Dudley Ward, whom he met in an air raid in 1917.

His informal clothes were sometimes thought 'rather common'. He experimented with a beret, tried to revive the straw boater, was photographed at Biarritz in a terrible check cap. He pioneered the cutaway collar and the 'Windsor knot' (afterwards known in America as the 'Bold Look Tie'), and the multi-coloured Fair Isle sweater. For a short time he wore a white waistcoat with a dinner-jacket, but it never caught on. Never mind what happened to him afterwards: the *Vanity Fair* assessment was right. What a guy! I wish I'd known him.

Florence Mills in 'Dover Street to Dixie'

(top left) (left to right)
Captain Latta, Captain of
the 'Empress of Australia',
Mr Stanley Baldwin,
Mrs Baldwin,
the Prince of Wales,
and Prince George,
July 1927

(top right)
The Prince of Wales
riding in after
a polo match at
Spring Hill
Farm,
August 1922

(above left) The Prince of Wales at the meet of the
Duke of Buccleuch's foxhounds at Minto House,
Scotland, December 1924
(right) The Prince of Wales seen arriving
at Meadowbrook in America for a polo match,
September 1924

The music front of 'Don't Know 'im?', 1920. The original of this photograph was taken in America between signing autographs. Its informality had immediate appeal resulting in it being reproduced in many different forms

By comparison, the other Royals seemed shadowy figures. Queen Alexandra, widow of the wayward Edward VII, the beautiful Danish princess who as a child had met Hans Christian Andersen and knew his fairy stories by heart, had given her name to Queen Alexandra Rose Day and an Imperial nursing service. In my childhood she was living in retirement at Sandringham, the Royal Family's country house in Norfolk, and when she died in 1925 most of the daily newspapers had purple borders.

George V, every inch a king and a sailor, and friend of John Masefield the merchant seaman who became Poet Laureate, was also happiest at 'dear old Sandringham'. He had become King only because his elder brother, the Duke of Clarence, had died – and he inherited his brother's fiancée, Princess Mary of Teck, the 'darling May' of his diaries and letters. Together they did slightly more democratic things than reigning monarchs had done before, such as riding on the scenic railway at the British Empire Exhibition, he grimly clinging to his grey bowler hat, she to her invariable pre-1914 toque. But they remained Edwardians, and were disgusted when George's cousin, Queen Marie of Roumania, wrote a newspaper article on 'My Ideal Man'.

King George's tastes were simple: next to his stamp collection he liked vaudeville, spectacular musicals, films and radio comedians. His favourite show was *Rose Marie*, which he and Queen Mary saw several times; but the star, Edith Day, could not be presented to them because 'her marriage had been dissolved'. George was something of a diplomat: in 1924 it was he who reconciled the first Labour Government to the constitution, and he put on a red tie to receive Ramsay MacDonald as his new Prime Minister.

He may not have 'liked abroad', but he had visited every dominion and most colonies. He may not have said (as was murmured) 'I won't knight buggers'; but he was genuinely perplexed by homosexuality and, on hearing that a man he knew well was so inclined, said 'I thought fellows like that shot themselves.'

When, in 1929, he seemed dangerously ill with pleurisy, and a Council of Regency was set up, the nation was inexpressibly relieved to hear that he had gone to Craigweil House, Bognor, a very average seaside resort in Sussex noted for its 'good air', to recover. By his special request, a pipe major woke him every morning with Scottish tunes. He 'knighted' Bognor by conferring upon it for evermore the title 'Regis'.

For two years, until she was eighteen, Mary had lived in Florence, where she acquired that taste for the fine arts which caused her to appear suddenly at antique shops all over London and add to her formidable collection of bric-à-brac. Was she prudish? I do not think so, but she was a stickler for the proprieties, even in the Twenties. A society lady refused to divorce her husband 'because if I did the Queen wouldn't ask me to tea any more'. And when, in 1925, *No, No, Nanette* came to the Palace Theatre, Mary ostentatiously turned her eyes away when Binnie Hale and the chorus came on in bathing dresses, a sight never before seen on the British stage. George loved her devotedly all his life, and in the middle of a speech, when he came to the words 'when I think of all that I owe to her', he was overcome with emotion. Mary herself never made a public speech, and was believed never to have used the telephone.

If George and Mary had a fault, it was that they could not communicate with their children. This was partly due to a tradition which George confided to Lord Derby, who thought the King was too hard on them. 'My father was frightened of his mother; I was frightened of my father; and I am damned well going to see to it that my children are frightened of me.'

Their eldest daughter, the Princess Royal, was always referred to by my elders as 'poor Princess Mary'. When, in 1922, she married 'poor Lord Lascelles', who looked like a dismal bloodhound but had three million pounds, they heaved a sigh of relief. She had humour, and did many good works; but it was difficult to believe that she had married for love.

There was no doubt about 'Bertie', Prince Albert, King George's shy, stammering second son, who, like the Pragga-Wagga, had gone through Osborne and Dartmouth but had gone up to Cambridge and, as a sub-lieutenant, had actually been in a battle at Jutland. With astonishing persistence he courted a girl who was full of the joy of the Twenties, Lady Elizabeth Bowes-Lyon, a commoner who had not even been presented at Court. She had grown up at Glamis, Scotland, in a castle where the ghosts of

Macbeth and his lady were said to roam. She was a Girl Guide. She could fish, but hated the sound of guns and the sight of piles of dead game. There is a story that when she was ten she consulted a garden-party palmist who said 'You will be a queen when you grow up.' Three years later she met Bertie and danced with him, but neither could remember the occasion afterwards. The all-important meeting was at Lord Farquhar's house in Grosvenor Square in May 1920, when she was twenty: he was twenty-four and in two weeks' time was to become Duke of York.

The following spring he proposed and she refused him. Elizabeth was, however, worried about him: 'He is a man who will be made or marred by his wife.' Queen Mary thought the girl's mind needed to be made up for her, and accompanied Bertie on his next visit to Glamis. But Elizabeth still resisted. Perhaps she knew that George V, whose favourite daughter-in-law she eventually became, 'dreaded the idea of daughters-in-law'. But hostesses such as Mrs Ronnie Greville of Polesden Lacey began to invite Elizabeth and Bertie to the same parties, and on January 13th 1922 a telegram was received by George and Mary at Sandringham. It said 'ALL RIGHT STOP BERTIE.'

They were married on April 26th 1923, in Westminster Abbey. The first two weeks of their honeymoon were spent at Polesden Lacey; the rest at Glamis, where Elizabeth developed, of all unromantic ailments, whooping cough. They went to live at 145 Piccadilly.

'The little Duchess' was quick to see that she could afford to be less formal than her husband. For one thing, she laughed more than any other Royal except the Prince of Wales, and said innocuously un-Royal things, such as (reported to me by two maiden aunts) 'Not another drink, dear – I mustn't be tiddly at the Palace.' In 1926, at Elizabeth's parents' house in Bruton Street, the future Queen Elizabeth II was born, we are told, 'feet first by Caesarian section', and the baby was officially said to be third in succession to the throne 'for the time being'. That year, too, Bertie, a useful tennis player, played at Wimbledon.

Next year the Duke and Duchess of York left on the inevitable Empire Tour, which was to include opening the Australian parliament in the new capital of Canberra. The Duchess had developed a technique of her own in establishing a rapport with crowds: she picked out one or two individuals and either spoke, or looked, straight at them. This led to a story that in Auckland, New Zealand, a local Communist leader who had been given this treatment was so bewitched that he said, in a press interview, 'I've done with Communism! She *looked* at me – and waved – and smiled!'

King George VI (then Duke of York) partnered by Louis Greig playing at Wimbledon, 1926

CHAPTER 5

Bobs, Shingles and Camibockers

The Little Duchess wore most of the Twenties fashions, except the extremes of thigh-length skirts and Eton crop, and in the middle of the decade she favoured the cloche hat. As she became more Royal, she had to wear 'off the face' hats, and the hat she was wearing when she sailed for Australia in H.M.S. *Renown* was an ingenious contradiction, an off-the-face cloche.

The cloche hat appeared in 1924, and reigned until 1930. It was often worn with a brooch in front. (Did I say 1924? But Cecil Beaton records that his mother had one in 1923.) The important thing about it was that if you wore it you had to cut your hair short. Once it had arrived, there was no future for the 'Greek' coiffure (with bun) which had prevailed in 1919–20. Bobbed hair was not new: Augustus John's portraits of Dorelia show that it was being worn before 1914, but only in Chelsea. It was 'arty', and it suggested 'Bolshevism' and free love. Hair was to become shorter yet, until by 1928, with the Eton crop at its full development, and with girls wearing trousers, it was not easy to tell them from boys. The year 1925 is usually

assigned to the Eton crop (but Cecil Beaton notes that Topsy, wife of F. L. Lucas, Fellow of King's College, Cambridge, had one in 1922). Perhaps we should say that 1925 was the year when *Punch* noticed it, in a joke which said 'Grow your hair, man, you look like a girl!'

There was a bob, then (1924) the shingle, then a mixture of both called the bingle. Girls with straight hair curled it with tongs heated on tiny methylated spirit stoves; or if they could afford it they had one of Vasco's or Marcel's 'permanent waves'. These took two hours and in London cost four guineas at Harrods for already shingled hair, or five guineas for long hair.

There are many theories to explain why women dressed as they did in the Twenties. Women had done men's jobs in Britain during the War, cut their hair short to work in factories and on the land; they could vote at thirty and (theoretically) become M.P.s at twenty-one. Only one, Lady Astor, had actually done so, and it almost goes without saying that she was an American.

Lady Astor arguing with a spectator, November 1923

(opposite) 'May in her Flower Garden', painted in 1929 at Thurlestone, Devon, by Edward Wolfe. 'Teddy' Wolfe, born in South Africa, first came to London in 1916. His palette shows a strong Matisse influence whose work he first saw in 1919. He was elected an R.A. in 1972, the first South African artist to be so honoured

(overleaf) 'Harper's Bazaar' cover design of 1929 – 'Nouveaux tissus, robes nouvelles', by Erté

1923

1927

1927

1927

1928

1929

59

Evening wear for 1924   **Day wear for 1924**

James Laver is one of several fashion historians who try to trace a rhythm in women's clothes and customs. After wars and plagues and other national crises, people want to dance, women wear thinner, sexier dresses, discarding anything that suggests motherhood, such as bosoms. So Mr Laver was not at all surprised to find, in the Twenties, 'no corsets, bad money and general moral laxity'. (Bad money? But the Twenties were the only period in living memory when, for Britain at any rate, the cost of living went *down*!) Another school of thought attributes the fashions of the Twenties, not to mannishness, but to a fear of emotion: there had been too much of it during the War.

Theories get us nowhere. In New York there was a theory that skirt lengths went up and down with the stock market, and that therefore the Wall Street Crash should have been easily foreseeable. Well, let us see what skirts actually did. Some time in 1920 a *New York Times* fashion writer wrote 'The American woman . . . has lifted her skirts far beyond any modest limitation.' Her skirts were, in sober fact, nine inches from the ground. A mathematician worked out a graph like this: in 1919 the hemline was 10 per cent of a woman's height from the ground; in 1920 it was 20 per cent; in 1923 back to 10 per cent; in 1924 up to 15 per cent; in 1925 over 20 per cent; in 1927, 25 per cent (and that still

Evening wear for 1927   **Day wear for 1927**

meant only to the knee). By the end of 1929 it was entirely possible to say that 'the skirt length came down with the stock prices.'

In straightforward physiological terms a British observer put it like this: 1919–23 – just above the ankles (1923 was the year of padded hips); 1924 – up to the calf; 1925 – just below the knees; 1926 – to the knees precisely (not higher). I do not quite believe this: *Punch* illustrators such as Lewis Baumer show girls with skirts well above the knee, and even I, as an observant schoolboy – well, enough of that; but you *could* see their suspenders and garters when they sat down.

In 1928 a beautiful thing happened. Skirts started lengthening *at the back*. This gave both the glamour of length and a backcloth for a good pair of legs, and the fashion was seen in the general 'back to romance' feeling of Noël Coward's revue *This Year of Grace!* and, in the following year, in the 'modern' scenes of *Bitter Sweet* in which skirts wholly covered the knees. The turning point was probably the Paris collections of 1929. At Patou's show, when he introduced longer skirts, it was reported that 'before the end of the show, the audience were already tugging at their skirts, trying to cover their knees.' Monsieur Patou was told by a member of his staff 'They are embarrassed by their skirts. Already they feel *démodé*.'

(above) **Smoking suits, 1922**
(below) **Pastel drawing of a 'Girl in Bloomers',
by Christopher Wood**

'Brevity', Dorothy Parker wrote when she was doing fashion copy on *Vogue*, 'is the soul of lingerie.' (Fashion copy, throughout the decade, remained euphemistic: 'hips' for bottom, 'figure' for breasts. And the invariable word for slim was 'svelte'.) With shorter skirts, the new tubular silhouette, the flattened bosom ('busts are *common*'), the deliberate lowering, almost the absence, of waistline, underclothes had to change. We have already seen the young throwing away anything that resembled a corset. Now came the camisole to banish the petticoat and flatten the breast, camiknickers (drawers plus chemise) in Jap silk and *crêpe de Chine* (usually pink), a strange 1927 hybrid called camibockers, and unnecessary garters purely to excite men. Ursula Jeans is believed to have been the first British actress to appear on the stage in camiknickers (in Miles Malleson's *The Fanatics*, 1927), beating, by a short head, Tallulah Bankhead, who did the same in Avery Hopwood's *Garden of Eden*.

The little boy look, the little girl look . . . Cecil Beaton, in *The Glass of Fashion*, has tried to describe a composite woman of 1926–7; one of those 'larger-than-life ladies who, with their short tubular dresses, cigarettes in long holders, cloche hats, bobbed hair, plucked eyebrows, bands of diamond bracelets from wrist to elbow, and earrings hanging like fuchsias'. He saw all this as 'an utter revolution in the concept of femininity . . . more than superficially related to cubism in art'. Towards the end of the decade, 'the accepted look had become as standardised as a prison uniform, and there was scarcely any difference between the styles for a child of eight, a flapper, or a woman of 18, 20 or 58 . . .'

In 1929 undies evolved a new trio: knickers, petticoat again, and brassière, a much more comfortable substitute for whalebone stays. Brassière, soon to become 'bra', was a fairly new word in 1929 (French dictionaries date it back to 1912, meaning an underbodice), for the simple reason that it had only just been invented. It accompanied the comeback of the corset, and its importance was that, for the first time in almost ten years, it recognized the existence of breasts. In England it cost 3s. 11d.

The Berlei Company, which in 1926 financed an 'anthropometric survey' classifying women into five basic figure types, may possibly dispute this; but the 'bra' seems to have been improvised by Polly Peabody of Boston, better known as Caresse

Head-dress for 1924

Tallulah Bankhead and
Robert Mawdesley in
'The Garden of Eden', 1927

Crosby, who, with her husband Harry, was a leading figure of the Paris American community and, among other selfless actions, published (at her Black Sun press) the work of Joyce, D.H. Lawrence and other controversial figures. Mrs Crosby was descended from Robert Fulton, the steamboat pioneer: 'I believe my ardour for inventing things springs from his loins. . . . I cannot say that my brassière will ever take as great a place in history as his steamboat, but I did invent it.' Before a dance, assisted by her French maid, Mrs Crosby quickly stitched together two handkerchiefs and some pink ribbon. She eventually sold the patent of what she called the Backless Brassière to the Warner Brothers Corset Co., for $15,000; and the words 'Kestos' and 'uplift' were born.

The profusion of undies, and the fact that every working girl now had more than two dresses (office and Sunday best), was largely due to the Swiss Family Dreyfus, who had developed a cellulose acetate varnish used during the war to cover aircraft fuselage and wings. Once called 'dope', it was then called 'rayon' and finally advertised as 'artificial silk', under the brand name Celanese. It looked particularly good in flesh pink and beige (beige was a colour invented by the Twenties), and caused a leg-revolution by means of sheer stockings. No more cotton, and not much wool.

There were in 1920 a few backless evening dresses, started by Teddie Gerrard in *Bric-à-Brac*; high heels (doctors said they were 'a threat to the birthrate'); flannel coats and skirts by young Norman Hartnell; jumpers (because people's aunts had made knitting their War work); a brief outburst (in 1925) of printed muslins and Batik scarves; Ciro pearls (synthetic), shown at Wembley Exhibition, where they fascinated Queen Mary; every kind of fur – especially silver fox, and even monkey-fur, pioneered by Princess Baba Faucigny-Lucinge – was worn. Russian boots, inspired by the Russian Ballet, were worn from the winter of 1924 onwards.

Through all this maze of fashion there walked, steadfastly, two consistent influences who left a permanent mark on styles until the Second World War: Coco Chanel, whose suits and dresses, free and comfortable, were designed for liberated women who played games, walked in the rain, drove cars; and Captain Edward Molyneux, who designed for Gertrude Lawrence.

(opposite) **Coco Chanel in a 'Chanel suit', 1929**

Never had so many people *talked* about fashion, and they were helped by fashion artists. These became personalities in their own right. I don't mean the art agency draughtsmen who covered the front page of the London *Daily Mail* with sketches when the sales were on at Barker's and Pontings and Arding & Hobbs, but men and women of genius such as Erté, Romain de Tirtoff, who is both artist and designer ('is' because, although his most famous work belongs to the Twenties, he is alive and well and eighty two, and there is now, indeed, an Erté revival). *Harper's Bazaar* was full of his work – fashion drawings, theatrical designs, house decorations.

(below) **'Harper's Bazaar' design of 1921, by Erté**

Erté in his Culver City studio, 1925

Bathing dresses were either two-piece (i.e. tunic and knickers down to the knees) or (for the more daring young) one-piece and skintight: you had to go to the north coast of Germany if you wanted to take your top off. In 1920 girls were still protecting their complexions with parasols. By 1930 sun-bathing was as important as sea-bathing and the very first beach pyjamas had been seen. Tight-fitting bathing caps had ousted the floppy mob caps in which women had entered the sea in the early Twenties.

What, meanwhile, were women doing to their faces? In the year 1929 someone worked it out that every American woman bought more than 1 lb. of powder and eight rouge compacts. There were 1,500 brands of face cream, and 2,500 different perfumes. There were only three basic shades of powder, and it was thought proper to use chalk-white powder if you were a blonde. In British upper-class society there was no teenage market at all, because a girl couldn't use makeup of any kind (or, for that matter, go to a party or a theatre) until she had 'come out'. Lipstick was in several shades, and you could give yourself a fashionable Cupid's bow mouth by using a different one on each lip. It is recorded of a Miss Baba d'Erlanger, in 1921, that she painted her mouth scarlet, her nails to match, and wore black under her eyes. Of Lady Lavery in middle age it was said that she wore so much make-up that you couldn't see her face at all.

Two mighty figures who hated each other took control of the cosmetics world – Mrs Tom Lewis, better known as Elizabeth Arden, and Mrs Edward Titus, better known as Helena Rubinstein. Both were eventually divorced and both married Russian princes. They never met. Perhaps the most famous

THE PLAY PICTORIAL

NO. 268

VOL. XLV

The double-breasted
dinner jacket was
introduced by
Jack Buchanan
in 'Toni',
Shaftesbury
Theatre, 1924

67

Arden product of this time was Ardena Skin Tonic, whose ingredients were said to be worth three cents, which retailed at $2·50.

Terrible new nouns were being added to the English language – 'facelift', 'facial', 'beautician'. The face-lifting movement was led by an American actress, Fanny Ward, who at sixty-plus wanted to look 'like a little girl'. Another new word was 'cosmetology', and young girls who had been trained in it could earn up to $60 (£15) a week plus tips, in an industry which was reckoned to be making $2,000 million a year.

Men, too, became fashion-conscious again. We have seen the Prince of Wales as fashion-leader, wearing a Fair Isle pullover on St Andrew's golf course. We could add Jack Buchanan, tap- and soft-shoe dancing star of many musical comedies, who introduced the double-breasted dinner jacket in a show called *Toni* at the Shaftesbury Theatre in 1924.

Most young Englishmen of any means at all could afford a tailor-made suit at £4–£8, but at the Fifty-Shilling Tailors a suit off the peg cost as little as 35s. ($10).

Suede shoes were regarded as homosexual; 'co-respondent shoes' (two-tone brown and white semi-brogues) were a bit caddish, but one knew people who wore them. Swimsuits were monotonously one-piece and navy blue, except on the Riviera and Lido, where you could wear very short trunks of any colour.

In England the top hat had disappeared from everywhere except the City (though the bowler became just as much a uniform). Soames Forsyte, strolling in Hyde Park in 1920, wore a Homburg – 'he had given up top hats – it was no use attracting attention to wealth in days like these . . . Manners, flavour, quality, all gone, engulfed in one vast, ugly, shoulder-rubbing, petrol-smelling Cheerio.'

British cabinet ministers and company directors (and, curiously, J. R. Campbell the Communist) still wore stiff butterfly collars, but lower down the hierarchy soft collars were slowly coming in, often with stitched holes for safety-pin-type gold tiepins. Plus-fours, a baggier development of the old Norfolk tweed suit, arrived about 1921, stayed for nearly twenty years, and survive today on golf courses. They were often worn with Fair Isle or college pullovers, especially at Oxford and Cambridge, where they became almost an undergraduate uniform. A few young men wore polo-neck sweaters: I can remember my mother pointing out a young man wearing one in the Popular Café (where everyone else wore ties) and saying 'That's Noël Coward'.

At school and elsewhere we wore rows of fountain-pens and Eversharp pencils in waistcoat and breast pockets. Wrist-watches, like silk handkerchiefs tucked into one's sleeve, were still rather caddish, and solid citizens had fob watches and chains, which of course meant wearing a waistcoat. You were expected to wear a hat, whether trilby, pork-pie, bowler or boater: my father, interviewing young men for the position of clerk in his insurance office, used to say 'Didn't seem to have a hat. Bit erratic, I thought.'

The typical male hairstyle was slicked-back with centre parting (the Bix Beiderbecke look). There were various moustaches, preferably the Ronald Colman fringe, and in simulation of Rudolph Valentino some young men sported sidewhiskers (this branded them, for their elders, as 'lounge lizards'), but only artists and very old men wore beards. Lytton Strachey must have been persecuted by small boys shouting 'Beaver!' after him in the street; they also shouted 'Bolshy!' after any man wearing anything brightly coloured. Matching tie and breastpocket handkerchief were O.K., but matching socks as well were too much. The Prince of Wales in 1929 had a double-breasted chalk-stripe flannel suit, with exceptionally wide reveres. This seems to have been *against* the late-1920s trend of single-breasted jackets worn with double-breasted waistcoats. Trouser creases tended to be knife-edged, and most fashionable young men had trouser-presses. You were expected to have a suit of tails as well as a dinner jacket, because a dinner jacket was too informal for most evening wear. Dinner jackets were sometimes double-breasted. With tails you wore a top hat, or a gibus which you could fold like a concertina and sit on instead of leaving it at the cloakroom, and gloves. It was bad form to offer cigarettes from a packet; correct to have a gold, or at least silver, cigarette case, often (*vide* Bulldog Drummond) Turkish on one side, Virginia on the other. If you had no Turks, you said 'I'm afraid they're only gaspers.'

Underclothes changed gradually in Britain,

under American influence: long underpants began to disappear, but many people, male and female, still wore combinations, known as 'coms'. The Men's Dress Reform Society, founded by the gynaecologist Norman Haire, the actor Miles Malleson and the psychologist Professor Flugel, tried to persuade everyone to wear open necks, knickerbockers and sandals. This made some headway among vegetarians but nowhere else.

Nobody, for many years, reformed the clothes of small middle-class children, who wore felt hats, kept on with elastic which cut you under the chin, and tight, pinching leather gaiters that had to be buttoned up with a button-hook (zips had not yet been invented). You can see them in Ernest Shepard's illustrations of Christopher Robin.

We have left till last the most outrageous of all male fashions of the Twenties: Oxford bags. Cecil Beaton was wearing them in Cambridge as early as 1922 (with 'fur gauntlet gloves, a cloth of gold tie, and scarlet jersey'), but it is reasonable to pinpoint 1925 as the year in which they reached ordinary mortals, in a width never seen before or since. They were generally light grey, but occasionally beige; and so wide that they flopped about like sacks, trailed in the mud and only the tip of the shoe was visible.

When, in 1932, I went up to Oxford, there were still one or two people wearing them, and among my first impressions of university life was one of a youth in Oxford bags, alone in the middle of Peckwater Quad, operating a yoyo. I knew then that this was the life for me.

Two-tone shoes

CHAPTER 6

A Dream of Fair Women

'We believed in Dream Girls' said Sam Behrman, in *Tribulations and Laughter*. 'It was a more guileless time.' Amid all the instant sex and apparent permissiveness girls were still put on pedestals, from which they frequently descended to become play-mates. (When we come to the songs of the decade, we shall see.) The Dream Girl who inspired Mr Behrman's observation was the unknown physio-therapist – a sort of Yankee Joan Hunter Dunn – whom George Gershwin never married. What was she like? Boyish, as Michael Arlen and other English novelists often made their heroines (frank, fearless, straight, true, green hats 'bravely worn', kissing and not telling)? How can you know, with other people's Dream Girls? The schizophrenia of the male mind was never better illustrated than in George F. Babbitt's Fairy Girl, who in his slumbers assumed the likeness of his friends' wives but never his own.

In England the 'English Rose' still grew, and, thanks to Coty and Chanel, smelled even sweeter. She was typified by Gladys Cooper, 1923's Peter Pan, often to be seen playing tennis at exclusive Frinton-on-Sea, Essex, and equally at home in London and New York. Like Lily Elsie, Gladys Cooper had an illusory unsophistication: men wanted to protect her, just as they wanted to protect Michael Arlen's heroine Lily Christine (because she was so short-sighted, which made nonsense of Dorothy Parker's couplet: protectiveness and pass-making were never far apart). You could say much the same of the Gish sisters, especially Lillian, who in *Broken Blossoms* made audiences almost faint with sadistic delight when she cried 'Please don't whip me, Daddy!' In the early Twenties an actress was first a beauty, and second an actress. It was probably Gertrude Lawrence and Edith Evans who broke this tradition, for neither could really be called beautiful.

More and more, due largely to theatre and movies,

Lillian Gish by Cecil Beaton

the beauties of the Twenties became international; the rose could be black and nobody minded. Anybody who had been to Paris or read magazines knew who Josephine Baker was and the fact that she appeared nude (chaps at school used to bring her to us in smuggled copies of *La Vie Parisienne*). Florence Mills, star of several Negro revues, who hit New York in *Dixie to Broadway* (1925), overwhelmed London in *Blackbirds* (1927) and launched 'I Can't Give You Anything But Love' on an endless journey.

Silent movies, assisted by publicity, created a breed of women called Vamps. Sometimes they were whores with hearts of gold; sometimes they had no hearts at all. They indicated passion with their bosoms, which went up and down like engines: nice girls, of course, didn't have bosoms, nor were they plastered with makeup like Theda Bara, Pola Negri, and (in her early days) Myrna Loy. Clara Bow, the redheaded 'It' Girl, 'collegiate flapper of the Jazz Age', is sometimes classified among the Vamps, but to me she is simply the rather fast girl next door who would say things like 'Hold me tight when we dance' and leave the rest to you. The 'It', I need hardly remind you, was invented by Elinor Glyn, author of *Three Weeks* and other sinful books, who also had red hair. 'Feast your weary optics upon this superflapper of them all,' cried *Vanity Fair*. 'In one person . . . we have the *genus* American girl, refined, washed, manicured, pedicured, permanent-waved and exalted.' A year after her screen debut Miss Bow saw fit to write her autobiography, thus outdoing even Beverley Nichols. It opened with the flat statement 'My father is the only person I care for, really.'

The year was 1927, and curves were coming back. Clara Bow was nothing if not curvy. So, eventually, were Charles B. Cochran's Young Ladies. Already, in Noël Coward's *This Year of Grace!*, they had worn long skirts for a number called 'Teach Me To Dance Like Grandma'; and Anna Neagle (who as Marjorie Robertson was one of them) has recorded that for his next revue, *Wake Up and Dream* (1929), Cochran actually forced his chorus to eat a fattening lunch to give them curves.

American actresses invaded London as never before. Was Teddie Gerrard really a beauty? Come to that, was she really an American? She appears to have been born in Argentina, and to have been launched by Wilson Mizner, playwright and Florida tycoon, and other opium-smokers, who used her, between rehearsals, to prepare the dope. She soared to fame on Broadway, and came to London, where she behaved badly in night clubs but woke up the town with that famous backless dress and a song to go with it, 'We're Glad to See You're Back'. In Paris she became La Belle Theodora and, we are told, accumulated as lovers 'a Russian grand duke, a Hungarian prince, a couple of titled Britishers, a New York real-estate baron, and the heir to one of America's large fortunes'.

There had never before been an actress (or, for all I know, anyone) called Tallulah. It couldn't fail, because hardly anybody remembered her surname, or if they did, it only confused them. Senator Bankhead, interviewed about his daughter's generally outrageous behaviour, was wont to say 'She has high spirits, but there's no harm in that.' Women liked her better than men did: men were rather scared of her. Hannen Swaffer, drama critic of the London *Daily Herald*, said 'London would be very dull without Tallulah, now that Mrs Meyrick is in jail.' Even in the famous drunk scene in *Fallen Angels* Tallulah was beautiful.

It was a two-way traffic: Britain sent to Broadway Gertrude Lawrence, Edna Best and Evelyn Laye. Hollywood sent Mary Pickford, the World's Sweetheart, everywhere, along with Norma and Constance Talmadge, and those forgotten pin-ups, Elsie Ferguson and Madge Kennedy. If I may indulge my own Child's Eye View again, at the age of twelve I would say that my idea of a beautiful woman was somewhere between Gloria Swanson (who became the Marquise de la Falaise de la Coudray) and Dolores del Rio; but all this somersaulted when I first saw Edythe Baker, a very refined blonde with a fashionable rosebud mouth. She was in Cochran's revue *One Dam' Thing After Another* at the London Pavilion, and she played the piano, in a nice, amateurish sweet-jazz way with triplets of fourths and big rolled tenths in the bass – the style that Carroll Gibbons afterwards turned into an art; and she made a famous record of Jessie Matthews's song 'My Heart Stood Still' (Rodgers and Hart) with 'The Birth of the Blues' on the flip side. Edythe Baker was almost a one-show star, for very soon afterwards she married a banker named d'Erlanger and was thenceforth seen only in the pages of *The Tatler*.

71

I like them fluffy, I freely confess,
With fluffy blue eyes and a fluffy blue dress,
And fluffy fair hair, and no brains at all . . .

The inferiority complex generated by blondes led many brunettes to bleach their hair.

Most of the ladies we have mentioned were on the right side of thirty. What, then, are we to make of Texas Guinan, who ran a New York nightclub, charged $30 for champagne that wasn't, and greeted guests with 'Hallo, sucker!' No wonder the columnist Heywood Broun called the Twenties 'Tex and the Coolidge Gold Rush'. She had a big mouth full of teeth, and every night from eleven till seven she sat on the top of a piano as entertainer and Master of Ceremonies rolled into one. Mary Louise Cecilia Guinan was thirty-one when the decade started. She went to early mass every Sunday, and six of her uncles were priests. 'She has been the subject of many sermons throughout the country,' *The New Yorker* noted without comment.

Topping girls, ripping girls – and Blondes. The Twenties had this thing about blondes. 'Blondes for weekends, brunettes for keeps', ran the saying. It wasn't all Anita Loos's fault. Gentlemen preferred them; Marlene Dietrich, whose *Blue Angel* was seen in Berlin in 1929, sang that one should Beware of them, proving it by taking off her panties as she ascended a backstage staircase and dropping them on Emil Jannings's head; and *Punch*'s A. P. Herbert wrote:

In London Society beauty was becoming organized into an industry, helped by the unashamed use of press-agentry. 'The most beautiful woman of the century' was of course Lady Diana Cooper, who played both Madonna and Nun in *The Miracle*, first in New York and then at the 1925 Salzburg Festival. She was not much noticed at her coming out, and was not considered a raving beauty until several years later. By 1926 she regarded her own beauty as finished: looking into her mirror after a

(above left) Edythe Baker in 'One Dam' Thing After Another'

(left) Marlene Dietrich in 'The Blue Angel'

bad dose of influenza, she said to herself 'That's over. Now it's nap on personality.' She was believed to sleep in black sheets, which was unusual and therefore decadent. Cecil Beaton, photographing her in Venice in 1928, says 'Her face was a perfect oval, her skin white marble. Her lips were japonica red, her hair flaxen, her eyes blue love-in-the-mist.' Another eye-witness, however, says her hair was pale gold and her eyes 'thrush blue'. She had a meditative trick of picking her nose.

But white skin was on the wane. From Mediterranean beaches, sun tan was coming in. Mark well the Spanish Duchess of Penaranda, deeply sunburnt, all in white, teeth, dress, pearls. Lady Plunket, who was rumoured to paint her skin with diluted iodine, kept her 'sun tan' all through the winter. There was talk of ultra-violet rays, based on a clinic in Switzerland run by a Dr Auguste Rollier, and people who had visted the north coast of Germany had noticed a good deal of *Nacktkultur*. Zelda Fitzgerald's sunburn was for real, from the age of sixteen onwards. Was she a beauty? She was 'the American girl living the American dream, and she became mad with it'. She was a Southern belle who used mascara at the age of fifteen. 'High in a white palace,' wrote Scott in *The Great Gatsby*, 'the king's daughter, the golden girl.' At school she was voted the Prettiest and Most Attractive Girl in her class. Yet Rebecca West found her 'very plain'.

The Marchioness of Londonderry, greatest of political hostesses; Lady Lavery, who modelled, in shawl and Irish harp, for the first Irish Free State banknotes in 1926; Viscountess Wimborne; the Duchess of Buccleuch who, as Countess of Dalkeith, had been voted the prettiest bride of 1921; Lady Louis Mountbatten and her sister Mary Ashley; Lady Ribblesdale, formerly Mrs J. J. Astor, most beautiful of the American hostesses on the London scene – these were the great ladies of the Twenties.

The technique of launching débutantes for the London Season was getting more elaborate and more expensive. With the presentation dress, other clothes for the season, a ball in a private house (*not* a hotel in those days) for 300 people, and miscellaneous expenses, bringing out one's daughter cost about £750. You were expected to start being a Dream Girl as soon as you left school. There were so many débutantes after the war that, to invite them all to one function, they had to be divided alphabetically

People Ashore at Cowes, 1926. Lady Louis Mountbatten and Lady Loughborough are seated next in front, the Hon. Mrs Lionel Tennyson behind and Miss Poppy Baring and Mrs Ronald Aird in the 'dickey'

(A–K, L–Z) and asked on two separate nights. Out of these, Fleet Street selected two or three who were likely to be news all through the Season, and of whom one was elected *Débutante of the Year* and became a national figure. Paula Gellibrand, who came out in 1919, was probably the first deb so ballyhooed. She lunched at the Ritz 'in a hat trimmed with wisteria', which was apparently enough for a gossip paragraph then. She was one of the first

Paula Gellibrand by Cecil Beaton

The Dolly Sisters

Adèle and Fred Astaire

'June'

debs who ever earned their living – as a mannequin. She was interviewed even more than the Archbishop of Canterbury. Her beauty, like Diana Cooper's, was still and spiritual and ladylike. She married the Marquis de Casa Maury. Most debs' weddings took place at St Margaret's, Westminster, where, for the marriage of Cecil Beaton's sister Nancy to Sir Hugh Smiley, hundreds of doves were released.

I have striven to prevent this chapter from becoming a catalogue, but I now capitulate. Henceforth let us be miscellaneous. The Dolly Sisters, for example, seem to have fascinated a large number of men, most of them millionaires. New York first saw them in 1924, but they had been around Europe for some time. Their real names were Jenny and Rosie Deutsch, and they were Hungarian. London first saw their famous black hair and fringes in Charles B. Cochran's revue *The League of Notions* (1921). Gordon Selfridge, the store proprietor, was in love with Jenny, whom he first saw in the Kit-Cat Club cabaret: it is said that he spent two million pounds on her, including the £40,000 which she lost in a single night at Deauville Casino.

June Howard Tripp became professionally and romantically known as 'June', star of musical comedy, and married Lord Inverclyde. Queen Marie of Roumania. Billie Burke, Mrs Flo Ziegfeld, for criticizing whom Dorothy Parker was fired from *Vanity Fair*, looked like a tiny doll and lived on to twittery, bird-brained comedy parts. Mistinguett, whom soldiers who had been on leave in Paris could remember, already fiftyish but indestructible: New York saw her in a Shubert revue in 1923, but for most of her life she was faithful to the Folies Bergère. Yvonne Printemps, one of the several Madame Guitrys, who made her New York debut in *Mozart*: she of the seductively nasal soprano. Adele Astaire, doing Oom-pah Trot with brother Fred in *Stop Flirting*, 1923: it was much the same show as *For Goodness Sake*, seen in New York the year before.

Was Isadora Duncan truly a beauty? She was photographed by Steichen on the steps of the Parthenon in a classical pose. She had tempestuous love affairs all over the place, and she was strangled by her own scarf while driving to see her newest young lover, a garage mechanic at Antibes, in September 1927. Nancy Cunard, the 'boy' figure of Michael Arlen's imagination – is it beauty or vitality in that face? (It was her back, 'like a weasel's', that excited

(opposite) 'The Black Venus', 1928, by Jean Gabriel Domergue. In 1929 or 1930 Josephine Baker, 'the Venus of Ebano' as she was then called, came to Buenos Aires to make her local début at the Astral Theatre. Charles Vibán was acting in her shows as a 'présentateur'. The friendship began there, and Josephine Baker gave Vibán this portrait of herself. Vibán died in Buenos Aires in June, 1971

Nancy Cunard, by Ambrose McEvoy

(left) Nancy Cunard by Cecil Beaton
(below) Marion Davies by Cecil Beaton
(bottom) Brigitte Helm as the female robot
in the film 'Metropolis', 1926

George Moore when she stripped for him.) Cecil
Beaton's sisters; the Paget twins; José Collins, star of
The Maid of the Mountains, who loved to eat tripe and
onions before a matinee, and became Lady Innes-
Kerr. Brenda Dean-Paul, who became a drug-
addict. Marjorie Oelrichs, who shocked New York
society by appearing in an advertisement for Lucky
Strike cigarettes. Marion Davies, W.R. Hearst's
girlfriend and photographer's favourite, whose
strangely empty face always looked so lifeless.
Colleen Moore, whose face invariably suggested the
word 'cute' . . .

In Germany there was Brigitte Helm, who in 1926
played a female robot in Fritz Lang's *Metropolis*;
in Hungary, Lya de Putti, who did erotic things
with a cigarette in D.W. Griffith's *The Sorrows of
Satan*.

Any Twenties girl who remotely resembled any
of these girls chose her model and imitated her style,
coiffure and makeup; and became either a Vamp or
a Dream Girl.

77

Woodrow Wilson

CHAPTER 7

Political Animals

'Nobody', said Scott Fitzgerald (odd how we keep coming back to him), 'was interested in politics.' In *The Crack-Up* he enlarged on this idea: 'The uncertainties of 1919 were over: there seemed little doubt about what was going to happen – America was going on the greatest, grandest spree in history . . . the whole golden boom was in the air – its splendid generosities, its outrageous corruptions and the tortuous death struggle of the old America in Prohibition.' WASP America, that is: middle and upper-class America, and Britain, that is.

On either side of the Atlantic, each in our own way, we avoided politics. To some (as it has always been to well-bred Frenchmen) it was a *sale métier*, especially once it was forced to depart from the dream of Universal Peace. Iris March declaims to Sir Maurice Harpenden towards the end of *The Green Hat*: 'To you, it seems a worthy thing for a good man to make a success in the nasty area of national strifes and international jealousies. To me, a world which thinks of itself in terms of puny, squalid, bickering little nations . . . is the highest indignity that can befall a good man, it is a world in which good men are shut up like gods in a lavatory.'

Well, now: how good a man was Woodrow Wilson? And, towards the end of his reign, Mrs Wilson? (For the *Zeitgeist* produced the Presidents, and the Presidents intensified the *Zeitgeist*.) To Europe, in 1920, Mr Wilson appeared as a sort of Nonconformist minister (like his father, who was one), waving his Fourteen Points and then disappearing, together with the United States, who seemed to have invented the League of Nations – and then

backed out of it. Beverley Nichols, visiting the States with an Oxford University debating team, saw him as a family dentist. To many Americans, for whom the fear of Bolshevism was worse than the fear of war, Wilson with his genuine concern for the underdog was a dangerous radical, a pro-German, a pacifist, an impractical high-minded academic. To the men around him, his leadership was magnetic. His international ideas failed in his lifetime, but they lived on after him, and his Nobel Peace Prize was not ironic after all.

To the Babbitts, what a relief Warren Harding must have been! 'America first.' 'Not nostrums, but normalcy'. (He was shaky in his use of words, and a victim of what Frederick Lewis Allen called 'suffix trouble'.) He was genial, Boosterish, handsome; he came from Blooming Grove, a small town in Ohio, and called people 'neighbour'. He didn't read books. He gave jobs to the boys from back home, because they were the only people he thought he could trust. He liked playing poker (and the stock market too), and despite Prohibition he made no attempt to conceal the supplies of whisky in his cupboard. His private life gave rise to rumours – girls in hotels, the famous affair with Nan Britton, the illegitimate daughter – but the whole truth did not come out until some years after his death. What did come out was the graft, and his reign is associated with the Teapot Dome scandal.

Back in 1914 President Wilson had designated an area of 9,500 acres in Wyoming as a naval oil reserve. In April 1922 Senator Kendrick of Wyoming received a telegram from the Rocky Mountain Oil and

Destroying wines
and spirits in
Boston during
Prohibition

(above) Contraband beer being tipped from barrels

(below)
Los Angeles
flushed with wine
when 33,100 gallons
were pumped
into the gutter

Gas Producers Association, alleging that one Harry F. Sinclair had been given the right to develop Naval Oil Reserve No. 3 without competitive bidding. Other irregular oil contracts were discovered, and the U.S. secret service worked on them for three years before their role became known. Not until 1929 was Albert B. Fall, Harding's secretary of the interior, convicted, together with Sinclair. Fall was found guilty of accepting a $100,000 bribe (called a 'loan') and jailed for a year and a day.

Whether Harding had any idea what was going on is not clear; at least he could be held guilty of failing to keep an eye on his Ohio friends, among them Harry Dougherty (Attorney-General), who had all betrayed him. He died suddenly of pneumonia (or was it apoplexy? – there were even rumours of suicide) in August 1923. At the beginning of his term he had said 'I cannot hope to be one of the great Presidents, but perhaps I may be remembered as one of the best loved.' At his memorial service, Bishop Manning of New York found it possible to say 'He taught us the power of brotherliness.'

He was succeeded by his Vice-President, Calvin Coolidge, a businessman's President if ever there was one, with, like Wilson, a touch of the Nonconformist minister: 'a Puritan in Babylon'. It was said of his nasal New England accent that he could make the word 'cow' have four syllables. He said memor-

Calvin Coolidge

able things like 'Work and save, save and work' (he himself managed to save out of his Presidential salary, which no other President ever did) ; 'This is a Business Government'; 'We need more religion'; 'We need more of the office desk and less of the shop window in politics'; 'If a man's out of a job, it's his own fault.'

This grim, pale, sandy-haired little man, who 'looked as if he smelt gas', ex-Governor of Massachusetts, pleased better-off people by reducing taxes. As a matter of irrelevant interest, we may record that he spent his honeymoon translating Dante's *Inferno*. He has been traduced by left-wing and 'lost generation' writers, but he was probably what America needed at the time. Unlike Harding, he had 'sound' men to help him run the country – Andrew Mellon, Herbert Hoover, Frank B. Kellogg. *He* knew whom he could trust. When the question of a third term came up, he said firmly 'I do not choose to run for President in 1928'. When Dorothy Parker (or it may have been H. L. Mencken) heard he was dead in 1933, she (or he) asked 'How could they tell?'

Unfair, of course. But this is not history: like *1066 And All That*, it is history as people remember it, and what we are seeing is the public faces recorded in press and folklore in an age of a little radio and no television.

With Herbert Hoover we are in mid-boom. Getting rich was still patriotic: the Dollar Decade was still very much on. Business was still to be independent, and 'we in America today are nearer the final triumph over poverty than ever before in the history of any land.' (The Wall Street Crash was two years away.) Eight years before his election as a Republican President there had been an attempt to make him run as a Democrat. In the 1928 Presidential election he had beaten Governor Al Smith of New York, the 'happy warrior' with his cigar and brown derby hat (he used to autograph brown derbies and give them away) who was 'wet' and Roman Catholic.

Mining engineer, wartime food administrator, war historian, Secretary of Commerce under both Harding and Coolidge, Hoover was a man who had *done* things; he had a grip on what he called the sitchee-ation. He had achieved much for Child Health, Better Homes and Mississippi Flood Relief, and his 'New Day' programme, frustrated by the Depression, was founded on the great possibilities he saw for America in the march of Science. He wrote as well as thought, and (like Coolidge) was a translator: with his wife he had done into English Georgius Agricola's *De Re Metallica*, published in Latin in 1556.

His statement of belief, *American Individualism* (1922), is worth quoting to show that for one man, at least, the Republican dream could be stated in almost Abe Lincoln terms: 'Our individualism differs from all others because it embraces these ideals: that while we build our society upon the attainment of the individual, we shall safeguard to every individual an equality of opportunity to take that position in the community to which his intelligence, character, ability and ambition entitle him; that we keep the social solution free from the frozen strata of classes; . . . while he in turn must stand up to the emery wheel of competition.'

'Nobody was interested in politics'; still less, it seemed, in foreign policy. In Britain, even Prime Minister Baldwin, when foreign affairs were being debated in the Commons, used to say to his neighbour 'Wake me up when this is finished.' But everybody knew about War Debts, and almost everybody was afraid of Bolsheviks, Anarchists, Reds, who were believed to go around with bombs in their pockets.

At the end of the War the European Allies owed the United States $10,000 million. Europe and America were of different viewpoints about this. Europe was for cancelling war debts altogether: Europe had given so much blood, and here was America exacting full payment with interest as if the whole struggle for democracy had been a business deal. Different countries negotiated their own rates of interest, and Chancellor of the Exchequer Stanley Baldwin, no horse dealer, arranged to pay Britain's $4,600 million over sixty-two years at the maximum rate, which was twice that paid by France, and eight times that paid by Italy. To certain countries America said wounding things like 'Little Finland pays – why don't you?'

'Make Germany Pay!' was a vindictive scream in Britain, and only economists such as Keynes saw anything ridiculous in fixing German Reparations at £6,600 million (plus interest). Germany paid a first instalment of £50 million promptly; but then inflation struck, and payments were suspended. In Germany the exchange rate rose from 280 marks to the dollar (70 times the pre-war rate) to 7,000 between June and December 1922, and in 1923 a rate of 60,000,000,000 marks to the pound was recorded. People hysterically bought things – diamonds, horse manure, cows, foreign currency, stocks and shares, anything to get rid of paper money. If you ordered a cup of coffee for 1,000,000 marks, you might not be able to pay for it by the time you had drunk it because the exchange rate had risen in the meantime.

Many victims of inflation turned to Nazism in their fury against the Weimar Republic. Hugh Walpole was at the Bayreuth Festival in 1924; the whole ten days cost him 3s. at the then rate of exchange. Cosima Wagner, nearly ninety and blind, was there, and Houston Stewart Chamberlain, Wagner's son-in-law and theorist of the Aryan master race, in a wheel chair. The younger Wagners supported a politician named Hitler, described by *The Times* as a 'Bavarian Royalist'; especially Siegfried Wagner's English wife, twenty-eight years his junior. Next year at Bayreuth Hugh Walpole met Adolf Hitler ('one of Winnie's lame ducks') who appeared in the Wagner box after dark: he was just out of prison and avoiding the police. 'Tears poured down his cheeks' Hugh recorded. 'I thought him fearfully ill-educated and quite tenth-rate – pathetic – I felt rather maternal to him!'

Meanwhile Coolidge had appointed General Dawes, a banker, chairman of the Allied Reparations Committee. To prevent bankruptcy and revolution, Germany was to be lent $2,475 million between 1924 and 1930. She was to pay the Allies $4,470 million, and the Allies were to repay the United States $2,606 million. General Dawes, for his labours, shared the Nobel Peace Prize with Austen Chamberlain. Round and round the reparations ran, involving Austria and Hungary too; Owen D. Young's 1929 plan by which German reparations (reduced to a quarter of the 1921 figure) would be paid over a period of fifty-eight and a half years never got off the ground; and the general financial collapse of 1931 and the advent of Hitler stopped them all.

To prevent revolution. Reds, Anarchists, Bolsheviks, Radicals, whatever they were, they were in our midst. Sacco and Vanzetti, for instance (we shall meet them in another chapter). The Reds were behind all those strikes. Bombs by post from 'Russian agents'. There were anti-Bolshevist riots, even some lynchings in the States. The Moscow Art Theatre, Balieff's *Chauve-Souris* Russian revue, Chaliapin himself, were all suspects. Charlie Chaplin and one or two other Hollywood stars were believed to be 'mentioned in Communist files'. Communists were mostly Jews, weren't they? So Jews were suspect too, and Henry Ford said they were manipulating international business. In the Southern States the Ku Klux Klan, giving themselves weird ranks such as Knight of the Invisible Empire, Imperial Wizard, King Kleagle and Grand Goblin, flogged and tarred and feathered. And who, if not Reds, wrecked the offices of the J. P. Morgan company, killing thirty people and injuring many more, in September 1920?

In Britain there was the notorious Zinoviev Letter. Britain's first Labour Government was unseated by the publication in the *Daily Mail* of a fairly obvious forgery: 'CIVIL WAR PLOT BY SOCIALISTS' MASTERS. Moscow orders to our Reds . . . and Mr Macdonald would lend Russia our money!' This document, dated September 15th 1924, purported to be addressed to A. MacManus, 'British representative of the Internationale', and was signed 'Zinoviev, Dictator of Petrograd'. The *Daily Mail*, as if this were not enough, published an ugly, Streicherish sketch of Zinoviev, claiming that he was a Jew whose real name was Apfelbaum, and that it was a plot to start an armed revolution in Britain.

There was an echo of this three years later, when the police raided the offices of Arcos, headquarters of the Soviet trade corporation in Kingsway, and opened safes with oxyacetylene drills searching for 'evidence of Russian espionage'.

In a strange way, Russia was *fashionable*. Bernard Shaw and Nancy Astor went there and were made much of. Film societies showed *The General Line* and other Russian propaganda films. 'When England goes Communist,' said Douglas Goldring, 'as usual, half the Government will be Old Etonian.'

To the British, still yearning for the good old days before 1914, anything that promised security and order was good. That fellow Mussolini, for instance – a bit thick, dosing your enemies with castor oil, but Lord Rothermere's newspapers were for him. In November 1925 a *Sunday Dispatch* leading article said 'In no country will Signor Mussolini's escape from the assassin's hand be welcomed more cordially than in Great Britain, for nowhere else, outside his native land, has the Italian leader more numerous or more ardent admirers.'

A historian, F. W. Hirst, saw the social conse-quences of war in terms of 'working class initiative sapped by obeying orders' during the War, which, however, had been 'an enriching experience'. The lack of discipline in youth could be attributed to fathers having been absent in the Army. 'Class distinctions have positively toppled down since the War. . . . A duke's daughter hoed turnips while her "social inferiors" were buying themselves fur coats out of their earnings in munition factories.' The *Punch* jokes about obstinate cooks and maids who would only do certain tasks around the house show that people really thought this: 'The new maid's a perfect treasure, but I wish she wouldn't call me "old thing"'; and (in 1926) a mistress (not yet called a housewife) asks her butler 'What is the cause of the servant problem?' 'Well, ma'am . . . you're going down and we're coming up.'

There were more than 300 millionaires in the United Kingdom, and it was reckoned that two-thirds of the national wealth belonged to $2\frac{1}{2}$ per cent of gainfully employed adults. But in 1921 there were 2,500,000 men who were not employed, and through the decade the figure was never lower than 1,100,000. If you were out of work, you drew the dole, which was 15s. a week for a family of five. Alternatively you hired a barrel-organ and played it in the street, wearing your war medals, with a chalked notice which said 'Ex-serviceman, wife and five kids to support.' If you were an unemployed Welsh miner, you walked to London or any big city and stood in the gutter singing *Cwm Rhondda*. Ex-officers, on their failing chicken farms, were not doing much better. No good taking up farming, on either side of the Atlantic. In Britain a scheme to guarantee grain prices went immediately wrong when prices catastrophically fell. Those farmers who hadn't gone bankrupt grew grass instead and went in for milk production. In America, efficiency and mechanization led to over-production.

One desperate method of drawing attention to poverty was born in the 1920s: the Hunger March. The first was in October 1922; the greatest in January 1929, when thousands of Glasgow workers gathered in Blythswood Square to give a send-off to 200 miners, shipyard, textile and fishing workers. With valises, haversacks and blankets, and a field kitchen to cook stew, they were led by a bagpipe band, marched to London, were sheltered on the way, warmed themselves with fires and hot tea at sympathetic points such as Ripon Constitutional Club, and arrived at last in Trafalgar Square, where 'Welcome To The Hunger Marchers' banners awaited them.

'People here, whether Protestant or Catholic, don't think with their brains,' said an Irish academic to a British journalist in 1920; 'they think with their solar plexus.' The Irish Republican Army, in an Ireland already partitioned, with two separate parliaments, were assassinating the Royal Irish Constabulary, who were being reinforced with ex-servicemen who became known as Black and Tans. The Southern Irish had an unrecognized republic, which almost made them Bolsheviks. The conduct of the Black and Tans worried everyone except *The Morning Post*: it seemed that Lloyd George was trying to out-terrorize the Sinn Fein terrorists. All the familiar events were there: Crown officers murdered in their beds; the seventy-four-day hunger strike which ended in the death of the Mayor of Cork, Terence MacSwiney; farms burnt in Lancashire and Cheshire; Downing Street barricaded. President de Valera, after a money-raising tour of America, returned in time for the Anglo-Irish Treaty, which gave him the Irish Free State with dominion status which he didn't want.

The 'troubles' entered their internal phase, and there was one further assassination on English soil – that of Field-Marshal Sir Henry Wilson, born in Southern Ireland, who had resigned from the Army, of which he had been Chief of Imperial General Staff, to become M.P. for North Down in Ulster, and Chief Military Adviser to the Northern Ireland Government. 'Ugly', as his troops called him, was shot dead by two Irish ex-soldiers, one a clerk in the Ministry of Labour, and both born in London, not Ireland. They were hanged in Wandsworth Prison. Why was 'Ugly' murdered? We do not know for certain, but it may have been a reprisal for the execution of a Republican in Belfast.

In an age before television, and with radio only just beginning, politicians appeared more than life size (in that few of their weaknesses were known) and yet less than life size (in that we had only newspaper articles and static photographs to go on). Lloyd George, the 'man who won the War', was losing Conservative support in coalitions and, far worse,

the support of his own party. A few colleagues (not friends – he had no intimate friends, and only Churchill used his Christian name) knew about Frances Stevenson. The middle class never quite trusted the man who had laid the foundations of the Welfare State. This man of genius was destined to put forth ideas from the Opposition, but never to rule again. And there were hints of scandal, which reminded some people of his share dealings during the Marconi Scandal of 1912: now it was the sale of honours, through a man named Maundy Gregory; and who was this man Zaharoff, an armaments dealer, who had been seen far too often around Downing Street?

Andrew Bonar Law, Prime Minister till 1923, born in New Brunswick yet regarded as a Scot, leader of the House who had lost two sons in the War – what a vague figure he now appears! Yet there were those who said 'He would have been the greatest Prime Minister we've ever had.' Lord Curzon, who had been Governor-General of India, a member of the War Cabinet, and then (till 1924) Foreign Secretary – and a very good Foreign Secretary, too, condemning as illegal the French occupation of the Ruhr to exact reparation payments – suffered, towards the end of his life, two big disappointments: it was Stanley Baldwin who got the Premiership in 1923, not himself (the news reached him at Montacute House, Somerset, by letter, because Montacute was not yet on the telephone); and Austen Chamberlain who in 1924 ousted him as Foreign Secretary.

Curzon married, for his second wife, an American lady, Grace Elvira Duggan, widow, and daughter of the U.S. consul in Rio de Janeiro; and his daughter married Oswald Mosley. Too bad that poor Curzon survives in our folklore for five stories: that, seeing some soldiers bathing, he remarked that he had no idea that 'the lower orders had such white skins'; that he was the subject of an irreverent verse which rhymed his name with 'a most superior person'; that he was habitually rude to his social inferiors, so that when Labour and Ramsay Mac-Donald came to power in 1924, senior Foreign Office people were heard to say 'What a comfort it is to have to deal again with a gentleman!'; that he kept one room at Kedleston, his stately home in Derbyshire, as an exact replica of his study at Eton; and that – an episode perhaps surprisingly well documented – he had as his one-time mistress Elinor Glyn, author of *Three Weeks* and heroine of certain alleged escapades on tiger-skin rugs, whose philosophy, Chips Channon tells us, was 'To live! To love! And to write! And to read the Bible!'

Baldwin? How much of his public face was a public relations campaign, carried out by himself? The cherrywood pipe. The shrewd industrialist who dressed like a farmer. His wife's terrible hats. His apparent motto 'When in doubt, do nothing.' His love of England, which meant the England of before 1914; his desire to 'read, live decently, and keep pigs'; in particular, to read the bucolic novels of Mary Webb, whose sales he quadrupled overnight by recommending them. It was said, as it was said of Henry Ford, that he had 'anonymously' given £125,000 to the Treasury, because this was the total dividend on his armaments investments during the War. Stanley Baldwin, most indolent of prime ministers, was the symbol of 'Safety First', and that was what most people wanted. If Baldwin had never achieved anything else, he would have gone down to posterity for his handling of the General Strike, as we shall see a few pages later. He was summed up thus by Harry Boardman, Lobby Correspondent of the *Manchester Guardian*: 'Crouching forward on the Treasury bench, elbows on knees, his stubby fingertips being severally and ruminatively examined by their owner with a look more perplexed than admiring . . . He got the Tory party to pass Liberal measures entirely repugnant to its ideas. He has never said a wounding word of an opponent.'

Winston Churchill, then a Liberal, was, as always in peacetime, not fully stretched, not quite trusted. He had got the Navy ready in good time for war, but the Dardanelles enterprise had gone wrong, and he had served in France briefly as Commanding Officer of the 6th Royal Scottish Fusiliers before being recalled by Lloyd George to office as both War and Air Minister. In the general election of 1922 he had lost his seat at Dundee to, of all people, a teetotaller named Edwin Scrimgeour, who, incredibly, was able to win an election in the land of Scotch whisky by his slogan 'Don't worry about Bolsheviks – worry about the pubs.' Hearing the result, the Manchester Stock Exchange sent Churchill a telegram: 'What's the use of a W.C. without a seat?'

Ramsay Macdonald (centre)

In 1924, calling himself a Constitutionalist, he was returned to Parliament as M.P. for Epping. Baldwin made him Chancellor of the Exchequer. There was an idea at the time that London must once again become the world's greatest financial centre, and that the way to do this was to return to the gold standard. Churchill did this, and also pleased a great many people by knocking 6d. off income tax. At a time when cigarettes were 10 for 6d., whisky was 12s. 6d. a bottle, and one could buy a bicycle for 30s., this really meant something. He had also begun to write *The World Crisis*, completed in 1929, which was to earn him enough money to buy Chartwell, his country house in Kent. 'Brilliant but erratic' was how most people summed him up. He played a short, sharp part in the General Strike of 1926, visited Cairo and Athens, talked to Mussolini, and returned to Chartwell to paint,

David Lloyd George, 1927, by Sir William Orpen

write, and lay bricks. It was not thought that he would ever dominate the nation's destiny.

How can we today imagine what Britain felt when faced with its first Labour Government? Livid fear – a capital levy – abolition of monarchy – Russian invasion – anything seemed possible. Of course, the Socialists had only got in by the back door, people said – because the Liberals had joined them against the Tories. King George V, to his surprise, found his new Prime Minister, Ramsay MacDonald, to be a gentleman, dropping no 'h's or 'g's, in spite of his being illegitimate. The man was completely at his ease, more so than any of his followers: he loved the aristocracy, he was happy in evening dress. He had a Rolls-Royce given to him by a director of McVitie & Price, the biscuit people, together with 30,000 £1 shares in the company. King George liked him.

Almost at once the topic of dress came up: everyone was wondering what the new Labour ministers would wear at the levees they would surely have to attend. Could they afford court dress even if they were willing to wear it? King George consulted his private secretary Lord Stamfordham, who consulted the Court Tailor, who advised that the full cost of levee dress would be £72. 2s. 6d. Lord Stamfordham thereupon wrote thus to the Government Chief Whip: 'I have ascertained from Messrs. Moss Bros., 20, King Street, W.C.2., which is I believe a well-known and dependable firm, that they have in stock a few suits of Household, Second Class, Levee Dress from £30 complete. This comprises trousers, coat, cock-hat and sword, and is the regulation dress.'

Labour came back again in 1929, and this time there were no real fears. The King's favourite Socialist was probably, by now, old George Lansbury, a Christian pacifist from the East End who had once edited the *Daily Herald*. They had interminable talks about their operations. The implacable enemy of Labour was a thrice-widowed multi-millionairess named Lady Houston, who set up on her yacht an electric sign which said 'To Hell with Ramsay MacDonald.'

Everything would be all right in the long run, even unemployment. What really mattered was the League of Nations. Of course, a store of arms had been found buried under a chapel at Gleiwitz, which must mean something. Of course, it was difficult, having neither America nor Russia in the League, and from New York and Washington it did rather look like an exclusively European institution, dominated by Britain and France. There were some splendid high-minded people behind it such as Lord Cecil and Professor Gilbert Murray. In some ways, the League's child, the International Labour Organization, seemed more effective: it included Germany, and it was directed by a man of vision, Albert Thomas. Could it not be said that the Locarno Pact of 1925, between Germany, Italy, France, Poland, Czechoslovakia and the United Kingdom, was the spirit of the League in action? It was hailed as 'the final peace settlement'. Stresemann had established the principle of German equality. Briand, for France, said 'We are Europeans. Away with rifles, machine guns, cannon.' There were thanksgiving services everywhere.

This was especially encouraging, because the League had taken a beating almost at its birth, when, in 1920, the Turks tried to win back Smyrna from the Greeks, and succeeded after two years of atrocities on both sides. (A Turkish mob tore out the beard of a Greek Metropolitan Chrysostomos, gouged out his eyes, and cut off his ears, nose and hands before killing him.) It has been said that the war was the work of Sir Basil Zaharoff, chief armaments salesman of Vickers, a Turk by birth, who was famous for his philanthropy towards the Great Ormond Street Children's Hospital. Asia Minor was a great deal further away than it is now, and the average newspaper reader took little notice of it: it was possible for a comedian named Milton Hayes, who recited monologues called 'The Meanderings of Monty', to make jokes about Turkish delight and 'even a Smyrn will turn'.

In 1928, the spirit of the League became greater than the League itself when fifteen countries met in Paris, to 'renounce war as an instrument of national policy in their relations with one another'. This was the outcome of negotiations between Aristide Briand (for France) and Frank B. Kellogg (for America). Any other country could join if it felt like it. There was a little embarrassment about asking Russia, but she too signed eventually.

In America and Britain there were new political animals, and they were female. On August 26th 1920 Secretary of State Bainbridge Colby had announced that 'the right of citizens of the United States to vote shall not be denied or abridged by the United States or by any State on account of sex.' The Nineteenth Amendment was in business, women were able to use their vote for the first time, in the Presidential Election of 1920 – and what they got was Warren Gamaliel Harding. Two years before, the principle of equal suffrage with men had been established in fifteen States, and this had been brought about by voters themselves wishing to give women the franchise – the only instance of this in the world.

Note the difference of speed and national behaviour between America and Britain. The sufferings of the Pankhursts and Emily Davidson (who threw herself under a horse at the 1913 Derby), the awful hunger strikes and forced feeding, were not what gave women the vote in Britain. It was the fact that they had done men's jobs during the War. But the British did not go nap like America: in 1918 they gave the vote to married women, women householders and women university graduates of thirty and over. Soon afterwards, someone realized that if women were given the vote, they would want to send women to Parliament, so that was made legal too.

Women were making news all through the Twenties. Helena Normanton, one of the first nine women barristers, had defeated Lord Birkenhead, the Lord Chancellor, who had once refused her petition to admit women to the Bar. She was not the first: Ivy Williams, an Oxford lecturer, had been called to the Bar in May 1922. Women, we have seen, were flying all over the globe, and swimming the Channel; they were also exploring lands where Anglo-Saxon women had never been before, and of these the most vocal was Rosita Forbes, who was riding camels, making films such as *From Red Sea to Blue Nile* (1925), and even trying to get to Mecca. In 1921, for the first time, women entered the Higher Civil Service. Yet – a *non sequitur*, of course – there was still, in 1927, a regulation at Lady Margaret Hall, Oxford, that a woman student could not go for a bicycle ride with a man, unless there were two other women in the party, and even so permission had to be obtained from the Principal beforehand.

We said some hard things, in an earlier chapter, about Sir William Joynson-Hicks. In 1928 he did something rather good, and he appears to have done it by accident. In the middle of a Commons debate about something else, he said something about the Conservatives planning to give the vote to all women of twenty-one and over. It looked like an election promise, and before long it was. The Equal Franchise Bill 1928 was passed on the day of Emmeline Pankhurst's funeral. So the Flapper Vote came into being (a flapper is solemnly defined in the *Oxford English Dictionary* as 'a young girl who has not yet "put her hair up"; sometimes with an implication of flightiness or lack of decorum'). So that when Britain's second Labour Government was returned in 1929, with the first woman Cabinet Minister and Privy Councillor, Margaret Bondfield, it was easy to blame the flappers, who had added 5,000,000 voters to the electorate. Hearing this good news before she heard its results, Lady Astor cried 'You may fool the men, but you can't fool the women.'

Nancy Witcher Astor was Britain's first woman M.P., elected for the Sutton division of Plymouth in 1919, a seat held by her husband Waldorf until he went to the House of Lords. It was a fairly Twenties-ish thing that she should be an American (she was one of the famous Langhorne sisters of Virginia), although she was almost pipped by Countess Markiewicz, elected by a Dublin constituency in 1918, who could not take her seat because she was a member of Sinn Fein and therefore a Republican. Nancy was a good M.P., although she occasionally drove the House up the wall with her filibustering and her obsessions. She was a teetotaller, nay more, a prohibitionist, and this was because her first husband, Robert Shaw, had been a drunk. Her second husband entirely disagreed with her: 'I should not have my excellent health today,' he said, 'had I not used stimulants freely all my life.' He died first, of course; but then, men usually do. Nancy was also a Christian Scientist.

She didn't think much of men: 'They are the nicer sex, but not the stronger.' She opposed a bill for easier divorce, because she thought it would make things easier for *men*: 'We are not asking for superiority, for we have always had that. All we ask is equality.'

Many and fearful are the stories of her electioneering repartee: 'You have enough brass to make a kettle' shouted a heckler. Riposted Nancy, 'You have enough water in your head to fill it.' 'How many toes are there on a pig's foot?' asked a farmer, trying to fault her knowledge of farming. 'Take off your shoe, man, and count for yourself!' Nancy replied. Only Winston Churchill seemed able to silence her. 'If I were your wife,' said Nancy, 'I'd put poison in your coffee!' 'If I were your husband,' roared Churchill, 'I'd drink it.'

When Lord Northcliffe died in 1922 J.J. Astor V outbid Lord Rothermere's £1 million offer and acquired *The Times*. The Astors already owned *The Observer*. So that, with Nancy's incessant entertaining at Cliveden, her forty-six-bedroom stately home on the Thames near Cookham, the power of the Astors was formidable indeed. Nancy and her friends were not yet known as the 'Cliveden Set', a term with sinister overtones invented by Claud Cockburn in the late Thirties. In the Twenties she had so many guests that her butler rebelled against allowing each guest only 1 ft. 6in. space at table, pointing out that at Buckingham Palace 2ft 6in. would have been allowed.

Nancy seldom read books, but she loved authors, and Barrie and Kipling, both shy men, would spend petrifying weekends at Cliveden. For Bernard Shaw she felt a special warmth, marred only by a fear of scandal lest anyone should think that her son Robert (by her first husband, whose name was also Shaw) was the illegitimate issue of her entirely innocent relationship with G.B.S. Another Shaw, T.E., 'Lawrence of Arabia', might occasionally be seen at Cliveden (Nancy used to go for rides on the pillion of his motorcycle); and you might even find yourself sitting next to Mahatma Gandhi. Guests were often required to play charades, an innocuous Twenties pastime practised also by both the Algonquin and the Bloomsbury sets; and one had to be prepared for certain eccentric practical jokes, such as Nancy's celluloid false teeth which she would suddenly put into her mouth in the middle of a conversation. Visiting her sons at Eton, she would cause fearful embarrassment by asking boys she did not know 'Have you cleaned your teeth today?'

The League, Locarno, the Kellogg Pact, the war that had made the world safe for democracy but had not yet created a land fit for heroes to live in – optimism was abroad, even more than at home. But the war that people really feared was class war. We have seen the Zinoviev letter, seen how jumpy America was about anarchists, Bolshevists, anything that threatened to upset, or even to alter, the established order. Reporting the Scopes trial for the *Baltimore Sun*, H.L. Mencken said 'To mention the Bill of Rights is to be damned as a Red.' As a grammar-school boy in the Twenties I remember seeing the only boy in the form whose father had voted Labour surrounded by a jeering mob who stamped on his cap and kicked it over a wall. When strikes in Britain escalated into a complete stoppage, it was easy – in 1926 – to imagine that revolution, possibly bloody, was at hand. Catholics were immediately told what line to take by Cardinal Bourne, who said that the General Strike was 'a sin against God'.

There were in Britain, in 1926, 5,000,000 members of Trade Unions out of a wage-earning population of 15,000,000: of these, 3,000,000 were involved in the General Strike. (So how general *was* the Strike?) The Strike, for which the Government was well prepared with troops, special constables and the Emergency Powers Act (1920), wasn't even deliberately planned. It seemed that the Trade Unions hoped to win by *frightening* the Government. The Government, although Prime Minister Baldwin's heart bled for the starving families of the miners, was never less frightened in its life.

The miners' case, stated by their leader A.J. Cook, Secretary of the Miners' Federation, and put on to a Pathé gramophone record, was this: 'We ask for safety and economic security. . . . Until (the miner) is given safety in the mines, adequate compensation, hours of labour that do not make him a mere coal-getting medium, and decent living conditions, there can be no peace in the British coalfields.' He was saying this at a time when German and Polish mines were undercutting our prices, and British miners were being asked to accept wage cuts to meet this competition. He was saying it to Lord Londonderry, one of the biggest coal-owners and husband of the most famous political hostess. Unfortunately Cook had also described himself as 'a humble follower of Lenin', which closed all middle and upper-class ears against him.

The miners were joined by the railwaymen, led by J.H. Thomas, and the transport workers, led by J.R. Clynes, including road transport; over all loomed the mighty figure of Ernest Bevin; then iron, steel, building, engineering and finally printing

(top) A bus in London carrying on with volunteer labour
(above) Mounted police armed with batons clearing the road after a riotous outbreak at the Elephant and Castle, London, during the General Strike

machinery, but by the beautiful hands of a voluntary helper named Lady Diana Cooper), described how supplies of milk and fish, brought into King's Cross, Euston and Paddington stations, were successfully distributed from an improvised food depot in Hyde Park. To enter Hyde Park, you had to have a pass signed by the President of the Board of Trade, even if you were Lady Louis Mountbatten, who was photographed for the one-page *Daily Mirror* carrying buckets about, in between 'Uncle Dick's Letter' for children and the adventures of Pip, Squeak and Wilfred, a comic strip which we shall examine in more detail in a later chapter. *The Times* of May 6th found space to cover the Stock Exchange: 'Calm Markets: General Decline in Prices' – but speculative shares such as gold mines were 'steady'. On May 7th *The Times* managed to produce a four-page paper praising the City's spirit and encouraging junior staff to volunteer for the Special Constabulary and other duties in 'the national emergency'.

Winston Churchill emerged as editor of the *British Gazette*, a truculent Government newspaper with a circulation of 2,000,000 printed by Viscount Hambledon, head of W. H. Smith's bookstalls, with the assistance of the true-blue *Morning Post* staff, and distributed by volunteer 'Bentley boys' in their sports cars. The *Gazette* never wavered from Sir John Simon's pronouncement that the General Strike was illegal. (Under an Act of William the Conqueror, some said; it was not a true trade dispute, but merely an attempt 'to make the public and Parliament and the Government do something'. *Was* it illegal? The point has never been resolved.) The Trades Union Congress had its own emergency paper, the *British Worker*. The Amalgamated Press went ahead with the launching of a new fiction magazine, the *Argosy*, and the editor, Clarence Winchester, distributed it himself to newsagents in his own car.

Had there been a complete shut-down of news, there might have been panic; but the new medium, radio, came to the rescue – it was in the Government's pocket, yet it managed, under John Reith's guidance, a reasonably impartial news service (though Churchill didn't think so).

The miners, who felt betrayed by the T.U.C., stayed out until August, and it took almost until Christmas to get everyone back to work. The

workers. Calling out the printing workers may have been the T.U.C.'s greatest mistake. The crunch came when machine operators at the *Daily Mail* refused to print a leading article which criticized the strikers. The *Daily Mail* made some attempt to print abroad and supply copies by air, but for most people newspapers disappeared for the nine-day duration of the strike.

If you were in or near a large city, you would probably get one of the single-page news-sheets flung together by volunteers and put out by the main Fleet Street offices. *The Times* of May 5th (a single flimsy page, 12 in. by 7 in., folded, not by

Winston Churchill, 1927, by Walter Sickert

General Strike left a slough of bitterness which has never really evaporated. 'The main cause of its peaceful defeat', wrote L. S. Amery of the General Strike some years afterwards, 'was that the public was with the Government, but without resentment against the strikers, while the mass of strikers themselves struck out of loyalty to the movement rather than from any passionate conviction of the justice of their cause.'

Lord Birkenhead wrote to the Viceroy of India that the miners' leaders were 'the stupidest men in England', with the possible exception of the mine-owners.

The Government passed a Trade Disputes Act in 1927 making general strikes illegal: it was repealed by the Labour Government in 1946. It was reckoned that the miners lost £60 million in wages; 500,000 men were kept out of work for months, and the national loss was put at £160 million.

For the middle class and above, the whole affair was rather a lark. It brought out what, fourteen years later, was to be known as the Dunkirk spirit. Despite the arrest of hundreds of strikers, a number of 'incidents' and the presence at key danger points of the Army, it was incredibly peaceful. The spread of private cars and the apparent plentifulness of petrol gave people a new freedom and mobility to fend for themselves.

Left-wing undergraduates at Oxford were few in 1926. One of them was Hugh Gaitskell, future leader of the Labour Party, who borrowed a car (a bull-nosed Morris) from Margaret Cole, wife and collaborator of the detective-story-writing economics don, and helped to distribute the *British Worker*. To do this, he had to have a Printers' and Papermakers' Union card to get through the pickets in Fleet Street. Returning to Oxford, he was fined £1 by the Warden of New College, H. A. L. Fisher, for climbing into college after midnight.

Most of the 'plus-four boys' from public schools and universities volunteered for driving buses and trains – sometimes in their plus-fours. Instead of the usual destination boards, there were notices saying 'This bus goes anywhere you like. No fares and kind treatment. Joy rides to the East End.' And 'The driver of this bus is a student of Guy's Hospital. The conductor is a student of Guy's. Anyone who interferes with either is liable to be a patient of Guy's.'

Sir Philip Gibbs, journalist and former war correspondent, went on such a trip to the East End of London, where cargoes of flour were being unloaded from the docks by troops and then escorted through pickets of strikers by armoured cars. He found the docks occupied by the Brigade of Guards, complete with military band, who were whiling away the time playing 'Poor Little Buttercup' from *H.M.S. Pinafore*. 'Doing our bit' said the officer commanding. Gibbs was able to get right into the dock only because the policeman on duty recognized him as a trench mate from the Battle of the Somme.

He then tried to get to Manchester. This was much more difficult. The driver of the train at Euston station wore a bowler hat, and walked along the train saying 'Good morning, everybody! I'm the engine driver. I hope to get you as far as Manchester.' It is sad to have to report that the train was derailed at Harrow. The bowler-hatted driver walked along the train again: 'That's torn it, I'm afraid. So sorry. Something went wrong.'

Meanwhile there were football matches between strikers and police; and there is evidence that the difficulties of volunteer-driven transport took middle-class people into districts they had never before visited, where shoeless children ran about streets strewn with horse dung, and where lived the very poor, still sometimes referred to as 'the great unwashed', for whom the Twenties never roared and were seldom gay.

Debutantes ran canteens. The Duchesses of Westminster and Sutherland, with Lady Maureen Stanley, drove lorries for *The Times*, while other Society women were 'newsboys' or switchboard operators for the *Express*. Fifty Cambridge undergraduates, led by the Olympic athlete Lord Burghley, organized food convoys between the Docks and the Hyde Park depot, and obliging strikers showed them how to lift heavy crates. Another Cambridge party, which included the Dean of King's, unloaded bacon and margarine at Grimsby.

Cecil Beaton, then working in the City, walked to his office from Paddington and noticed 'lorries piled high with giggling typists; old carts were chock-a-block full of women dangling legs and loving it all. "Such a lark", they seemed to be saying, "so new, so amusing, so bohemian."' When he arrived at his office, he found a typist who had walked all the way from Clapham, and in a nearby teashop a waitress who had walked for four and a half hours. At home, hearing a lorry backfiring at night, 'all the servants hurried in fright to hide in one another's rooms. They thought a revolution had started!'

Authors were also 'doing their bit' (that old wartime phrase!). Hugh Walpole became an Information Officer, but seems never actually to have done anything because the Strike was over too soon. Somerset Maugham, Arnold Bennett tells us, was a 'sleuth' at Scotland Yard – possibly because of his Intelligence experience during the War. Whatever he was doing had to be done at night, from 11 p.m. to 8.30 a.m.

On the first day of the Strike, Bennett noticed 'many more motors about'. He walked to Victoria Station, found it shut (although 'a train had gone somewhere during the morning') but all the bookstalls open though there were no newspapers. 'The populace excited and cheery . . . News from the wireless at very short intervals, $\frac{1}{2}$-hour intervals at night up to midnight.' A week later he was ready to call the Strike 'a political crime that must be paid for.' It was truly revolutionary because the T.U.C. 'had the infernal cheek to issue permits to goods and vehicles to use the roads and railways'. By next morning the Strike had become 'pitiful, foolish – a pathetic attempt of underdogs who hadn't a chance when the over-dogs really set themselves to win'. Tube trains were being driven 'by swagger youths in yellow gloves who nevertheless now and then overran the platform,' and passengers were handled by 'University porters with gold cigarette cases and an incredible politeness and fatherliness towards you for your safety'.

On the day before the General Strike was called off a group of Northumberland miners, to register a protest against owners, unions, Government and everyone else, unbolted and removed a length of railway track by Cramlington colliery. They succeeded in derailing the famous *Flying Scotsman* – incredibly, without any loss of life.

When it was all over, there were thanksgiving services in churches, including one at Windsor at which King George V was heard to say to the Dean 'That was a rotten way to run a revolution. I could have done it better myself.' Ernest Bevin, General Secretary of the Transport and General Workers' Union, the biggest trade union in the world, saw that employers might use their victory harshly, and had a private meeting with the Prime Minister, who said in the House of Commons 'I am not out to smash trade unions, and I will not allow the strike to be made a pretext for the imposition of worse conditions.' A portrait of Prime Minister Baldwin, 'The Man who led the Nation through the Crisis', was the Royal Academy's picture of the year, and Baldwin with his cherrywood pipe enjoyed for the next ten years or so the image of 'The Man Who Kept His Head'.

Mr and Mrs Stanley Baldwin at Ascot, June 1926

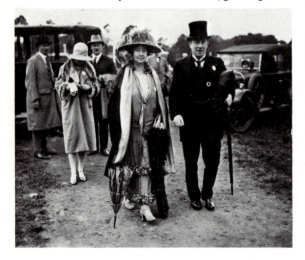

(opposite) – 'Danseuse de Kapurthale' – a characteristic Art Déco figure in bronze and ivory, of a dancer in a sequined cat-suit, by D. H. Chiparus, whose figures reflected the decorative modes of the Twenties, especially the stage extravaganzas of 'George White's Scandals', the Ziegfeld Follies and the Folies Bergère

CHAPTER 8

Elusive Cadences

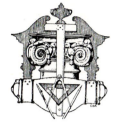

America never had a General Strike; but then, Britain never had a Florida Boom.

'Go to Florida . . . where the whispering breeze springs fresh from the lap of the Caribbean and woos with elusive cadence like unto a mother's lullaby.' I do not know who wrote this copy for an advertisement, in 1925, for the Sunshine State. It may have been Ben Hecht, then publicist, at $2,500 a week, for Key Largo City (described as 'a combination of Tahiti and Newport'); or Harry Reichenbach, 'the most gifted mob psychologist since P.T. Barnum', who earned $3,000 a week; or P. Jocelyn Yoder, head of Coral Gables publicity department, who employed, among other eminent writers, Rex Beach.

The Florida Boom of 1924–6 could only have happened in America, and in the Twenties. There is nothing else like it in Anglo-American history, with the possible exception of the South Sea Bubble. In 1920 you could say that most people knew three things about Florida, apart from the sunshine: its State tree was the palmette palm; its State flower the orange blossom; and its State bird the mocking bird. One or two people might have associated Florida with coconuts and avocados. Oh, just one other thing: there was no State income tax.

In Miami (a city of 30,000 souls in 1920) there were suddenly 2,000 real estate offices and nearly 6,000 house agents, and a population by 1925 of 75,000. Mangrove swamps and a hinterland of panthers, alligators, mosquitos, rattlesnakes and vermin were being turned into 'Venetian' cities – Venetian cities with skyscrapers. 'Elusive cadences' – well, the actual sound you could hear was that of riveters as the steel-framed buildings soared. (If you want a mild present-day parallel, look what has happened at Torremolinos, Costa del Sol, and certain beaches in Majorca.) Somehow, with an acute shortage of gas, electricity and telephones, a strip of coast south of Palm Beach sixty miles long was staked out in fifty-foot lots.

Many of those lots were bought only to resell. It was not unusual for one bought for $1,000 to be sold eventually for $200,000. Even the promoters – men such as George Merrick, of Coral Gables, the converted citrus grove; J.W. Young of Hollywood-by-the-sea; and D.P. Davis, of Davis Islands – believed their own publicity: if you visualized something, it existed. Thus a property called Manhattan Estates was described as being 'three-quarters of a mile from the fast-growing city of Nettie', which city not only did not exist but there wasn't even a stake in the ground to show where anyone proposed to build it.

The Sunshine State, up to 1920, was where many people in delicate health went to die. Taking Palm Beach as the fashionable centre, despising all others, the three great developing personalities had been Henry M. Flagler, J.D. Rockefeller's right-hand man at Standard Oil, hotel and railroad builder (it was he who had pushed the railroad to Key West in 1912); Colonel E.R. Bradley, civic leader and gambling (especially roulette) promoter; and Paris Singer, of the sewing-machine family, a wealthy dilettante, patron of the arts and amateur architect. Singer, one of the lovers of Isadora Duncan and 'Lohengrin' in her autobiography, had also come to Florida on his doctor's advice, and thought he had only a few years to live.

So too had thought Addison Mizner, who, in 1918

'Gelmeroda IX', 1926, by Lyonel Feininger. Feininger was born in New York in 1871 but aged sixteen went to live in Germany and remained a resident in Europe until he returned to America for the last nineteen years of his life. He died in 1956. He was the first artist to be chosen by the architect Walter Gropius for the staff of the school that became the Bauhaus

when he was forty-five, had arrived in Palm Beach from New York on a stretcher. As a boy of fifteen he had celebrated the Fourth of July in his home town of Benicia, California, near San Francisco, by leaping over some exploding fireworks, which had fractured his leg, with gangrene supervening. The one positive result of this mishap was that, in convalescence, he had started painting. Addison Mizner, on his stretcher, was now suffering from mortification of a leg bone; his lungs weren't too good either; nor was his heart. It should perhaps be mentioned that he was 6ft 2in. high, fat, and weighed 310 lb. Once off his stretcher, however, he was astonishingly strong, and liked walking on his hands and holding a table aloft with a single hand. He had arrived in Palm Beach on borrowed money, and was $60,000 in debt.

Addison was about to become one of the three great 'society architects' in America. The other two were Stanford White, shot by a millionaire sadist named Harry Thaw for raping one Evelyn Nesbitt who afterwards became Mrs Thaw; and Richard M. Hunt. All Addison needed was Paris Singer's money, with which he transformed Palm Beach into a rhapsody of neo- (or possibly pseudo-) Spanish architecture. His only serious competitor was Joseph Urban, designer of the Ziegfeld Theatre and several super-cinemas. Seeing their work, Harry Thaw, who had escaped the death penalty after a series of trials which turned on the question of his sanity, is said to have cried out 'My God, I shot the wrong architect!'

In all that follows, Addison was accompanied by his brother Wilson, dope-addict, failed playwright and witty conversationalist, who had recently served a jail sentence for running a gambling joint, and whom we last met as a sponsor of Teddie Gerrard.

It seems niggling to point out that Addison Mizner was not a qualified architect. He had never even taken a correspondence course in architecture. But he could draw, the human imagination was the only limit, and money (for his clients) hardly mattered. The 'artist's impression' of a building was all. So the Everglades Club at Palm Beach and the Cloister Hotel at Boca Raton came to be thought 'among the most beautiful buildings in America'. Paris Singer was more than satisfied that his money was well invested: 'Each house that Addison builds is more beautiful than the one before, so I am waiting to get

the last of them.' Frank Lloyd Wright liked Addison's work, too, so it must be O.K.

In New York, it seems, you could set up as an architect without a licence; but in Florida you had to pass examinations. However, Addison's examining board was faced with a man who had already designed buildings which everyone could see, so they admitted him on the grounds that 'he had a happy faculty of combining the illustrated works of other countries with the draughtsmanship of his associates to bring about a most pleasing and successful architectural renaissance which suited the Palm Beach taste of the period.' In return for this gesture, Addison gave a lecture on how to make a client spend more than he wanted to. It had to do, he said, with the eternal triangle of ambitious wife, cowering husband and dominating architect. He generally referred to the client as 'the sucker'.

During the boom years of 1924–6 the Mizner brothers were multi-millionaires, and the half-imaginary city of Boca Raton ('Beaucoup Rotten', rival promoters called it) was what Wilson called 'a platinum sucker trap'. It was Venice with electric gondolas and steam yachts and a chain of ocean-front estates, parks and gardens, south of Palm Beach. Or, according to another description, it was a blend of 'Venice and Heaven, Florence and Toledo', with 'a little Graeco-Roman glory and grandeur thrown in.' A former United States ambassador to Spain was quoted as saying 'It is more Spanish than anything I ever saw in Spain'. A cynical reporter called it 'Bastard-Spanish-Moorish-Romanesque-Gothic-Renaissance-Bull Market-Damn-the-Expense-style.' Lots worth $11 million were sold on the first day of business.

One of the wonders of Boca Raton was the 219-foot-wide highway, El Camino Real, which led to it. This, the widest highway in the world, had twenty traffic lanes, lighted by concealed lamps in the kerbstones (Wilson's theatrical idea). Down the middle ran a Grand Canal, with Rialtos, landings and electric gondolas manned by gondoliers who sang to guitars and used dummy oars (because you need two hands to play a guitar). There was only one thing wrong with El Camino Real: it didn't lead *from* anywhere, because it was only half a mile long.

Acting on Harry Reichenbach's principle of 'get the big snobs and the little snobs will follow', the Mizners for some time specialized in American celebrities. Soon du Ponts, Vanderbilts, Elizabeth Arden, Irving Berlin, Herbert Bayard Swope and Marie Dressler ('the Duchess of Boca Raton') were all listed as owners of property in Florida. To these was added the name of the Rev. Maitland Alexander, described as 'the multi-millionaire clergyman of Pittsburgh'. British names were also infiltrated: rightly or wrongly, Lady Diana Manners (whose name had been Cooper for the last five years), Lord Ivor Spencer-Churchill, Lord Glenconner and the Duchess of Sutherland were quoted as patrons of the 'new Riviera', the old Riviera being now 'almost deserted' except for the Scott Fitzgerald set. Among aristocratic developers from Europe were the Duc de Richelieu and Countess Marie of Wittelsbach (billed as 'the only woman in the world who knows the inside story of Mayerling'). The fact that Al Capone had a Miami property complete with swimming pool was played down.

So far, Florida was still a playground for the fairly rich. But the real boom ('development' was the preferred word) started with Miami, rather looked down on by Palm Beach. What was about to happen was an exercise in 'opening up the mass market'. 'Miami', said William Jennings Bryan, who was running 'the world's greatest Bible class' at the Royal Palm Hotel, 'is the only city in the world where you can tell a lie at breakfast that will come true by evening.' Gold and oil rushes were never like this: it is estimated that of the 2,000,000 people who surged into Florida during the boom years, 300,000 concentrated around Miami. There was every prospect of a solidly built-up city 70 miles long between Miami and Palm Beach – or 150 miles, if you counted the chain of islands between Key West and the mainland. Or why not 300 miles, all the way north to Jacksonville? Florida had enough lots to provide homes for 80,000,000 people, half the population of the United States.

At this point the stories get wilder and wilder. The retired railroad worker who, by buying and selling land, made $2 million. The hot-dog man who made $4 million. P. Jocelyn Yoder went to the barber, asked for his usual man, and was told 'Oh, he quit – he's a millionaire now.' Raymond Schindler, a former private detective, ran a business for making artificial islands by forcing sand into steel frames. The traffic jams were so bad that street-peddlers sold novelties to drivers who couldn't move.

One man sold ten-line poems about Florida at $50 apiece. Another man sold life memberships of non-existent yacht clubs. Outside real estate offices, each 'opening a new town', were queues in which you could sell your place to someone else for $100. This was no place for conventional businessmen: 'the wild man with a shoestring', said Alva Johnston, one of the historians of these times, 'fared better than a careful investor with a bank roll.' Within three years thirty-three advertising agencies sprang up in Miami. Most of them regularly bought space in the *Suniland Magazine*, which had 256 pages. Probably the most dismayed people in America were bank managers in the North whose clients were withdrawing their money to spend in Florida.

In the real estate offices there were sometimes cabaret shows to encourage the customers, and Coral Gables hired Paul Whiteman's Band for a sales rally. On street corners were evangelists and paid orators, all praising Florida. Above their heads were aeroplanes sky writing. Song writers were hired to write songs about cities not yet built. Golfers such as Bobby Jones and Walter Hagen endorsed new enterprises while playing. Tex Guinan had a Miami nightclub where a glass of crushed ice cost $2.50.

The time has come to study Addison Mizner's style of architecture. In his autobiography, *The Many Mizners*, he says that his father was Minister Plenipotentiary to five Central American countries. It seems to have been a young Guatemalan priest who taught him about Spanish architecture, and he did eventually study in Spain at the University of Salamanca. His mother hoped that he and Wilson and two other brothers would become priests or ambassadors. Architecture was not ruled out, but Addison showed no sign of studying it seriously. He wanted to wander about the world first, and went to China. He then got a job in the office of Willis Polk, the architect who designed many skyscrapers and exhibitions in a 'Spanish Renaissance' manner. We next find him (in 1897) working on a gold mine near Delta, California: Addison's explanation of this sudden switch was that he had been commissioned by President Barrios of Guatemala to design a $2,000,000 government headquarters, but Barrios was assassinated before Addison could get to Guatemala City. However, Addison's dates are wrong, for Barrios was not killed until 1898.

(top) The 18-mile-long automobile road which connected Jacksonville with its sea beaches (above) The sea front at Miami in 1926 showing a few of the gigantic hotels and apartment houses in the course of erection

98

The Venetian pool at Coral Gables

(above) An aerial view of Miami

(left) Orange-crush at 11 a.m., Miami

(below) The Patio Restaurant of the Antilla Hotel at Coral Gables

Addison, accompanied by Wilson and two other brothers, now moved up to Klondike for the gold rush. He then wandered alone around the Pacific and Indian Oceans, spent some time in Hawaii, and returned to Guatemala to grow coffee. Here he seems to have spent most of his time buying up altars, crucifixes and other religious *objets d'art* from many churches left in ruins by earthquakes, to sell to wealthy people in New York. Eventually he started a practice as a landscape architect on Long Island, but claimed that the War destroyed his business.

A man who had done all these things must be fitted for something, and a man who could draw and paint could at least put his ideas on paper, leaving other more specialized talents to carry them out. It was Kid McCoy the prizefighter (the original 'real McCoy'), then physical fitness instructor at Gus's Baths, Palm Beach, who invited Addison to build his first 'Saracen-Spanish masterpiece', the Everglades Club. At Palm Beach Addison built a house for Harold Vanderbilt, and another for William K. Vanderbilt Jr; at Biltmore, North Carolina, one for George Vanderbilt. 'The Towers', designed for William M. Wood, head of the American Woolen Company, had a log-burning fireplace in the bathroom. To anyone who said 'This is going to cost a lot of money, Mr Mizner' Addison was apt to reply 'You'd hate it if it didn't.' Occasionally Addison forgot details like doors and staircases, but these problems could be solved later: his principle, quite seriously, was 'Construction first – blueprints afterwards', even if this meant tearing down walls in the course of construction to accommodate a new idea. Moorish patios, frescoes, porticos, loggias, baroque staircases, a touch of neo-Byzantine, colonnades, orangeries – you could have all or any of them in the truly beautiful house; and Addison, at one point in 1925, was working on a hundred buildings at once.

Sometimes each room was in a different style or period (like a Cunard liner). A house Addison designed for himself was to have had secret staircases, oubliettes, a moat, a dungeon, a drawbridge, battlements with X-shaped holes for bows and arrows to shoot through, and turrets galore. But the boom collapsed before the house could be completed.

Having learned Spanish from his early Guatemalan background, Addison could talk to Spanish-speaking Negro workers in their own language. This helped him to set up a factory in West Palm Beach for making (and faking) furniture, tiles, and wrought iron: his wrought-iron expert had once been the village blacksmith. Faking could include an effect of age contrived by soot on the ceiling, broken tiles, a statue with a chipped nose, and woodworm holes made with Wilson's airgun.

Yet Addison really knew about Spanish art, and went to great trouble to collect genuine pieces. In the mid-Twenties he met Alec Waugh, the English novelist, who was at first shocked by his affectionately blasphemous language but grew to like and admire him. Waugh thought Addison's taste almost infallible, and that if any building of his was guilty of excessive ornamentation, it was probably the client's fault for insisting on it, which was only possible on a day when Addison's ulcers were bad.

Together they went to Spain to buy old furniture and other antiques. It seemed that Addison knew King Alfonso well enough to call him 'you old son of a bitch'. He knew the Duke of Alba, too, and more than once proved him wrong on points of Spanish architecture and history. Somehow Addison was allowed to take the fourteenth-century panelling out of a room in the University of Salamanca ('the very room in which King Ferdinand and Queen Isabella had commanded Columbus to discover the New World') and install it in his own house on Via Mizner. (The clients had to make do with imitation panelling.) Addison's bed was also supposed to have been Ferdinand and Isabella's: it eventually went to the Mizner Museum at Driftwood Inn, Vera Beach.

Addison Mizner was now running three inter-related businesses: his architectural practice, his factories for making or faking tiles, wrought iron, stained glass and anything else the customers wanted, and the sale of genuine antiques from Spain. He was employing Spanish painters and decorators and Italian copiers of old masterpieces. He and Wilson owned Mizner Mile, a strip of nearly 1,000 acres near Boynton, 15 miles south of Palm Beach. It seemed that the boom would never end.

Apart from the natural cycle by which, psychologically as well as economically, a boom is inevitably followed by a slump, it is not easy to trace just why and how the collapse started. Collective madness has its flashpoint at which it must explode. The advertisers' and press agents' claims became curiouser and curiouser. At Coral Gables there was going to be a University of Miami where classes would be held in the open air, like those of the ancient Greeks. Fulford-by-the-Sea and Hollywood-by-the-Sea were also planning universities, presumably to hold classes in the sea. Sun-propaganda had gone beyond ultra-violet rays, which were now called actinic rays and were said to keep the arteries supple. Copywriters now used a kind of Orwellian Newspeak by which everything contained the seeds of its opposite. Thus 'by-the-sea' meant 'remote from the sea'. 'Heights' meant anything more than two feet above sea level. (Cecil Roberts wrote a whole book on his search for Alcantara Heights, 'the loveliest city ever turned out by a printing press'.) Coral Gables, several miles inland, advertised '40 miles of waterfront'. Sometimes lots were advertised as being near a 'proposed city'. Will Rogers mocked them by inventing a real-estate deal whose attraction was that 'all these lots are by our Proposed Ocean'.

If the property market was declining, then industry must be stimulated. 'Pensacola has 97 industries' said one advertisement. There were carefully instigated reports that the film industry was about to leave Hollywood, California, for Florida, and it was true that Lewis Selznick did actually look around the beaches with plans for a Picture City; but already the real-estate men were using the slogan 'Live next door to the stars!' There was a 'proposed rubber boom' too; only the rubber was going to be a substitute manufactured from sunflower sap, in which Edison, Ford and Firestone seemed more than mildly interested.

The sudden reports of 'buried treasure' in 1926 suggested that the bottom of the barrel was being scraped; yet hundreds of people came to dig, and indeed there *was* buried treasure, put there by Wilson Mizner.

Things were going wrong. For one thing, the 'suckers' were not keeping up their payments (most lots were sold for a down payment and three annual instalments). There was a new Treasury ruling that income tax must be paid on all transactions. Urgently needed goods and materials were not arriving because there simply weren't enough freight trains to carry them, and sea transport was temporarily out of action because an old Danish warship, which was being turned into a hotel, sank and blocked the Miami channel so that no other ship could get in or out. Even neo-Spanish architecture seemed to be going out of fashion; it wasn't new,

Addison Mizner hadn't invented it, and it had been a strongly promoted feature of exhibitions and fairs since before the War. A sort of chauvinism set in: 'After all, our ancestors were Anglo-Saxon'; perhaps imitation Elizabethan taverns were going to be the new thing. 'Have-Faith-In-Florida' Clubs started up, and Wilson Mizner began to invent European financiers who were said to be putting money into Florida.

It was about this time that one of the 'big snobs' pulled out. General Coleman du Pont, president of E.I. du Pont de Nemours, was famous for two things other than for being a du Pont: he had lent Tallulah Bankhead $1,000 to start her on her stage career, and he was a great man for awful practical jokes such as electric-shock handshakes and exploding cigars. Du Pont found out that Wilson Mizner had once been in prison, and started wondering about the company he was keeping. He also found out that Wilson was using the du Pont name in publicity without permission; and as the General said, in the understatement of the decade, 'Advertising firms are apt to exaggerate.'

Other 'big snobs' followed. Frantic attempts were made to revive interest in neo-Spanish houses by installing Wurlitzer organs at anything up to $45,000 each. Ben Hecht packed up and went to Hollywood; he had never invested a nickel in Florida, never trusted a Florida bank. In 1928 there were thirty-one bank failures in Florida; in 1929 fifty-seven. There were two severe hurricanes in September 1926 which reminded the world that, around the Caribbean, you cannot have 'elusive cadences' and 'soothing tropic winds' all the time.

Splendid buildings were abandoned unfinished. Paris Singer's seven-storey hotel, which he was building on his own Singer's Island, was invaded by wildfowl, who used it as a roost. Another hotel was converted into an egg-and-broiler farm.

Addison Mizner, it is not easy to imagine why, found he was broke, and lived mainly by borrowing. Wilson Mizner went to Hollywood, where he wrote scripts and for some time ran a restaurant. *Cosmopolitan* Magazine tried to make him write his autobiography, and there was even talk of making a film about him. When Cecil Beaton went to America in 1931 he found Addison friendly and keeping fashionable company still, and Wilson 'much too lazy to do anything except hang around the Brown Derby and gossip'. Two years later they both died.

CHAPTER 9

Mad Dogs and Englishmen

I am thirteen. It is Sunday evening, after supper, and we have been invited next door for coffee and Albert Sandler. Sandler, a violinist, for many years led the orchestra in the Palm Court of the Grand Hotel at Eastbourne, and he broadcast for an hour on Sundays. The pianola was used no more: everything now was radio, called 'wireless'.

Sandler always had two guest singers, one of whom would probably be a baritone such as Peter Dawson or Harry Dearth; and it was more than probable that Peter or Harry would sing 'The Road to Mandalay'. This had more than a musical significance to the Grand Hotel people, whose chatter and clinking coffee cups and brandy glasses we could actually hear from the loudspeaker; it gave a special glow of pride in the Empire on which the sun, even if they didn't realize it, was at last setting. Sometimes Peter or Harry would sing 'Rolling Down to Rio' instead, and when he did, you could be pardoned for not being able to remember whether Rio wasn't British too.

The British still had a sense of mission about this Empire. It represented things as far apart as the Gilbert and Ellice Islands, where Sir Arthur Grimble had had to fight an octopus under water (not only to prove his courage to the natives he ruled, but because it was regarded by them as his privilege), and Mother India at Viceroy level. Here is Earl Winterton on life in Simla, the summer residence of the Viceroy and staff of the Indian and Punjab Governments:

> Colleagues saw too much of each other and too little of the rest of the population. This propinquity produced

considerable malice below the surface. What A or A's wife said of B or B's wife in private was usually repeated by C or his wife to B. Since the leading officials of the Government were men of intelligence who worked at high pressure, their wit at each other's expense had a lacerating quality.

But not before the natives; certainly not at an official dinner party at Viceregal Lodge:

> As the Viceroy and his wife walked slowly into the dining room preceded by two aides-de-camp marching in step, the band crashed into the National Anthem and the brilliantly attired Indian servants, to the number of a dozen or more, standing behind chairs buried their heads in their hands as a mark of respect.

Meanwhile Arthur Grimble, as an Assistant Resident Commissioner in the Gilbert and Ellice Islands earning £600 a year, had to serve six years without his wife and family before he qualified for three months' home leave. 'In the Colonial Office,' he was told, 'we know nothing officially of wives and families.' There were no regular air services, and his 700-mile-long chain of atolls was nine to twelve weeks from London by sea, changing ships at Sydney, so that home leave could mean nine months' absence on full pay. There was not even the consolation of letter writing: there were only three mails a year. So Grimble ruled by sympathy and laughter: learned the local language, translated native poetry into English, studied rainmaking, absorbed values long forgotten by Western civilization. The Islanders had one great criticism of the British: 'The white man can fly; he can speak across the ocean – but he has no poets like ours.'

What did the Empire mean? To Grimble,

Not the imperialism of Britain, but the liberalism of individual Britons, plugging along at their jobs in the field, was the force that held the affections of simple peoples true to the mother-country throughout the long era of autocratic rule. In its own way our system worked, on the whole, with real benevolence among simple peoples. When we got into the field we saw it inspiring many of our senior officers to earnest work, and often deep self-sacrifice, in desolate places.

But in India not all the peoples were simple. That there was much to be learned from their values was the belief of a non-political minority, and their feelings and doubts were expressed by E. M. Forster, whose *A Passage To India* appeared in 1924. Could the twain ever meet? On the polo field perhaps:

They reined up again, the fire of good fellowship in their eyes. . . . Nationality was returning, but before it could exert its poison they parted, saluting each other. 'If only they were all like that,' each thought.

Correlli Barnett, one of the younger British historians, thinks that the British lost their Empire through the influence of nineteenth-century evangelical religion, which they absorbed at their public schools. They had lost the 'hard as cannon' realism of the eighteenth century, and had accumulated an Empire which left them technologically backward and un-self-sufficient. They had withdrawn into the imperial fantasy. Especially in India.

There were at this time about 320,000,000 Indians (the Muslims would not be known as Pakistanis for another twenty-five years), of whom perhaps 5 or 6 per cent knew who the British (*bilati-lok*) were. Lord Chelmsford, Viceroy until 1920, had introduced reforms, with the Secretary of State E.S. Montagu, giving a certain measure of self-government known as 'dyarchy'. He was succeeded by Lord Reading, formerly Rufus Isaacs, who, after trying his hand at fruit-broking, had run away to sea, been a jobber on the Stock Exchange, read for the Bar and somehow become Attorney-General, survived the Marconi Scandal of 1913, and had become Lord Chief Justice and Special Ambassador to Washington.

Reading inherited a load of trouble. Educated Hindus and Muslims both rejected 'dyarchy' and pressed for *purna swaraj* (complete self-government). Mahatma Gandhi, one of the most extraordinary personalities of all time, whose mind was formed by reading Ruskin, Tolstoy, the *Bhagavad Gita* and the New Testament, was able to persuade millions of Indians to boycott everything British and resist passively by *satyagraha* or 'soul force'. The Punjab rebellion and the Amritsar massacre had infuriated those millions in ways which no visit by a Prince of Wales could mend. Reading in 1922 authorized Gandhi's imprisonment for six years – but the Mahatma was released in 1924 after an operation for appendicitis.

Swaraj became the slogan of all the younger generation of Indian leaders, particularly Jawarhalal Nehru, educated at Harrow and Cambridge, whose Anglophilia had changed overnight after Amritsar. In 1927 Britain appointed a commission under Sir John Simon to find out how Indian self-government could be extended – but did not invite any Indians to sit on it.

Yet Indian officers were being trained at Sandhurst (ten a year); and the Indian Civil Service was being opened to Indians; but too slowly for India. There were bombs, assassinations, killings of policemen.

Egypt became an independent kingdom in 1922. In the same year, Iraq became a mandated territory, which lasted for ten years. What did all these imperial terms really mean? The vague phrase – perhaps more of an ideal – 'British Commonwealth of Nations' was being used. We first hear of it from Lord Rosebery, in a speech at Adelaide, Australia, in 1884; and again from General Smuts in 1917. It was used in the Anglo-Irish treaty of 1921, and again at the imperial Conference of 1926. Did it mean the whole Empire? or did it mean the United Kingdom plus the self-governing Dominions?

And Dominion Status? Did it mean that the Dominions would automatically follow the mother country wherever she went? It did not, indeed.

In September 1922 the Chanak Crisis blew up, and Lloyd George asked the Dominions for both moral and military support in order to prevent Turkish violation of neutral zones in the Greco-Turkish war. To his surprise, the Canadian Prime Minister, Mackenzie King, mildly pointed out that his government had had no prior information about the matter, and could not anyway take action without consulting the Canadian parliament. South Africa seemed to feel the same. Three years later the Dominions Office was created, and described by

Walter Runciman as 'a Foreign Office with a family feeling'. And in the Balfour Report of the 1926 Imperial Conference, Dominions were defined as 'autonomous communities within the British Empire, equal in status, in no way subordinate one to another in any aspect of their domestic or external affairs, though united by a common allegiance to the Crown, and freely associated as members of the British Commonwealth of Nations'.

Native education was much discussed, beginning with tropical Africa. Natives, it was said, were being prepared for self-government: it seemed to be assumed that they would react democratically, and be absorbed into the system as the Britons had once been absorbed into Rome.

The War had been 'a triumph of Empire'. The British Empire had not only defeated Germany; it had shared out her colonies among some of the victors. The Treaty of Versailles had 'settled Europe for good', and British strategic thinking was Empire-based still. Strong 'buffer states' had to be maintained to protect India. In London within the stone half-moon of Aldwych, Australia House had risen, soon to be followed by India House. In India Sir Edwin Lutyens had been building a grandiose new capital city, New Delhi, since 1911, on a site somewhat larger than Washington D.C.: it was barely completed in time for independence.

In Malaya and other outposts east of Suez the Somerset Maugham people were planting rubber, drinking gin pahits and stengahs (in Singapore hotels the Chinese bartenders still write 'stengah' on your bill when you order a whisky and soda), looking forward desperately to the Christmas issue of the *Illustrated London News* which had been posted to them in September, and to ultimate retirement to a cottage in Devon, coming home on leave every few years (and, if single, proposing to the first girl they met so as to be able to return to the East with a wife); occasionally putting a pistol to their heads to end it all. And in Burma a young Bengal-born Indian Imperial Police officer named Eric Blair, one day to call himself George Orwell, was finding that his duties included shooting an elephant and witnessing public hangings.

The Commonwealth had another purpose in those days: to relieve the high British level of unemployment. Ex-officers whose chicken farms had failed, former private soldiers who were sick of play-

ing barrel organs in the streets, youths fresh from school who could not find a job, all looked hopefully overseas. About 56,000 emigrants a year sailed for Canada, Australia and South Africa, even if they had nothing but their white skins to offer. In 1925 the S.S. *Minnedosa* left Glasgow for Canada loaded with Scots, who carried a banner saying 'We've got jobs in Canada – we don't want the dole!' Most people in Britain at this time knew perhaps three things about Canada: the Prince of Wales had a ranch in Alberta, there were some Indians, and there were Mounted Police; and the last two facts had probably been gleaned from the spectacular musical *Rose Marie*. Two of my cousins, knowing nothing of New Zealand except Canterbury lamb, emigrated there and found themselves, in 1929, standing in much the same kind of dole queue that they would have seen in Britain, before eventually getting jobs in a cheese factory.

Sensing this ignorance of the Empire at home, the Government encouraged a British Empire Exhibition at Wembley, a rural area in Middlesex, seven miles from London, which had just been connected to the metropolis by underground railway and was about to become a suburb. For the first time the Empire was coming to Britain, instead of the other way round. This coincided with Empire Free Trade and an Empire Marketing Board. Most of the administrators of the Wembley Exhibition, which opened in 1924, were generals and colonels, and the architecture they favoured inevitably reminded people of Australia House in Aldwych and Sir Edwin Lutyens in New Delhi.

There is no American parallel to this until the Chicago Century of Progress in 1933. 'Wembley' was not a large exhibition, if you compare its 220 acres with the New York World Fair's 1,216, but it had cost £4,500,000 and was the biggest Britain had ever had. There was a stadium for 125,000 spectators. There were fifteen miles of streets, with evocative names like Anson's Way, Drake's Way, Dominion Way. Each building flew so many flags that you could hardly see the shape of its roof. Biggest of all was the Palace of Engineering, 'the largest concrete building in the world . . . six and a half times the size of Trafalgar Square'; second biggest was the Palace of Industry (which included a coal mine with real pit ponies). There was a Palace of Arts, a reconstruction of Old London Bridge, real

Map of the British
Empire Exhibition

'Tomb of Tutankhamen'
at Wembley

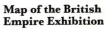

'Punch',
July 16th, 1924

Country Parson (visiting Wembley and much impressed by the tomb of TUT-ANKH-AMEN). "EXCUSE ME, COULD YOU TELL ME—IS THIS THE REAL THING?"

live Maoris, a Hong Kong Chinese restaurant, an Indian Pavilion which seemed to owe something to the Taj Mahal, a Queen's Doll's House designed by Lutyens. In the Canada building you could see a reproduction of the Niagara Falls. The Gardens contained 100,000 tulips and 5,000 delphiniums. At night all this was 'floodlit' (a new word in 1924). 'You cannot see it all in one day,' proclaimed the Official Guide (price 1s.); 'it will be open for 150 days.' The London & North Eastern Railway built a special new station near Wembley Hill, to handle 16,000 passengers an hour, and the London General Omnibus Company built an eight-platform bus station for 20,000 passengers an hour.

There were conference halls, for films and discussions, and facilities for large parties of schoolchildren. What did they remember of Wembley? I can tell you. The Amusements Park, especially the Dodgem cars, with which Billy Butlin, pioneer of holiday camps, was making his first big money. Models of the Prince of Wales and Jack Hobbs in Canadian and Australian butter. The Tibetan musicians, with their enormous alpenhorns, and dancers (Tibet was in the news because the ascent of

Everest had just been attempted). My music master at school took them to a nearby dance band which was playing 'Yes, We Have No Bananas', and asked them what they thought of Western music. 'It is so sad' they said.

So Britain knew little about Canada? One answer was the Rodeo (advance publicity taught us to pronounce it Ro-DAY-oh), a cowboy championship for Wild West riders, rope spinners, horses and cattle. Some of them came from the United States, but no matter. Two shiploads of them arrived at Tilbury, organized by Tex Austin and master-minded by Charles B. Cochran. They ran wild in the City, lassoing stockbrokers' top hats. It was all wonderful publicity.

On the first afternoon of the Rodeo 80,000 people brought in £10,000 to the Wembley Stadium. But in the evening a steer broke its leg and had to be shot. This released an outbreak of fury which had been building up in the R.S.P.C.A. for some time. Cochran and Austin were prosecuted – and eventually acquitted. But the harm had been done. Roping steers, thought people who regularly ate roast beef for Sunday dinner, was cruel. People stayed away,

The Never Stop Railway

H. M. Bateman's comment in 'Punch', May 28th, 1924

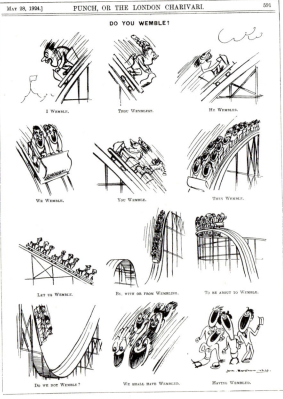

The 'Gold Coast' section

the Rodeo made no profit, and Cochran went bankrupt – at a meeting of creditors which closed with everybody singing 'For He's a Jolly Good Fellow'.

Punch made fun of Wembley, notably in H. M. Bateman's series of sketches. We have seen how the Bright Young People behaved at Wembley. It was also fashionable among anti-imperialist intellectuals to sneer at it and to refuse to go to it, or if they went to it, not to admit they had enjoyed it. Some of them formed a league called W.G.T.W. – 'the Won't-Go-To-Wembleys'. Never mind: 27,000,000 people *did* go, in spite of an exceptionally rainy summer; and it only lost £1½ million.

Perhaps its greatest moment was its opening on St George's Day, April 23rd 1924, when Sir Edward Elgar, Master of the King's Musick, conducted massed choirs and bands in 'Land of Hope and Glory'; and as they sang A.C. Benson's words – 'mother of the free . . . wider still and wider . . .' they meant every one of them. The Exhibition, whose President was the Prince of Wales, was opened by King George V, whose speech was relayed by the B.B.C. to nearly 7,000,000 people who for the first time heard a monarch's actual voice.

When at last Wembley closed, a Mr Arthur Elvin bought most of its buildings and made it a centre for international sport, especially the newly fashionable greyhound racing.

Had the Exhibition succeeded in stimulating the interest of the British public in the Empire they were already beginning to lose? Difficult to say. It certainly impressed Karel Čapek, the greatest writer of a new small country, Czechoslovakia, who called it 'the Biggest Samples Fair' in the *Letters from England* he wrote home to Prague. The Palace of Engineering frightened the man who had invented the word 'robot' from the Czech verb *robotiti* (to work), and for whom all machines were fearsome animals. He was unable to reconcile the wealth of Empire with the poverty of a blind, scabies-ridden beggar who had sold him a box of matches in a London street.

'I've brought you here to see the wonders of Empire' says a harassed father in Noël Coward's film *This Happy Breed*, 'and all you want to do is go on the Dodgems'.

Cigarette cards recording the British Empire Exhibition

107

CHAPTER 10

The Sporting Life

Athletically and socially, leaving aside ephemera like pogo sticks, yoyos and Mah-jongg, the Twenties game was – tennis. If you were lonely and had no one to take you dancing, you joined a tennis club. Tennis was a game at which women, shingled, short-skirted, enfranchised, could and did excel. Tennis also lent itself, like Hollywood, to the star system.

Lawn tennis is just a hundred years old. It is fairly typical of the twentieth century that it should have been invented by an Englishman, developed by everybody else, and excelled in by Americans. When Major Walter Wingfield in 1874 patented 'a new and improved portable court for playing the ancient game of tennis', it was shaped like an hour-glass. Nobody welcomed the idea more than the All England Croquet Club at Wimbledon, a suburb of London, which was doing badly. The Wimbledon Croquet Club laid down several grass courts – and lawn tennis was in business.

It must have spread pretty quickly, because an American lady, Mary E. Outerbridge, saw it being played by British officers in Bermuda in the winter of 1874, and took it home to the Staten Island Cricket and Baseball Club. It was all friendly pat-ball at this stage. In 1900 a Harvard undergraduate, Dwight F. Davis, donated a cup for international competition, and science and aggression began to enter the game. Should you or should you not play at the net or the baseline? The matter was partly decided by Maurice E. McLoughlin, a Californian who was used to asphalt courts; he invented the cannonball service, which changed the speed and character of the game and helped to make it a

William Tatem Tilden II, 1927

lucrative spectator sport. Garden-party tennis was over, except at garden parties.

By 1920 Wimbledon was ready for William Tatem Tilden II, a twenty-seven-year-old giant from Philadelphia. He was to dominate international tennis for the next ten years. You could say, perhaps, that 'Big Bill' had an intellectual approach to tennis (he wrote plays and books, and was a passable actor). After losing the U.S. singles final in 1919, he spent the whole winter remodelling his backhand. When, in 1922, he had part of one finger removed, he simply changed his grip. He won the Wimbledon title in 1920, 1921 and 1930; was in eleven Davis Cup teams, and led the fight to keep the Cup in America for seven years. He won seven international championships, six in a row, and the last in 1929.

What was the secret of this winner of seventy United States and international championships, who was perhaps the greatest player of all time? Experts assure us that he had the 'perfect tennis build – powerful shoulders, light frame and long legs.' His great weapons were 'a paralyzing forehand and backhand'. The British players, raised on the less concentrated game of cricket, in a wet climate, seemed unable to reach this standard. Perhaps there was still too much friendly amateurism.

'Big Bill' was a tremendous team man as well as a star. In 1920 he and William Johnston, a Californian, went to New Zealand, beat the Australasians and took the Davis Cup back to the States. (Three years later Johnston became the first Californian to win the men's singles at Wimbledon.) Tilden, Johnston, Norris Williams and Vincent Richards for several years seemed an unbeatable team: Australians, Japanese and French could do little against them until 1927, when the 'four Musketeers', Borotra (who in 1926 had won the men's singles at Wimbledon, in his famous beret), Lacoste, Cochet and Brugnon, took the Davis Cup to France – the first Latins ever to beat the Anglo-Saxons at their own game.

The old wooden-roofed premises at Worple Road, Wimbledon, could no longer cope with the crowds, and a brand new concrete stadium for 15,000 people was opened by King George V in June 1922. That summer Wimbledon was host to players (many of them ex-soldiers) from sixteen countries. Next year Forest Hills, Long Island, not to be outdone, built a concrete stadium of about the same size – and opened it with the first Wightman Cup matches.

Hazel Hotchkiss Wightman, born of covered-wagon stock in Healdsburg, Northern California, in 1887, has been called the 'Queen Mother of American tennis' – especially women's tennis. Famous as a performer in her own right (she partnered Tilden, Borotra, Norris Williams, Helen Wills and others in mixed doubles, and had won four U.S. Women's Singles Championships since 1909), she somehow tutored and mothered and kept the peace among the leading women tennis stars of the Twenties. Her own technique was based, it is said, on 'brilliant footwork and anticipation'.

She was a little hearty, perhaps. Her book *Better Tennis* contains an alphabet of tennis maxims

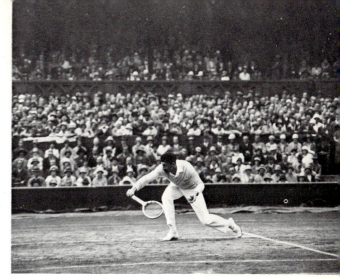

Jean Borotra, 1926

beginning with Always Alert, Be Better, and Concentrate Constantly, and ending with Xceed Xpectations and Zip Zip. Well, it seemed to work. She told Sarah Palfrey, one of her protégées, she could easily win her match if only she would Quash Qualms. She coached Helen Wills in volley and footwork, and Helen Jacobs in Constant Concentration. The only trouble was, the two Helens were seldom on speaking terms.

Mrs Wightman and Sarah Palfrey won five National Indoor Doubles Championships. Mrs Wightman and Helen Wills won two Wightman Cup doubles matches, two U.S. Championships, the 1924 Olympic tournament and an All-England Championship at Wimbledon. At Wimbledon Mrs Wightman earned undying fame, in a country

Helen Wills

which believes in playing games in silence, by one constantly-shouted phrase: it was 'Run, Helen!'

'Until Hazel Wightman came along,' veterans have told me, 'mixed doubles was quite an ordeal for the female half of the team. Remember, none of us had ever seen a girl who could smash or volley like a man.'

Although Mrs Wightman described Helen Jacobs as her 'most responsive' pupil, it was to Helen Wills that most of the glory came. (In Britain, as the years went on, we got a little confused about her changes of name – Wills – Moody – Roark.) All her strokes had

Suzanne Lenglen playing at Wimbledon, 1925

'Punch', July 2nd, 1924

power. She won the American title seven times in nine years, and the Wimbledon title six times in seven years. She was handsome, too, what you could see of her face, which wasn't much, because she wore an eye-shade (it became her brand image, like Lenglen's bandeau). Like all tennis girls at Wimbledon, she wore white stockings, because Queen Mary hated bare legs. Only in California and South Africa could you play bare-legged.

The Americans played, but the French *performed*. They were dramatically fascinating to watch, even if you knew nothing about the game. They threw temperaments – I mean, principally, Suzanne Lenglen. She was the Tilden of women's tennis. She had won her first championship at St Cloud when she was fifteen, and first appeared at Wimbledon in 1919 when she was twenty. In the next six years she carried off six Wimbledon titles. In 1925 she played five matches, losing only five games. Whole sets were won to love, and Suzanne (she was always called by her first name) beat Kitty McKane in the semi-finals without losing a single game.

In a singles match she was never defeated. Day after day the Royal Family (King, Queen and Princess Royal) watched her from the committee box. 'Suzanne is playing today' sighed an American hostess in London. 'I guess my mah-jongg party is sunk.' Suzanne played with her whole suntanned body: 'She has raised lawn tennis to an acrobatic art' said a mesmerized sports reporter. In order to be acrobatic, she dispensed with the traditional blouse, tie and long skirt, and wore usually a thin, one-piece loose-fitting dress, but sometimes a jumper (a new word then for jersey or sweater). Girls everywhere copied her pleated short skirt and rolled-top stockings, and tied back their bobbed hair in bright-coloured (often orange) bandeaux like hers. She leapt and ran and dived and volleyed and smashed. She hardly ever served a fault. Poor Mrs Lambert Chambers, a pre-war champion who still played around the baseline, simply couldn't cope with her. If ever Suzanne had an off day, it was said that this was due to the fact that her Svengali father wasn't among the spectators. In 1926 Suzanne retired from Wimbledon after a row with the referee.

In that same year professionalism crept in, and Suzanne, Vincent Richards, Mary Brown and Howard Kinsey (often regarded as the inventor of the dropshot) all accepted offers of money.

The Twenties were a golden age for cigarette cards. In the top row: Grimmett, Chapman, Sutcliffe and Gregory – from a series by Rip (Players 1926). Wakefield (Harlequins) and Dimmock (Spurs) are from a similar series. Papyrus, winner of the Derby in 1923 (Turf). 'Lawn Tennis Celebrities': Brugnon, Betty Nuthall, H. W. Austin and Mrs Mallory (Gallahers 1928). The golfer, Roger Wethered, (Gallahers 1923)

Painted in Chelsea today
before Donoghue left it
for Kempton June 4 - 1921

A.J. Munnings.

Stephen Donoghue -
rode the Derby Winner
1921.

'Steve Donoghue, June 4th, 1921', by Sir Alfred Munnings

Only two British names are to be found in 'the world's first ten players' during these years – A. R. F. Kingscote and Bunny Austin; and the women were led by Kitty McKane (Mrs Godfree), the only player ever to beat Helen Wills at Wimbledon (1924).

Boxing, too, was largely dominated by Americans. Irish-Americans, Jewish-Americans, Italian-Americans: did race matter? (It apparently did for Dempsey, who, promoted by Tex Rickard, refused to fight Harry Wills, a Negro). To this American ascendancy there was one glaring exception: Georges Carpentier, 'the great French gentleman', heavyweight champion of Europe, whose physical beauty seized women and men alike, beginning

(above)
The Jack Dempsey and Georges Carpentier fight at Boyle's Thirty Acres, July 2nd, 1921
(left)
The reach of Jack Dempsey
(right)
Georges Carpentier

with Bernard Shaw, who had seen him knock out Joe Beckett, the heavyweight champion of England, in 1 minute 15 seconds, in 1919.

Heywood Broun, watching him in training for his fight with Jack Dempsey, world heavyweight champion, in 1921, wrote: 'One of the most beautiful bodies the prize ring has ever known.' A girl reporter in the New York *Evening World* wrote: 'Michelangelo would have fainted for joy with the beauty of his profile, which is almost pure Greek.' A *New York Times* reporter compared him to Orlando in *As You Like It*, about to throw Charles the wrestler. Bernard Shaw and everyone else was rooting for Carpentier. There was even a smear campaign, encouraged by Rickard for publicity purposes, alleging that Dempsey had dodged the draft in the War while Carpentier had served in the French Air Force.

They met at Boyle's Thirty Acres, an arena built on a marsh in Jersey City. Tex Rickard noted with satisfaction that the gate receipts from 80,000 people were nearly $1,800,000. In Paris a signal system had been arranged by which six Army aircraft were to fly over the city flashing red lights if Carpentier won, white lights if he lost. The lights were white. In the first round Dempsey broke Carpentier's nose. In the second round Carpentier broke his right hand on Dempsey's jaw – and his left had always been weak. In the fourth round Carpentier was knocked down twice and counted out the second time. The whole business had lasted ten minutes.

Two things were happening to boxing: it was trying to become more scientific (which was what attracted Bernard Shaw and other intellectuals), and it was becoming big show business. The second trend was winning. Women, as well as men, came to the big fights; what the crowd wanted to see was plenty of slugging followed by a knockout; and not too quickly, either, or it wasn't getting its money's worth. To many people this was the golden age of boxing, when the prizes were vast and taxation light.

Dempsey's style, revolutionary in its day, was well suited to all this. Margery Miller Welles, one of the few women writers on boxing, said of him: 'A beautifully coordinated athlete who kept on the offensive almost continually. . . . His constant movement and the speed of his attack constituted his defence. He had little patience with the jab and less with long-range fighting, preferring the infighting to which his powerful, short hooks were adapted.'

Dempsey retained his championship until Tunney took it from him in 1926. Tex Rickard promoted five fights for him, and each made over $1 million. There were two against Gene Tunney (1926 and 1927), one against Luis Angel Firpo in 1923, and one against Jack Sharkey (1927).

The weirdest fight in which Dempsey was ever involved was at Shelby, Montana, in July 1923. Shelby was a cattle- and sheep-farming town of under 500 people. Just north of it was an oilfield, which doubled the population almost overnight. What Shelby needed, Mayor James A. Johnson thought, was publicity. Why not stage a fight between Dempsey and Tom Gibbons, of St Paul? They would need about $100,000. Somehow, mainly by underwriting it with land and oil leases, Mayor Johnson raised the cash and also built an arena. It now appeared that they needed another $200,000. The honour of Montana was at stake. Nobody was buying tickets because nobody was certain that the fight would take place.

Nerves were taut, trigger fingers itchy. Would Dempsey and Kearns, his manager, decamp with the money they had so far collected? There is not the slightest evidence that they contemplated any such thing, but Shelby had taken a dislike to them. On the afternoon of the fight, Dempsey arrived late and bottles were thrown at him as he entered the ring. Gibbons survived for fifteen rounds (a record against Dempsey) and honour was felt to have been satisfied when the referee decided for Dempsey. When Dempsey boarded the train for Salt Lake City at Great Falls, the crowd shouted 'Don't hurry back!' Soon afterwards four Montana banks failed, partly because of the end of the oil boom and partly (so Shelby believed) because of the fight.

The name of Luis Angel Firpo, named the Wild Bull of the Pampas by Damon Runyon, comes down to us from the golden age of boxing because of the most violent four minutes in its history. He fought Jack Dempsey at the Polo Grounds in September 1923. Firpo, heavyweight champion of South America, an almost penniless Argentinian who did well enough in the ring to become the millionaire owner of five cattle ranches, drove Dempsey right through the ropes in the first round, but was knocked down seven times. In the second round Dempsey knocked him out. The four minutes had been watched by more than 80,000 people paying up to $27·50 for ringside seats, who did not seem to want their money back. The moment of crisis in round one, showing Dempsey landing in the lap of a sportswriter, has been caught forever in a painting by George Bellows.

Dempsey's furious tigerish attacks met an immovable object in 1926 – James Joseph ('Gene') Tunney, who four years before had won the American light heavyweight championship from Battling Levinsky. Tunney defeated Dempsey for the title, and in the following year fought him again. This was the famous 'battle of the long count' in which Dempsey, after half a dozen smashing blows to the jaw, knocked Tunney down; but instead of retiring to neutral ground, stood over him. This gave Tunney about five seconds before the referee began to count, so that he was able to get on his feet by 'nine', and won the decision. Tunney married a socialite named Polly Lauder, corresponded with Bernard Shaw, and after his retirement lectured at Yale on Shakespeare.

Cricket, we were taught at school, was more than a game: it was meant to teach fair play, not only to us, but to natives in the British Empire. I was once taken to see Jack Hobbs at Canterbury, but remember nothing about it except the strawberries and cream we had for tea. Everybody wondered whether he would beat W. G. Grace's record of 126 centuries, and in 1924, on August 17th, he made 101 against Somerset, scored another century in the second innings, and was congratulated by the King.

In English county cricket Yorkshire and Lancashire stayed at the top, excelling in aggressive bowling and fielding. In Gentlemen v. Players, the Players usually won. In the 1926 Test Match, England won the Ashes ('the symbolic remains of English cricket taken back to Australia') for the first time since 1912, and they did it again in 1929. These came as welcome revenges after our being outclassed by Australia for the first years of the decade: there was, to uphold our honour, the great batting partnership of Hobbs and Sutcliffe, and the bowling of Maurice Tate. In the 1928–9 recovery, the other great names in the side led by A. P. F. Chapman were Larwood, Geary, White, Hendren, Jardine and Hammond; and, for Australia, a new name destined to dominate cricket for the next twenty years – Don Bradman.

Jack Hobbs   **Don Bradman**

Herman 'Babe' Ruth

Had I been an American schoolboy, my horizon would have been filled by the personality of George Herman Ruth, the 6ft 2in. left-handed Sultan of Swat, who restored to baseball the prestige it had lost through the Chicago White Sox scandal, in which eight players were accused of accepting bribes to 'throw' the 1919 world series. And next to 'Babe' Ruth came Ty Cobb.

There was still a good deal of controversy about the origins of the game. Had it been invented by Abner (later General) Doubleday in 1839? Or did it owe something to the old English game of rounders, and to another game called baseball mentioned by Jane Austen in *Northanger Abbey* as a favourite pastime of Catherine Morland in her childhood? (Soviet Russia once claimed that *Beizbol* was an old Russian game.) The Spalding Commission of 1907–8 had no doubt that Doubleday and the cadets he was instructing at Cooperstown had played the first game of baseball, and so, in September 1920, the original ground became hallowed as Doubleday Field and ratified as such by a New York Supreme Court three years later. The year 1923 also saw the building of the Yankee Stadium.

Ty Cobb

Babe, an orphan from the slums of Baltimore, where he attended a reform school, played for Boston Red Sox until New York Yankees bought him for $125,000. He was a rags-to-riches hero who wasn't always a man you would want your child to meet. He ate like a boy who'd never had enough; sometimes he drank too much, until Mayor Jimmy Walker told him that he owed it to the nation's youth to behave himself. Babe promised to reform, and did it so successfully that in 1927 his major league record for home runs in one year was 60 in 154 games.

His fame was such that any headline containing Babe, Bambino, Bam, or Slam was known to be about him: 'Babe Conks 36' = Babe has hit his thirty-sixth home run. Why Babe? No baby was ever so ugly. 'Everything about him is big,' wrote Paul Gallico. 'His frame, his enormous head surmounted by blue-black curly hair, his great blob of a nose spattered generously over his face, his mouth and his hands – only his ankles are strangely thin, like a woman's. . . . He talks like a sailor whose every third word is an oath.'

Babe drew crowds of 60,000 to 70,000, who were as delighted by his misses as by his hits: 'When he misses the ball, the force of his swing whirls him around until his legs are twisted like a German pretzel' said one spectator. Another said 'When he was playing in the Yankee Stadium, he would point right over the middle flag of the grandstand to show where he was going to hit the ball out of the park, and the next ball he hit right over the flag.' Nearly always in trouble with the baseball authorities, umpires, speed cops, and lawyers, he was equally capable of tear-jerking sentimental journeys to the bedsides of sick children. By 1930 he was getting roughly the same salary as the President of the United States; and in an age of lenient taxation that meant something.

In England most schoolboys could tell you what had won the Derby and who was going to win the Oxford and Cambridge Boat Race. The Derby was broadcast by the B.B.C., but the occasion was ruined by the announcement 'In accordance with the B.B.C.'s licence . . . we may not mention the name of the winner.' You went to the Derby by car more often than by coach, and you yelled 'Come on, Steve!' because Steve was Steve Donoghue, already in his forties, who won the Derby six times. The

horses? Well, there was Captain Cuttle, and Manna. But who cared about the horses except the owners? Well, the R.S.P.C.A. did, especially in the 1929 Grand National, when an outsider called Coregalach (100–1) won in a race in which only ten out of sixty-six horses finished.

As for the Boat Race, Oxford used to win sometimes in those days; but not in 1925, when the Oxford boat ignominiously sank.

There was polo at Hurlingham; car racing at Brooklands (dominated by Bentleys); dirt-track racing (an Australian idea) at new stadiums called speedways; ice rinks; above all, greyhound racing, which, it was reckoned, over 13,000,000 people were regularly attending in 1929. America's Gertrude Ederle, eighteen years old, was the first woman to swim the Channel in 1926.

Golf, hated by H. L. Mencken in America and Osbert Sitwell in England, claimed more recruits than ever, and clock golf began to appear in public

(right) Gertrude Ederle is crowned Queen of the Waves after swimming the Channel in 1926

(overleaf) 'The Jockey's Dressing Room at Ascot', 1923, by Sir John Lavery

parks and at seaside resorts. We spoke of mashies, and niblicks, for clubs did not yet have numbers, nor were their shafts until 1929 allowed to be of steel. The great names were Hagen, Diegel, Sarazen, Jones, Tolley and Roger and Joyce Wethered. The last three were British, and it is nice to be able to claim that American prowess after the First World War was partly due to the influence of Scottish golfers who had emigrated to the States.

All through the Twenties Bobby Jones, from Georgia, the greatest amateur golfer of his age, played for America against Britain in Walker Cup matches, and in 1930 he brought off his 'grand slam' by winning both British and American

Bobby Jones

amateur *and* open in the same year. Robert Tyrer Jones Jr's advice to golfers was 'Use your instinct . . . the more thoroughly we can divest the subjective mind of conscious control, the more perfectly can we execute our shots.' That way, too, you haven't time for nerves. Often he couldn't remember having hit the ball at all. Bobby, the great gentleman of golf, once penalized himself two strokes for picking out of a wood, and lost the match by one stroke. Praised for this piece of sportsmanship, he said 'You might as well praise me for not robbing a bank.' He retired at twenty-eight.

At my school, where we happily played association football, we were suddenly told that in future we were to play rugger, because rugger was a gentleman's game; and a special master was imported from South Wales to teach it to us. To this day I still prefer to watch soccer, and several million people in Britain and Brazil and many other countries are with me.

Soccer was still one of the games at which the British could beat foreigners; but it was much more local rivalries that drew the cloth-capped crowds to the big matches (J. B. Priestley uses those caps, at the beginning of *The Good Companions*, to introduce us to Jess Oakroyd). It was a swifter game than it had been before the war, with more heading, less dribbling and (in 1928) a new offside rule that altered tactics fundamentally. The new Wembley Stadium drew crowds in special trains from all over the country 'up for the Cup'. And its first Cup Final was nearly a disaster.

As Bolton Wanderers prepared to meet West Ham United on April 28th 1923, the 91,000 or so ticket-holders were swollen by hordes of people – there seem to have been at least 35,000 of them – who rushed the turnstiles, broke through the barriers and streamed on to the ground. Even the ritual singing of 'Abide With Me' failed to control them, and soon a thousand people (including policemen) had been injured, sixty quite seriously. Fortunately the mounted police were there, and they took forty minutes to restore order. The hero of the day was P.C. George Albert Scorey, a former troop-major of the Scots Greys, who was largely responsible for getting the mob back beyond the touchline. Nobody gave him a medal or promoted him; but 'the policeman on the white horse' became a folk hero. The match, incidentally, was won by Bolton, 2–0.

Walter Hagen

CHAPTER 11

People Like Us

In a decade which was fast rejecting corsets and every other kind of constraint Judd Gray was a corset salesman. In an age which didn't much care for orthodox religion Judd Gray was a churchgoer; and he lived in Queens Village, Long Island. A smallish man, he was in love with a biggish Norwegian girl named Ruth, who was inconveniently married to Albert Snyder, art editor of a magazine devoted to the rising pastime of sailing. Ruth called Judd 'Lover Boy'; Judd called Ruth 'Momsie', which tells us a little bit about both of them.

Albert Snyder was a Christian Scientist, and it was a matter of sorrow to him that he could not convert his wife to his own faith. It was his remedy for everything, even for her desire – which he must surely have suspected – to kill him. Or was it just part of her fantasy life that she had given him drugs, and gas, and tried to choke him to death? Too many movies, perhaps?

Eventually Ruth and Judd planned one of the most ineptly clumsy killings in the annals of crime. Judd prepared the weapons and hid them in one of his corsets, which was fashionably pink: they were a heavy weight, for bashing the victim, a length of wire, for garrotting him, and a bottle of chloroform, for minimizing his resistance. They then set to work, trying to make it look as if the job had been done by persons unknown, with robbery as the motive.

Nobody believed this for a second; and the two accused alienated a good deal of sympathy by accusing each other of doing the actual violence. Or so it seemed to the spectators in court, who included such celebrities as Aimée Macpherson,

the hot-gospeller, and D. W. Griffith, the film maker. Judd and Ruth went together to the electric chair, and the execution, according to American custom in those days, was witnessed by the press, one of whom secured a scoop photograph of the actual moment of death by strapping a vest-pocket camera to his ankle.

For this was a Twenties murder, blown up big by the mass media; not a gangster killing, but something with which average readers could identify themselves; especially an average woman reader, daydreaming of a secret lover. Why else should millions of people in at least two continents have followed it so avidly? A crime which many must have committed in their hearts, so that, for some, Ruth must have been a heroine, and Judd a sympathetically weak man, like so many men. Looking at their faces, you would have sworn that the main butchery was done by Ruth. How could this mild, bespectacled little man have brought himself to do it?

But it was Judd who interested H. L. Mencken, who reported the trial for the *Baltimore Sun*. He recognized that spectre of Anglo-American life, the Nonconformist Conscience. 'His (Judd's) initial peccadillo [adultery]', Mencken wrote, 'shocked him so vastly that he could think of himself thereafter only as a sinner unspeakable and incorrigible. . . . Sin is a dangerous toy in the hands of the virtuous. It should be left to the congenitally sinful, who know when to play with it and when to let it alone. Run a boy through a Presbyterian Sunday school, and you must police him carefully all the rest of his life, for once he slips, he is ready for anything.'

The press, especially the New York *Daily Mirror*, never let anything alone: the Hall-Mills murder, for example. It happened in 1922, was reopened in 1926 after much newspaper agitation – and still nobody was found guilty. For 'Lover Boy' and 'Momsie', read 'Babykins' and 'my Gipsy Queen', for these were what Mrs Eleanor Mills and the Rev. Edward Hall called each other in intimate moments: in particular, in letters, which James, Eleanor's husband, eventually sold to a newspaper for the by no means princely sum of $500.

Dr Hall, forty-one-year-old Rector of St John the Evangelist, New Brunswick, N.J., and Mrs Mills, thirty-four, who sang in his choir, were found shot dead under a spreading crab apple tree in De Russey's Lane, not far from the church. Mrs Mills had been shot more thoroughly, and her throat had been cut too. The bodies were surrounded by pages of letters which were full of compromising phrases.

At the trial no fewer than four people were accused of murder: the Rector's widow, Frances Hall, who was seven years older than her late

Photograph showing the actual moment of death by electric chair of Ruth Snyder

husband; her two brothers, Henry and Willie, an amiable nutcase whose hobby was riding around on the local fire-engine; and her cousin Henry Carpender, a highly respectable member of the New York Stock Exchange. Mrs Hall denied all knowledge of her husband's affair with Mrs Mills, though she knew Mrs Mills well and had generously paid for her recent kidney operation. Both she and the three accused men denied being anywhere near the scene of the murder on the day or night in question.

At this point black comedy enters the story. If you were to ask almost any American over forty, in a TV quiz, 'Who was the Pig Woman?' you would get an answer which referred to the Hall-Mills murder, even if the name had been forgotten. The name in fact was Jane Gibson, and she gave her evidence from a stretcher, for she was dying of cancer. Mrs Gibson, who lived near De Russey's Lane and kept pigs, made a practice of riding her mule at night, 'looking for corn thieves', and she claimed she had actually seen the murder being committed. The effect of her evidence was ruined by her aged mother, who kept interrupting with 'She's a liar.' The court also formed the impression that she was a liar.

This raised the question why Mrs Hall had sent a brown coat to Philadelphia, some fifty miles away, to be dyed black. Was it bloodstained? Certainly not, Mrs Hall replied: she needed a black coat for mourning. The jury accepted this story, and as the Pig Woman had been the key witness for the prosecution, there was nothing to be done but acquit all four accused. After more than fifty years we are unlikely ever to know who killed the Rector and his paramour under the crab apple tree. Apart from the *Mirror*, Alexander Woollcott believed that 'the world's interest in the Hall-Mills case was immeasurably enhanced by the romantic flavour of the phrase 'De Russey's Lane'.'

'To think this should happen to *us*!' – 'people like us!' The crimes which most fascinated the Twenties, and the media of the Twenties, were those committed either by or against ordinary people, whatever 'ordinary people' means. The phrase was used in bewilderment by Mr Grayson, father of Edith Thompson, and immortalized by Beverley Nichols in a world scoop: the sort of assignment that only a young reporter is tough enough to undertake – interviewing the murderess's parents the day after she has been hanged. *People Like Us* was also the title of a play by Frank Vosper, which could not be publicly performed in the lifetime of Edith Thompson's parents.

A week or two after the Hall-Mills murder, on October 3rd 1922, Percy and Edith Thompson caught the last train home from Liverpool Street Station, London, after going to see a farce by Ben Travers, *The Dippers*, at the Criterion Theatre. They did not often 'do a show' together: being childless, they both had jobs, he as a shipping clerk, she as bookkeeper-manageress at a wholesale milliner's in Aldersgate Street in the City.

As they walked from their local station to their house in Kensington Gardens, Ilford, Essex, a young man appeared from the shadows, shouted something like 'Why don't you divorce your wife?' and stabbed Thompson twice. Edith was heard, by someone in a neighbouring house, to cry out 'Oh, don't! Oh, don't!' Thompson, who, although only thirty-two, had had several heart attacks, died within a few minutes, and the assailant disappeared.

Next day Thompson's brother told the police that a young man named Frederick Bywaters had been making trouble between Percy and Edith; and Bywaters was found, and arrested, at Edith's parents' house in Manor Park, North London.

Bywaters was eight years younger than Edith, who was twenty-eight. He had been the Thompsons' lodger when he was not at sea (he was a steward on the P. & O. liner *Morea*), and had accompanied them on a holiday to Shanklin, Isle of Wight, where they had all taken happy snaps of each other. There had been a row, and Bywaters had moved out of the house; but he and Edith continued their association on Bywaters's infrequent shore leaves, and by letter.

Bywaters's letters were generally addressed to Edith's Aldersgate office, and most of them she wisely destroyed. In this case, he was the hoarder, and the letters from Edith which followed his ship to Marseilles, Port Said, Aden and Bombay were produced in evidence. They have been thought, by some, worthy of inclusion in anthologies of Great Love Letters. Well, they weren't quite that, but they were moving and literate and full of the romantic books she read: *The Shulamite* (about Abishag, last addition to the aged King David's harem, inherited by the young King Solomon);

The Guarded Flame, John Chilcote, M.P., The Fruitful Vine – how many of their authors can we even remember today? And *Bella Donna*, by Robert Hichens – about a wife poisoning her husband.

> We ourselves die and live in the books we read while we are reading them and then when we have finished, the books die and we live – or exist – just drag on through years and years, until what? Who knows? . . . We are not the shapers of our destinies.

The letters were not always on this level: sometimes she is making jam and chutney; or – 'Darling, your own pal is getting quite a sport. On Saturday I was first in the egg and spoon race . . .' And some of them hanged Edith Thompson; for they contained explicit details of attempts to poison Percy. 'Digitalin,' she wrote, after reading *Bella Donna*, 'is a cumulative poison . . . the same dose, harmless if taken once, yet frequently repeated becomes deadly.' And Percy had a heart condition: if this method had been used, would we ever have heard of Thompson-Bywaters? In cross-examination Edith admitted that she had wanted, not to kill him, but to 'make him ill'; thus undoing a great deal of Sir Henry Curtis-Bennett's defence of her.

But digitalin would not have been dramatic enough. She says, in other letters, that she has been putting powdered glass in Percy's porridge, and then actually smashing up an electric light bulb so that the pieces shall be bigger. Sir Bernard Spilsbury, the pathologist, who did the *post mortem* on Percy Thompson, found no evidence of poisoning, and thought the whole thing was self-dramatization. Spilsbury seems also to have thought that Edith Thompson was guiltless of any conspiracy to murder her husband, and one of the passages he sidelined in his copy of the report of the trial is from one of her letters to Bywaters: 'I like you deciding things for me. I've done it so long for myself . . . I want you so badly to lean on and to take care of me . . .' There are also masochistic declarations of love in which Edith seems to be seeking the he-man, the demon lover, the whip of Valentino, all so fashionable in the 1920s.

Bywaters had confessed, and there was nothing the law could do to save him from the rope. Mr Justice Shearman's summing up seemed to browbeat the jury into condemning Edith Thompson to death for adultery more than for murder. He took particular exception to a sentence in one of her letters about her husband: 'He has the right by law to all that you have a right to by nature and by love.' This simply ennobled adultery, he told the jury: 'I am certain that you, like other right-minded persons, will be filled with disgust at such a notion.'

The appeal against the verdict on Edith Thompson was dismissed, and she was hanged at Holloway Jail in circumstances of such horror that one of the warders had a nervous breakdown and committed suicide. Several novels and plays have been based on the case, notably F. Tennyson Jesse's *A Pin to See the Peepshow*, whose heroine gets right inside the world of Edith Thompson when she considers what her lover means to her: 'He was as much a part of her life as the Indian Love Lyrics.'

'People like us.' Back to Beverley Nichols, in the Graysons' sitting room: 'People who had neat little houses in dreary suburban crescents. People who had a pair of Staffordshire dogs, very brightly polished, on each side of a clock with a glass case over it. People who had an upright piano with a piece of beaded silk on the top, and a pile of songs which included 'Because' and 'Friend of Mine' . . .'

George Orwell, with his eyes on this same decade, tried to construct, from a *News of the World* reader's viewpoint, a composite murderer. He should be 'a little man of the professional class – a dentist or a solicitor, say – living an intensely respectable life in a suburban detached house (so that the neighbours could hear suspicious noises). He is probably Conservative, Nonconformist, Temperance. He will be in love with his secretary or another professional man's wife, and he will choose murder only because it is less damaging to his career than adultery. The means chosen should, of course, be poison.'

Like little Major Herbert Rowse Armstrong, M.A. (Cantab.), fifty-eight, weighing only ninety-eight pounds, solicitor and clerk to the Justices of the Peace in Hay, Breconshire, Wales. In 1922 he was charged with the murder by arsenic of his large, bullying wife Katherine Mary, after she had made her will, leaving him £2,300. Mrs Armstrong had spent some time in a lunatic asylum. We do not know of any particular 'other woman' in his life – but he seems to have been suffering from V.D. at the time of his trial: there had been certain weekend excursions to London, where, whatever else he was up to, he had bought large quantities of weedkiller

The jury arriving at the Armstrong case, 1922

containing arsenic, ostensibly to eradicate dandelions, of which there were only twenty in his garden.

There was a legal argument, at the trial, about admissible evidence. Had the poisoning of Mrs Armstrong anything to do with the attempted poisoning of Oswald Martin, a rival but friendly solicitor in the town, who was dunning Armstrong for £500 paid as deposit on a sale of property? Armstrong sent him chocolates injected with weedkiller; then pestered him with invitations to tea at which he offered him buttered scones, after one of which he was extremely ill. To make sure his guest ate the right scone, he picked it up and put it on Martin's plate, smiling 'Excuse fingers.'

Norman Thorne, hanged in 1925 for the murder of Elsie Cameron, fulfils some of the Orwell requirements. He taught in Sunday school, belonged to the Band of Hope, helped to run boys' clubs. He scraped a living from a small chicken farm at Crowborough, Sussex, where the neurotic Miss Cameron visited him on December 5th 1924. For weeks she had been imagining herself to be pregnant and pestering him to marry her. Unfortunately he was more interested in a local girl, Elizabeth Coldicott, whom he seems to have taken to the cinema immediately after killing Elsie (by bruising resulting in shock, Spilsbury said). Thorne seemed to enjoy the press publicity, and actually asked to be photographed feeding chickens at the hen run where Elsie's dismembered body was eventually dug up. His story that Elsie had hanged herself, and that panic had made him cut her up with a hacksaw, was discounted by the pathologist's evidence. If only he had stuck to the truth – that he had struck her during a quarrel – he might have got away with manslaughter. But then, of course, he would have had to resign from the Sunday school.

Very British was the public reaction to the shooting, on September 26th 1927, of P.C. George William Gutteridge, the village policeman of Stapleford Abbots, between Romford and Ongar, in Essex. The shooting of a policeman, much rarer then than now, provoked an outburst of horror: in every village up and down the country people thought 'Suppose it had been *our* bobby.' And the names of Browne and Kennedy have come down to posterity as among the most hated in our criminal history. You can poison your wife, chop up bodies, swindle people out of thousands of pounds, and people will feel sympathy and even admiration for you; but if you kill a policeman, you are damned by all but professional criminals.

Men like Frederick Guy Browne, with a long record of violence, car thief and proprietor of a garage near Clapham Junction, where he employed a much pettier criminal named William Kennedy. Together they had stolen Dr Lovell's Morris-Cowley car from Billericay, Essex, and driven it to London through back lanes, avoiding the main road, which was why they were flashed down by P.C. Gutteridge's torch at Stapleford Abbots. 'May I see your licence, sir?' And as he pulled out his notebook, Gutteridge was shot through the face, and again through both eyes as he lay on the ground.

Much nearer to Orwell standards were the goings-on at Birdhurst Rise, in the most sedate middle-class quarter of South Croydon, Surrey. In April 1928 Mr Edmund Duff, fifty-nine, a retired Commissioner of Northern Nigeria, returned from a fishing holiday to his home in nearby South Hill Park Road. He ate the cold supper his wife Grace had left out for him, felt extremely ill, was told by the family doctor, Dr Binning, he was suffering from colic, and died next evening. The following February his unmarried sister-in-law, Vera Sydney, forty, who lived with her mother, Mrs Violet Sydney, the comfortably-off widow of a

barrister in Birdhurst Rise, was violently ill. Dr Binning's diagnosis of gastric influenza was confirmed by a specialist. Miss Sydney died about thirty-six hours later.

Less than three weeks later, Mrs Sydney, sixty-eight, took a dose of a tonic prescribed by Dr Binning, said it tasted nasty, and in a few hours died. Dr Binning was inclined to explain this as food poisoning. If criminal poisoning ever occurred to him, he would have dismissed it because he was a friend of the family; as for inquests, they meant publicity, and nobody in South Croydon wanted publicity. But now the Home Office intervened, and the bodies of Mrs Sydney, Vera Sydney and Edmund Duff were exhumed. The details of what was found, and the complications arising from the mutual dislike of two pathologists, Spilsbury and Brontë, are too many to cover here; but it was almost certain that arsenic had been taken in each case, always in a liquid – beer, soup and tonic.

Mrs Sydney's son Thomas, a concert entertainer, lived with his family in South Hill Park Road, near the Duffs' house, and was always popping into his mother's house; he had been there the day before Mrs Sydney's illness: they had discussed her will. Vera Sydney had about £4,500, and by her will her mother received a life interest on £2,000. In the event of Mrs Sydney's death this sum was to be divided between Thomas Sydney and Grace Duff. Grace also popped in a lot. Thomas Sydney used arsenical weedkiller in his garden, but so did thousands of other people.

Verdict: murder by some person or persons unknown, after a series of inquests and adjournments, lasting until August 1929, reducing the coroner almost to nervous prostration. It was said that the police had opinions about the case which were more than theories, but the problem of the crimes, if they were crimes, has never been solved.

Into no theory or category of crime does the death of Starr Faithfull conveniently fall. Hers was a Twenties life, a Prohibition life, a John O'Hara life, maybe a Vladimir Nabokov life; and I quote it as a link between two worlds – people-like-us and the others; or between British and American crime of the Twenties at the point where they differed most widely; yet her death overlapped the Twenties by eighteen months.

On June 8th 1931 the body of twenty-five-year-

Starr Faithfull

old Miss Faithfull was found washed up on Long Beach, N.Y., wearing a silk dress and nothing else. She had drunk veronal, but no alcohol, before her death, which was due to drowning and had taken place at least two days before. Due to drowning alone? Her lungs were full of sand as well as water, and it was suggested that this was consistent with her having been held down under the waves near the shore.

No alcohol: this was strange, for Starr was a drunk, and had been admitted to Bellevue Hospital, New York, about twelve months before, suffering from 'acute alcoholism' and 'contusions on face, jaw and upper lip' after being beaten up in a hotel room by a man who may or may not have been a client. Not that Starr was a prostitute in the ordinary sense: she seems to have got her kicks from tormenting men without enjoying the final consummation; and above

all from the wild parties that used to take place on board transatlantic liners before they sailed for Europe. A kind of nymphomaniac, and yet she wrote to a friend: 'It's the preliminaries that count with me.' Of those 'preliminaries' she kept an obscene diary.

Yet about some things she was curiously prudish: in an era of thigh-length skirts she preferred them ankle-length, and disapproved of contemporary bathing-suits as indecent. The stories about her multiplied after her death: she had been seduced at the age of eleven by a former mayor of Boston, she was an ether addict, she was a culture-vulture, she had a death wish. (Is any of this beginning to sound familiar? Lolita, perhaps? Gloria Wandrous in *Butterfield 8*, certainly.)

Because all liners went past Long Beach, about four miles out, and because it was known that Starr had been on the Cunard liner *Mauretania* during part of June 5th, it was tempting to assume that she had fallen (or thrown herself) overboard. But there were witnesses that she had gone ashore long before the ship sailed.

It was not the *Mauretania* that was the centre of Starr's life: it was the *Franconia*, or rather the ship's surgeon, George Jameson-Carr. Starr had had two glamorous trips to England in the luxury liners of those days which were the nearest approach to the fantasies of Hollywood come true. Dr Jameson-Carr by no means reciprocated Starr's feelings for him. On May 29th, after a good deal of drinking, she had expressed a desire to stay on board and sail with him to England. The ship's company had shoved her into a small boat and taken her ashore. She then wrote two letters to Jameson-Carr, containing among other things the following sentences:

> Life is horrible . . . I take dope to forget and drink to try and like people . . . I know it will soon be over . . . the only thing I dread is being outwitted and prevented from doing this . . . No ether, allonal or window-jumping. I don't want to be maimed . . . It's a great life when one has twenty-four hours to live.

Emotional blackmail – or genuine intent to commit suicide? On June 5th her family in respectable St Luke's Place, Greenwich Village, reported to the police that she had not come home the previous night. If it was suicide, it couldn't have been emotional blackmail. If it was murder, it might have been. It didn't matter – least of all to Starr.

CHAPTER 12

People Unlike Us

'I was T.T. until Prohibition,' said Groucho Marx. So were a lot of other people, including Robert Benchley, as befits a good Nonconformist. But soon even Benchley, on coming out of a swimming pool, was liable to say things like 'I must step out of these wet things and into a dry Martini.'

Many American parents, downing their last high-balls in the year 1919, felt relieved that their children would be spared this addiction to alcohol. They would drink instead the soda-pop, ice-cream, candy, sundae confections that made the Babbitt children's faces so pasty. Some States were already dry, had been so since before the War. The Anti-Saloon League and other temperance bodies, female-dominated, had been hard at work – one of them, the National Prohibition party, since the Civil War. What was about to happen was regarded as 'the greatest social experiment of modern times'. Or, in the words of the Anti-Saloon League, 'an era of clear thinking and clean living'.

In 1919 the Volstead Act, implementing the Eighteenth Amendment, made it illegal for anyone to manufacture or drink any liquid with more than $\frac{1}{2}$ per cent alcohol. Theoretically this could admit a weak kind of wine or beer; but wine and beer were still largely the drinks of immigrants. America had been founded on stronger stuff. Among many antici-pated benefits it was thought that Prohibition would help to avoid trouble with Negroes in the South. Many great men of the time gave praiseworthy reasons for a dry America: 'The speed at which we run our motor cars, operate our intricate machinery, and generally live, would be impossible with liquor' said Henry Ford. And Dr Charles Foster Kent deleted all references to wine in the Bible. He was paralleled, in Britain, by Arthur Mee, editor of *The Children's Newspaper*, who, reprinting great poems for the edification of his young readers. substituted the word *lemonade* for wine, beer, ale, etc. What he made of 'the true, the blushful Hippocrene' is not recorded.

Certain people were 'good and ready' for Pro-hibition. Within a year of the Volstead Act becoming law, portable one-gallon home liquor stills were on sale at $6–$7. Rum was arriving from British Honduras or the West Indies by motor launch. Canadian whisky was entering the country through Detroit. J. & B. Rare Scotch built up a brand loyalty during these years which gave it the dominance it enjoys today. Foreign labels were copied and stuck on to cans, stating that no others were genuine; as the contents were often made from wood alcohol, which was said to result in blindness if not death, or from dilute sulphuric acid, this could be serious. The three great operating points for illegally im-ported liquor were Vancouver, from which a fleet of ships worked the West Coast; Nassau, Bahamas, which supplied Florida and the South East; and St Pierre de Miquelon, West Indies, where huge ware-houses sprang up to supply the East Coast. Overland, a certain amount came in through Windsor, Ontario. In Europe, Hamburg and Antwerp were among the main collecting points, at which some of the biggest bootleggers owned their own ships.

British businessmen visiting New York were generally greeted at their hotels with an internal

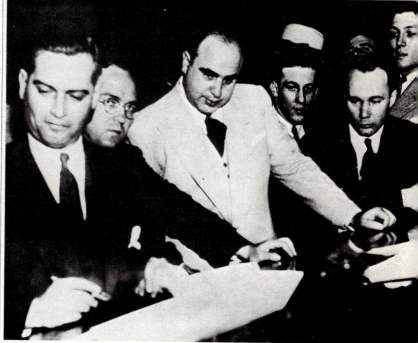

(above) Federal agents Izzy (Einstein)
and Moe the Peerless (Smith)
confiscating liquor
(right) Al Capone (centre in light suit)

telephone call, 'Want any liquor, pal?', or had a card pushed into their hands by a bell-hop which said 'Sam Mordecai, Interior Decorator' – and you knew, of course, that it was *your* interior Sam wished to decorate. Sam then delivered bottles in brown paper parcels.

What happens when crime and law become indistinguishable, and *Untermensch* becomes *Herrenvolk*, was about to be seen in Chicago, 'the wickedest city in the world', where every citizen could tell you who the following people were: Orazio 'the Scourge' Tropea, Murray 'the Camel' Humphries, Spike O'Donnell, Sam 'Golf Bag' Hunt, Dingbat O'Berta, Jake 'Greasy Thumb' Guzik, Hymie 'Loud Mouth' Levine, and Machine-Gun Jack McGurn.

Johnny Torrio was an established gang leader when America went dry. He had started life as personal bodyguard to Diamond Jim Colosimo, multiple brothel owner, whom he eventually 'bumped off' and to whom he gave a 'swell funeral' which was attended by all Chicago's top brass, including judges, aldermen and police. Kenneth Allsop, in his definitive work *The Bootleggers*, gives a map showing the 'gang areas' of Chicago, and the pattern of the next few years he sees as divided into three main phases: Torrio organizes the areas and profit-sharing; O'Banion breaks it up; and Capone moves in as dictator of all.

Already in 1920 Torrio was aiming at the monopoly of all booze in the city. It seems that he and Capone (a Neapolitan, not a Sicilian) had grown up together in the Five Points gang in New York, and he first sent for Capone (then twenty-three) to 'take care of the competition'. Soon Mr Capone had visiting cards printed: *Alphonse Capone, secondhand furniture dealer, 2220 S. Wabash Avenue.* Before long he had superseded Torrio, who fled to Italy after an attempt on his life, installed his own Mayor, and was said to have his own employees in 161 bars and gambling houses. With sawn-off shotguns, Thompson sub-machine guns and occasionally bombs, he 'took care of' the O'Banions, the Gennas, the Aiellos. His annual income during these years has been put at $30 million, the proceeds of gambling houses, dog tracks, laundries, garages, fish markets, dairies, vice, dance halls, liquor and protection rackets. 'Protection' meant that you paid gangsters to avoid having your place smashed up by an 'education committee'.

How heavily was Big Bill Thompson, Republican Mayor of Chicago, involved in all this? The British knew only one fact about him – that he wanted to punch King George's nose. They therefore enjoyed raising their brows when, on Thompson's death in 1944, an unexplained hoard of $1,750,000 in banknotes was found at his house. The *Encyclopaedia Britannica* (which is of course published from Chicago) says, with embarrassed understatement, that during Thompson's mayoralty 'the growth of the gang system subjected Chicago to wide criticism'; and that the four-year reign of his successor, William Dever, a Democrat, 'did not appreciably stem the tide of lawlessness'. By 1927 Big Bill was back in City Hall, and in Capone's office his portrait shared the walls with those of Abe Lincoln and George Washington.

'I own the police' Torrio had said, and in 1923 it was reckoned that 60 per cent of Chicago cops were actually in the liquor business. It was possible, in the 1924 municipal election, for voters in the suburb of Cicero to be ordered how to vote at pistol point. These quiet suburbs, Capone said, were 'virgin territory for whore-houses'. He was, as always, 'supplying a public need'. His mass executions, he maintained sorrowfully, were made necessary by the unreasonableness of his competitors – men like the Gennas who were offering raw alcohol at half price: 'We were making a shooting gallery of a great business, and nobody profited by it.' And when it was church-going Hymie Weiss's turn to be rubbed out, Capone said in despair 'Forty times I've tried to arrange things so we'd have peace and life would be worth living.'

The trouble was that Capone, with his $30,000 bullet-proof armoured Cadillac, a machine-gunner seated beside the driver, with a scout car in front and a posse of armed henchmen in another car behind, and his mansion at Miami with accommodation for seventy-five guests, had glamour. At school in England we spoke gangster language – 'Muscling in on my racket', 'Sez you', 'Put him on the spot', 'Know him? I shot him!' and 'He shall have a swell funeral'. We queued eagerly for gangster films and Edgar Wallace's play *On the Spot*, with Charles Laughton as Toni Perelli (the third-act curtain of which came down on Perelli, about to be bumped off, on his knees in front of a crucifix, screaming 'Donna Maria!').

For the customers, the great speakeasy life was in full swing. You had your own bar behind a bookcase at home, and if you were a big enough shot your bootlegger called on you personally, and of course you carried a hip-flask. But there was nothing to touch the excitement of speakeasies. 'There was an unholy joy', Donald Ogden Stewart, the veteran screenwriter now living in London, told me, 'in going down some steps to a dingy door, sliding back a panel and saying 'I'm a friend of Bob Benchley's – can I come in?'

John O'Hara has listed them for us in New York, in one of his nostalgic catalogues in *Butterfield 8*: some of them were run by Owney Madden, who had a secret system for disposing of every drop of liquor between the first knock of a police raid and the time they entered the room. He said 'youse' and 'dese' and 'dem', not because he came from Brooklyn but because he was Liverpool Irish. The Dizzy Club, Hotsy-Totsy, Chez Florence, the Type & Print Club, Basque's, Michel's, Tony's E. 53rd Street, Tony's W. 49th, 42 W. 49th, Aquarium, Mario's, the Clamhouse, the Bandbox, W. 44th Street Club, McDermott's, the Sligo Slasher's, Newswriters', Sam Schwartz's, Frankie & Johnny's . . . At some of them you were expected to wear a tuxedo. Even the Stork Club was a speakeasy, and I have met an octogenarian who still has his membership card. And if you belonged to the Algonquin Set, you patronized Jack & Charlie's Luncheon Club (the same as the 42 W. 49th listed above), which sold real imported wines and spirits.

Speakeasies, the Prohibition era itself, nowadays have glamour too. Kenneth Allsop discovered, in 1960, a Gaslight Club on North Rush Street, Chicago, which was a faithful reproduction of a 1920s speakeasy; and Alistair Cooke, in the mid-1950s, visited Princeton and found a 'revive the 20s' cult whose members made their own bath-tub gin in the correct manner with distilled water.

The crimes of Chicago were mostly unsolved (and there were some 500 gang killings altogether, 227 of them believed to be of Capone's 'competition'); that is to say, everyone had a good idea who did them but nobody could prove anything. I have selected three, because they tell us more about People Unlike Us than the others.

Diamond Jim Colosimo was rising fifty when the Twenties began. He had hauled himself up by his

Two speakeasy bars

sock-suspenders (which, like most other parts of him, were inlaid with diamonds) from shoeshine boy to a commanding position in the vice industry, which he was able to do because he had squared a number of Chicago politicians and presumably also the police. His ostensible calling was restaurant proprietor, and his place on Wabash Avenue and Twenty-Second was patronized by stars of music and show business, especially of opera, which Big Jim loved better than anything. At Big Jim's you could expect to meet Caruso, Tetrazzini, Galli-Curci and Flo Ziegfeld.

In 1920 he left his wife Victoria and went off with Dale Winter, a singer who had had a few lessons with Caruso. There had been a number of smallish gang murders previously, but the death of Colosimo is usually regarded as the first true gang execution of the post-war years. Yet was it a gang killing, in the usual sense of 'taking care of the competition'? Or were the police using hoodlums to accomplish their own ends, having failed to pin anything on Diamond Jim? And if so, was Victoria, the deserted wife, the chief informant?

Whatever the reasons, Diamond Jim, on May 11th 1920, went to a 'business appointment' and was never again seen alive. Torrio, the bodyguard, took over his empire, assisted by Capone. At Diamond Jim's funeral, Torrio wept real tears and made a speech in which he said 'We was like brothers.'

One man who profited from every killing, because he had a share in Schofield's flower shop on North State Street and was thus in the market for wreaths, was Dion, Deanie or Gimpy O'Banion, who had graduated from being an altar boy at Holy Name Cathedral through safe-blowing to controlling all bootleg liquor on the North Side of Chicago. He seemed to have a genuine conscientious objection to being involved in the vice racket, and might have survived for many more years if he had not fallen foul of the Torrio-Capone syndicate. He sold Torrio his interest in a brewery and, as soon as he had done it, Torrio was arrested – double-crossed, it was said, by O'Banion. O'Banion was Irish, and therefore not familiar with the power of the Unione Siciliano or Mafia, to which Torrio and also the Terrible Gennas, who ran the West Side booze area, and even Capone, although he was a mere Neapolitan, belonged. So that when O'Banion was heard to say 'To hell with them Sicilians', he had signed his own death warrant in five words.

When, on November 8th 1924, Michael Merlo, president of the Unione Siciliano, died, Torrio and Capone between them spent $18,000 in floral tributes at O'Banion's flower shop. Two days later a bunch of customers turned up at the shop and put six shots into O'Banion. There seem to have been three of them: the one in the middle shook him by the hand and held on while the other two pumped lead into him. He, too, had a swell funeral, with floral tributes (orchids) on a scale never seen before. The flower shop thereafter became the gang headquarters for O'Banion's successor Hymie Weiss, and then a gangster named Drucci, and finally Bugs Moran.

Five years later 'them Sicilians' tried to find a final solution to the Irish in what has come to be known as the St Valentine's Day Massacre in 1929. Apparently planned at Capone's headquarters at the Lexington Hotel, the executions were actually carried out while Capone was in Florida. Five O'Banion men had gone to a garage on Clark Street to meet persons unknown to discuss a big consignment of whisky. The persons unknown were in police uniform, but no one really believed they were policemen; and they had machine-guns. With the O'Banion boys two other men were killed – a doctor and a *Chicago Tribune* reporter named Jake Lingle who seems to have been a part-time gangster, or was at least in the pay of Bugs Moran. Bugs Moran may have been the real target of the exercise, but he wasn't there. He wasn't there on numerous other occasions, and miraculously survived until 1957.

Various explanations have been offered by sociologists and psychologists for Chicago gangsterism. Wops and Micks and Yids, we are told on one level, couldn't assimilate. Their education was non-existent, they didn't understand the normal American goals, the right way to pursue happiness; they knew no way out of slums and ghettos without violence. 'The gangster of the Prohibition Era', Max Lerner said in an often-quoted (but not otherwise explained) observation, 'was almost invariably a Sicilian, an Irishman or a Jew'. Were they 'emotionally deprived'? It seems not: the common denominator between them, it has been said, was that they all loved their Mommas.

Of the bootleggers themselves, the men who got the stuff for the gangsters to distribute, we know less. What did they do in their retirement? Well, one of them, Charles Guttman, actually did a bit of good in the world: he spent some of his millions on starting an institution in New York for screening women for the early detection of breast-cancer.

No explanation seems to suffice for the mass-killings in Chicago, and we have known far worse since. But how to explain one isolated killing (also, it happens, in Chicago) which defies classification? In Colin Wilson's *Encyclopedia of Murder* it has a heading of its own: 'Murder for Experiment'. It belongs to the Twenties, not only chronologically,

but psychologically and philosophically, and in the ensuing trial many technical terms from the new young science of psychiatry were hurled about the court room. The only crime in British annals which remotely approaches it was the Moors Murders in the early 1960s, and then only in the fact that in each case a murderer's mind had been influenced by a writer: de Sade, in the case of Brady and Hindley; Nietzsche in the case of Leopold and Loeb.

Nathan Leopold, nineteen, and Richard Loeb,

The St Valentine's Day Massacre, 1929

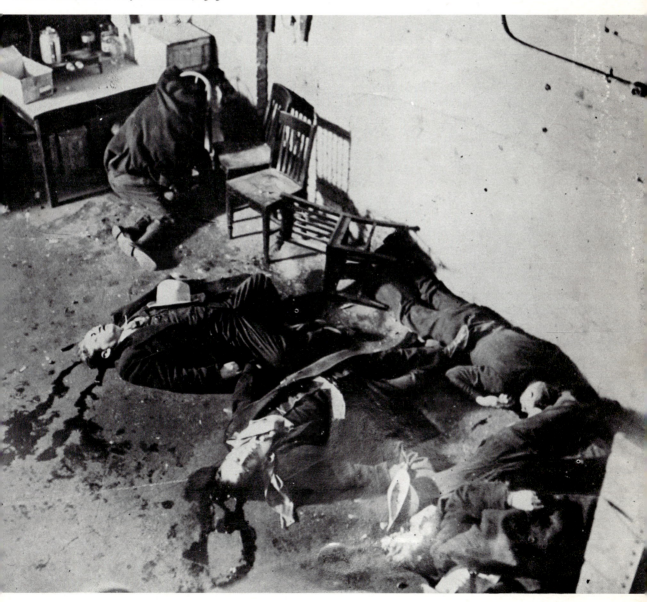

eighteen, were law students at Chicago University. Much has been made of their intellectual precocity, and Leopold in particular has been credited with the highest I.Q. ever known. He was certainly the dominating partner in what appears to have been a homosexual relationship. They were rich, bored and fascinated by the theory of the Superman – beyond morals, beyond the law; and by murder – the perfect murder – as an intellectual exercise.

Bobbie Franks, a boy of fourteen known to Loeb's family, came out of his school in South Side Kenwood, on the afternoon of May 21st 1924, to find Leopold and Loeb, all smiles, waiting with a hired car. Would he like a ride? Bobby got in and was instantly done to death with four blows of a chisel. The two students then held his head under water to make sure he was dead, tried to obliterate his features with hydrochloric acid, and stuffed his body into a drainpipe near the Pennsylvania railroad.

They then ate a good dinner at a restaurant and drove to Leopold's home where (note the leisurely order of events) they drank a good deal of whisky, played cards, washed the blood off the car and (using the name of Johnson) telephoned Mrs Franks to inform her that her son had been kidnapped but was 'at present well and safe'. The Frankses would receive a ransom note for $10,000 with instructions on how to convey the money to Mr Johnson. The police, of course, must not be informed.

In fact, notifying the police was the first thing Mr Franks did. The police told him next day that Bobby's body had been found. They also found a pair of spectacles belonging to Leopold. Leopold's explanation was that he had dropped the spectacles weeks ago while bird-watching, which was his hobby, and that on May 21st anyway he had been out with Loeb and two girls named Mae and Edna, who could not be traced.

Meanwhile two *Chicago Daily News* reporters, Goldstein and Mulroy, had compared the ransom note with some other samples of Leopold's typewriter and found them identical. Under police interrogation both Leopold and Loeb confessed, but each accused the other of striking the lethal blows.

At the trial both men were defended by Clarence Seward Darrow, then sixty-seven. It was still an age of 'great advocates', men like him, and Sir Edward Marshall Hall and Sir Patrick Hastings in England, who could move juries to tears and set aside the directions of judges. Darrow believed in pity, charity and love, but thought of himself as an agnostic. He thought that the criminal himself was never wholly responsible, that jails should be transformed into hospitals, and that capital punishment should be abolished; that everybody married too young and that divorce should be made easier. He had read more widely than any other advocate of his time. He wrote books about crime, about Prohibition, about himself. He came from Kinsman, Ohio, where he was born the son of a miller. He nearly always needed a haircut. He always *defended* – and not one of his clients was ever executed.

Leopold and Loeb, on Darrow's advice, pleaded not guilty. Darrow gave one of the great performances of his life. He quoted A. E. Housman, Omar Khayyam, the Bible. He moved not only the jury, but the two defendants, who began to weep hysterically. He told Judge Caverley that this whole court stood between love and hatred, between the past and the future; and how the mothers of the accused had once gazed into their babies' eyes, wondering about their future. Above all, he used words such as schizophrenia (for Loeb) and paranoia (for Leopold) which nobody who had not read Freud and Krafft-Ebing could possibly have understood at that time.

The horrified public wanted the death sentence; but the killers of Bobby Franks got life imprisonment for murder and ninety-nine years for kidnapping.

In our last crime, it is difficult to decide who was on trial – the defendants or the American conscience. Again, it is something which could only have happened, in the way it did happen, in the Twenties – or possibly during the time of Senator Joseph McCarthy, thirty years later.

On April 15th 1920 F. A. Parmenter, paymaster of the Slater & Merrill Shoe Factory, South Braintree, Mass., and Alessandro Berardelli, his bodyguard, were shot by two men who escaped in a car with the $16,000 payroll. Three weeks later Nicola Sacco, a shoe worker, and Bartolomeo Vanzetti, a fish seller, were arrested: both were armed (Sacco with a loaded .32 Colt and Vanzetti with a .38 revolver). Vanzetti was charged with another robbery, despite an alibi sworn to by thirty witnesses, and sentenced to fifteen years in prison. Then both Sacco and Vanzetti were tried before Judge Webster Thayer of the Massachusetts superior court for the

South Braintree killings and found guilty.

Sacco, when arrested, had in his pocket a revolutionary pamphlet announcing an anti-capitalist meeting at which Vanzetti was to speak. It was also noted that both men had been in Mexico during the War and were therefore draft-dodgers. Had they been tried for murder or for being anarchists? Was not the trial blatantly unfair? Had not Judge Thayer been heard, at his golf club, referring to them as 'dagoes' and 'anarchistic bastards'? Had he not (as counsel for the defence alleged) been 'carried away by his fear of the Reds'? Was it even certain that Sacco and Vanzetti had been at South Braintree on April 15th?

During the next seven years all attempts at securing a retrial failed. In November 1925 a man named Celestino Madeiros, already under a sentence for murder, claimed that the crime was the work of a gang led by one Joe Morelli of which he had been a member.

On April 9th 1927 Sacco and Vanzetti were sentenced to death by Judge Thayer. The last declarations of both men, moving as they were, did little to help them against the Red scare: Sacco – 'I know the sentence will be between two classes, the oppressed class and the rich class'; Vanzetti – 'I am suffering because I am a radical.'

Bernard Shaw, Einstein, Galsworthy and Wells were among intellectuals all over the world who pleaded against the sentence. An independent committee headed by President Lowell of Harvard investigated and agreed that there was legally no case for clemency. There were demonstrations all over the world, and protest bombs in New York and Philadelphia. In London 200,000 people gathered at a mass meeting in Hyde Park the day before the executions on August 23rd 1927; and on the day after, another mass meeting had to be dispersed by a police charge. Not all of them were Communists: some were People Like Us.

Nicola Sacco and Bartolomeo Vanzetti

CHAPTER 13

Music Ho!

Jelly Roll Morton

'Chicago, Chicago, you toddlin' town...' Yes, we are still there; only now we are listening to a new kind of music at the Dreamland Café; and if Capone's boys drop in and shoot the place up, the musicians just go on playing, pausing only to take a slug of bootleg gin or a whiff of marijuana. With any luck, the thoughtful gangsters will dish out $100 bills before they leave.

These musicians are, many of them, coloured, for in the last few years there has been a steady stream of Negroes from the South to the booming prosperity of Chicago and Detroit (some of them have jobs at the Ford factory). When the New Orleans brothels were closed down jazz musicians had to find somewhere else to earn a living.

Joe King Oliver, the cornet-player, had arrived in 1918, and soon sent for his old friend Louis Armstrong. Influenced by them, a group of largely white musicians developed what came to be known as Chicago-style jazz, more of a free-for-all than New Orleans style (which Chicago knew already through Jelly Roll Morton and others). They included Pee Wee Russell, Mezz Mezzrow, George Wettling, Eddie Condon, Muggsy Spanier, Bud Freeman, Joe Sullivan, and Bix Beiderbecke, and they joined up with such black musicians as Coleman Hawkins, Don Redman and Fletcher Henderson. Some of them couldn't read music. Some were, in their own lifetime (Bix, for example) known only to aficionados. What they were playing, jazz (originally 'jass'), had once had an obscene meaning, but very few people knew it; and it gave its name to a whole era.

(opposite) Detail from 'Nightclub, Marseilles', 1928–29, by C.R.W. Nevinson. The figure with a beard in the top right hand corner is Augustus John

(overleaf) Design for the 'Rhapsody in Blue' set of 'George White's Scandals', 1926, by Erté

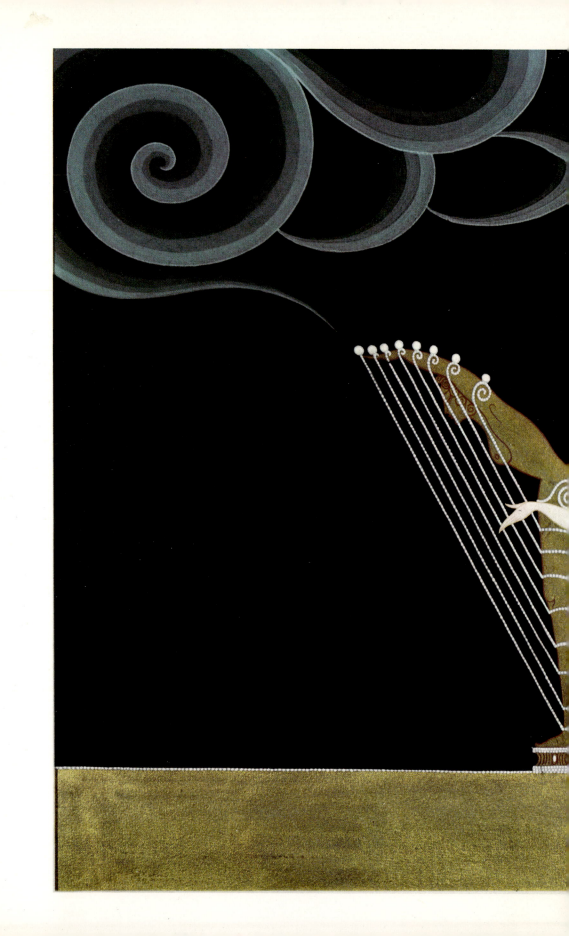

It would be possible to show the progress of jazz by a map, very much as medical officers of health trace the spread of a cholera epidemic: New Orleans – Chicago – New York – (with branches out to Pittsburgh, Cincinnati, and Atlantic City) – back to Chicago – on to California, London and Paris (but not much before the Thirties).

In Oxford and Cambridge in the middle Thirties the great debate was white jazz versus black jazz: Bix—Red Nichols—Casa Loma versus Armstrong—Ellington—et al. (Their records were only just beginning to be released in England.) I had been converted to black jazz by a single record, Duke Ellington's 'Stevedore Stomp', made in the last ten minutes of a recording session, containing the most extraordinary improvisation (especially Bigard's clarinet) that I had ever heard. To me, much white jazz was amateurish, dilettante, with a slack beat. But an Indian friend, with whom I played piano duets, couldn't stand the naked emotion of the Negro style. We were influenced, in our tastes, by Spike Hughes, who had helped to make a jazz cult in Cambridge during the Twenties, and was writing every week in the *Melody Maker*.

One trouble was that the Twenties expected all jazz to be danceable, and all Negro players to be funny black men (the logical end to which came in the Thirties with Cab Calloway hi-de-hi-ing, and Louis Armstrong singing 'You Rascal You' clad in a tiger skin). Unless a Blues could be 'swung' its full significance never got across. In England only a very small minority had ever heard of Ma Rainey, Bessie Smith, Blind Lemon Jefferson or Sleepy John Estes. Never mind: we were learning a new language, words like 'wa-wa mute', 'plunger', 'flutter-tonguing', 'riff', 'lick'. And people who had heard the Original Dixieland Jazz Band, with its slack rhythm, on its London visits in 1919 and 1920 might have formed a faint idea of the possibilities of jazz, while noting that its pianist, an Englishman named Billy Jones, was the only member of the group who could read music.

In Chicago all was glory. King Oliver had Armstrong on second trumpet, Honoré Dutray on trombone, Johnny Dodds (clarinet) and his brother Baby on drums, Lil Hardin (whom Louis Armstrong married) on piano, and Bill Johnson (bass). Between 1922 and 1924 they produced what was still largely New Orleans music – 'Dippermouth Blues' (which

'Louis Armstrong's Hot Five', 1926

in another form came to be known as 'Sugar Foot Stomp'), 'Canal St Blues', 'High Society' – but it was acquiring a Chicago polish. The old choppy phrasing and after-beat stress was beginning to go.

New York was already becoming a 'big band' city, and the bands were formed by ballrooms like Roseland and the Savoy. In those days Harlem was in the main a middle-class Negro quarter: you went there to dance and hear jazz, and to see the high-yellow (half-caste) dancing girls at the Cotton Club. In 1924 we find Armstrong here, with Fletcher Henderson's Band: his *legato* trumpet style was new to New York, and he was developing as an entertainer, 'scat' singing for the first time in 'Everybody Love My Baby', and performing 'stunts' such as 250 high Cs ending on top F.

In November 1925 Louis was back in Chicago, at the Dreamland, but (strangely) still earning only $75 a week. To this period belong the records made by 'Louis Armstrong's Hot Five' (sometimes Seven) all of them ex-New-Orleans except Lil Hardin, with Kid Ory on trombone, Johnny Dodds, and Johnny St Cyr (banjo) – 'Cornet Chop Suey', 'Potato Head Blues', and that landmark in jazz, 'West End Blues', made in 1928, which has been studied by musicians of every kind all over the world as, technically and emotionally, the most astonishing instrumental improvisation ever produced by jazz.

This same period gave us 'St James Infirmary',

(opposite) **Constant Lambert, 1926, by Christopher Wood**

and here Louis had with him Earl Hines (piano), Zutty Singleton (drums), Fred Robinson (alto sax), Jimmy Strong (clarinet), Don Redman (alto sax), and Mancy Cara (banjo). Hines, his right hand in tremolo octaves imitating trumpets, his left hand often eccentric with unusual harmonies, developing a fast, light style that was to influence all future jazz pianists, had had a fairly orthodox musical training. He came from a reasonably prosperous home in Pittsburgh where his father, a crane foreman, ran a brass band and played a parlour organ. Like Benny Goodman, who had suddenly appeared from Chicago's West Side in 1922 when he was only thirteen, Hines rather despised the 'back-room boys'

Benny Goodman

who couldn't read their notes.

To Chicago from Davenport, Iowa, came Bix Beiderbecke, the eternal adolescent (like so many Twenties personalities) who was destined to die of bath-tub gin and other excesses at the age of twenty-eight. He and his friends had a peculiar appeal for students at Northwestern University, where the Dixieland style, outdated almost everywhere else, still had many adherents. So were born the Wolverines. With his individual cornet-playing ('like shooting bullets at a bell' someone said) Bix, whether he knew it or not, had far outclassed Dixieland's Nick la Rocca. He could play piano, too, and the eclectic Ravel-Debussy progressions of his famous solo 'Bixology' were a new noise in the jazz world. A bit of an intellectual, even though he had been a drop-out at school? Frankie Trumbauer thought so, his evidence being that Bix knew who Proust was.

There was a more intellectual appeal, too, in Red Nichols and his Five Pennies; Joe Venuti, classically-trained jazz violinist, and Eddie Lang, Segovia of the jazz guitar (the last two had started together with Bert Estlow's Quintet in Atlantic City).

It was now 1928, and Louis Armstrong, broadcasting regularly from the Savoy Ballroom, was making $200 a week, having meanwhile become leader of 'Louis Armstrong and his Stompers' at the Sunset Café, with Earl Hines as pianist and organizer. The Sunset, whose proprietor Joe Glaser charged patrons $2.50 merely to get in, served illegal liquor but, for reasons he alone knew, was never raided. It had showgirls, too.

In New York an entirely new, rich, brassy, jungle sound was beginning to be heard: elegant Ellington, with his famous seldom-changing team of Johnny Hodges (alto sax), Barney Bigard (clarinet), Harry Carney (baritone), Joe Nanton (trombone) and Bubber Miley (the wa-wa 'crying trumpet' specialist) and others; playing from superb arrangements numbers like 'Black & Tan Fantasy', 'The Mooche', 'Creole Love Call' and 'Cotton Club Stomp'.

Edward Kennedy Ellington came from Washington, D.C., where his father (like King Oliver's) was a butler. Although his parents wanted him to study fine arts, he had been playing the piano professionally from the age of seventeen. After one or two false starts in New York he assembled the core of his famous band at the Kentucky Club, moving on in 1927 to the Cotton Club, where his reputation for a

Fats Waller

unique blend of jungle violence and refined sweetness became established for ever.

Since it was possible at this time to leave school at fourteen, nearly all the great names of Twenties Jazz were absurdly young. At fifteen, Thomas 'Fats' Waller was organist at the Lincoln Theatre. His father, pastor of Harlem's Abyssinian Baptist Church, was pleased; but about his son's leaning towards jazz he had the worst misgivings. The excellence of Fats's piano-playing might never have won recognition had he not also been both an entertainer and a prolific composer of popular songs. It is possible to see, in recorded numbers such as 'Handful of Keys' and 'Numb Fumblin' the influence of his piano-teacher Leopold Godowsky, who took him through the Fugues and Inventions of Bach. As for the songs, who does not know 'Ain't Misbehavin', 'Honeysuckle Rose' and 'My Very Good Friend the Milkman'?

Britain knew many of the tunes, but was much slower to be invaded by jazz. Most people in the Twenties would have agreed with Paul Whiteman, who preached 'Symphonic Syncopation'. The kind of New Orleans—Chicago improvisation, with wrong notes, of which Pee Wee Russell used to say cheerfully 'you've got to get lost once in a while', was not for Whiteman, who around 1925 declared that it was finished. Whiteman, once principal viola-player in the San Francisco Symphony Orchestra, hired arrangers and put on the first big show band: 'I figured that if I wrote down the things that we played well, then at least we would always play them well.' He was a large, round man, and I am not surprised to learn, on the authority of my daughter's American godmother (whose uncle played saxophone for him) that he had an inordinate fondness for chocolate fudge, which she as a very small child used to feed to him on his visits to London. He hired a number of music-reading jazz stars to play for him, and in 1924, at New York's Aeolian Hall, gave the first performance of Gershwin's *Rhapsody in Blue*, conducting, as no back-room jazzman ever conducted, with a long white baton. From this example all the big bands we knew in the Twenties, including the English Jack Hylton and Jack Payne, were born.

George Gershwin, who had studied the piano with Charles Hambitzer and harmony with Edward

At rehearsal: (left to right) Jack Donahue, George Gershwin, Sigmund Romberg Marilyn Miller and Florenz Ziegfeld

Kilenyi and Rubin Goldmark but never mastered orchestration (*Rhapsody in Blue* was arranged by Ferdie Grofe), came up like anyone else through Tin Pan Alley, musical comedy and revue – *La La Lucille, George White's Scandals, Lady, Be Good!* and *Tip-Toes*. In 1922 he had unsuccessfully attempted a one-act opera, *Blue Monday*, and in 1925 wrote his *Concerto in F* for the New York Symphony Orchestra, going on in 1928 to *An American in Paris*, which Eric Blom (in Grove's Dictionary of Music) condemned for its 'excessive commonness'.

But, until *Porgy and Bess* in the 1930s, no work of his ever swept the world as *Rhapsody in Blue* did. Its first-night audience included Walter Damrosch, Victor Herbert, Heifetz and Rachmaninov, Mengelberg, Stokowski and Kreisler. We do not know what they thought of it, but Samuel Chotzineff, music critic of the *New York World*, thought it had 'made an honest woman out of jazz'. Gershwin was now on top of the world. He became a personal friend of Prince George, afterwards Duke of Kent, who gave him a photograph signed 'To George from George'. With engaging simplicity Gershwin said of his mother 'The extraordinary thing about her is that she's so modest about me.' Such was his national importance that in 1927 The New Yorker commissioned a profile of him from Sam Behrman.

There might have been a minor Gershwin in Fred Elizalde, a rich dilettante Cambridge-educated band leader of Filipino origin who spent a good deal of time in London. Remembered now mostly for a piano solo called *Vamp Till Ready*, he too composed a 'symphonic jazz suite' called *Heart of a Nigger*. The word 'nigger' seems to have been more affectionate than offensive in those days (witness Van Vechten's novel, *Nigger Heaven*), but the substitution of the word 'Coon' for its London performance was meant to be tactful.

Jazz was very much a minority cult in Britain – and American records were not easy to get. There were crude imitators of the Original Dixieland Band who seemed to be debasing it even further; and, among intellectuals, only musicians seemed seriously interested, and even then they seemed Gershwin-Whiteman-orientated rather than going back to the basic Negro material. Arnold Bennett, invited to the press début of the Savoy Orpheans, noted that they 'play strange instruments all looking like silver and gold . . . they play bad music well.' The publicity manager pointed out 'Count G., the finest saxophone player in the world'. Under Count G.'s chair was a canary in a cage: 'It's the only canary that has crossed the Atlantic alone. Count G. gets £83 a week. The band costs between £430 and £460 a week.' But to Aldous Huxley 'modern popular music is more barbarous than any folk art has been for hundreds of years.'

Young British composers in the Twenties, looking around for ways of expressing the spirit of the age, seized on jazz, half seriously, half humorously, and wove it into their work. Young William Walton made fun of popular syncopation in his music for Edith Sitwell's *Façade*, but under Constant Lambert's influence he would dash straight from a Queen's Hall concert to hear Paul Whiteman at the Hippodrome, or to the London Pavilion to hear Florence Mills, the blues singer (on whose death Lambert wrote an Elegiac Blues for piano). It is also said (but Walton has not confirmed this) that he earned some spare-time cash by writing orchestrations for the Savoy Orpheans.

But the Twenties knew Walton for his *String Quartet* (1922), a *Piano Quartet*, written in 1918–19, which somehow got lost in the post for two years, and his *Portsmouth Point* overture. The *Viola Concerto* (1929), first performed at a Promenade Concert in October 1929 with Paul Hindemith as soloist, had its jazzy moments; but the great *Belshazzar's Feast*, with words by Sacheverell Sit-

well, in which one could again trace a tiny jazz influence, did not come until 1931.

On the eclectic Constant Lambert the jazz influence was deeper. While at the Royal College of Music, where he was studying under Vaughan Williams, he met the painter Edmund Dulac, who introduced him to Diaghilev. The great impresario immediately commissioned a ballet from him – the first time an English composer had been so honoured – and the result was an updated *Romeo and Juliet*, in which the hero and heroine are at a ballet school and finally elope in an aeroplane. It was produced in Monte Carlo in 1926.

Lambert was already famous as one of the reciters of *Façade* and as a protégé of the Sitwells, who were talent spotters of the first order: he stayed with them at Renishaw in Derbyshire while writing another ballet, *Pomona*, first performed in Buenos Aires in 1927. The same year saw the performance of his *Music for Orchestra*, which had a liberating effect on all young composers; and in 1929 came the famous *Rio Grande*, to a poem by Sacheverell Sitwell, first performed in Manchester and immediately followed by a second performance the next

William Walton, 1925, by Christopher Wood

day at the Queen's Hall in London, with no less a personage than Sir Hamilton Harty at the piano. For the first few bars you seem to be listening to a recently discovered concerto by Gershwin, completed by Stravinsky; the tinkling consecutive fourths seem to belong to Zez Confrey, and the Charleston beats to everyone; and at one point the chorus sings four complete bars of 'I Can't Give You Anything But Love, Baby'.

In France, jazz was penetrating Les Six – or were they Sept? or only Cinq? or, if you include Roger Désormière, Maxim Jacob and Henri Cliquet-Pleyel, les Huit? Anyway, young (except Erik Satie, who died in 1925 aged fifty-nine) composers in revolt against they knew not what. It is to be doubted whether any French musicians really understood what jazz was about until the Hot Club of Paris in the Thirties.

Like many young composers of apparent brilliance but no settled direction, some of them wrote ballets for Diaghilev. Thus Henri Sauguet's *La Chatte* was produced in 1927 when he was twenty-six, and Francis Poulenc's *Les Biches* (retitled *House Party* for London) was produced in Monte Carlo in 1924. Poulenc, despite a pleasing melodic invention, seemed to be rebelling against romance and refinement, and cultivated a kind of deliberate vulgarity. His music, like that of others of Les Six, was first heard at a concert organized by Satie, friend (but how different!) of Debussy and a dabbler in all the fashionable 'isms' of the day – cubism, surrealism, dadaism.

Darius Milhaud, more serious, less dilettante than others of this group, tried in 1923 to organize some of them into another group, the Ecole d'Arceuil, named after a peculiarly dreary industrial suburb of Paris. Milhaud had written music of real quality, notably *Socrate*, a symphonic drama for four sopranos and chamber orchestra, whose austerity had an influence on Stravinsky. It is perhaps in his *Création du Monde* that the jazz idiom stands out most prominently.

All these younger men were studied by Maurice Ravel, most of whose best work was already done; he had given lessons to Vaughan Williams and (in orchestration) influenced George Gershwin (from whom, in return, he afterwards borrowed liberally in his *Concerto in G*). Fashionably, he wrote ballet music, including the ever-popular *Bolero*; and he

Nikitina and Lifar in the London production of 'La Chatte', 1927

made a four-month tour of the United States in 1928, which confirmed rather than began his interest in the jazz idiom. There are 'blues' phrases and rhythms in the second movement of his violin and piano sonata, and echoes of Harlem in his piano concerto for the left hand.

Elsewhere in Europe jazz took root, if only temporarily – in Stravinsky's *Ragtime*, Hindemith's *Kammermusik No. 1.*, Krenek's *Johnny Spielt Auf*, Weill's *Mahagonny* and *The Threepenny Opera*. The *Threepenny Opera*, generally regarded as the first opera in which jazz rhythms can be discerned, ran in Berlin for five years, and re-creates, as nothing else does, the corrupt hopelessness of post-war Germany.

In America there seemed to be two other trends in 'serious' music – one in the Macdowell tradition, rooted in the American past, yet having no truck with Negro music; and a wild experimentation. Samuel Barber, still in his early twenties, was respectful of tradition, yet set three of James Joyce's *Chamber Music* lyrics to music. Aaron Copland's five-part concert suite *Music For the Theatre*, written a few years before *The Threepenny Opera*, shows both the fascination jazz had for him and the fact that it never really became a part of him. He just enjoyed it while it was there. Charles Ives, rising fifty, senior partner of Ives & Myrick, New York insurance brokers, had done most of his composing before 1920, and it is probably true to say that hardly anyone at that time understood him: in his symphonies we can now see that he was a pioneer, anticipating later Stravinsky, even atonality (Schönberg's first twelve-note experiments were being carried out in Vienna). Virgil Thomson, teaching at Harvard before he moved to Paris in 1925, did much to make Ives's work better understood.

By contrast, Walter Piston and Roger Sessions seemed to be going back almost to the Middle Ages in an attempt to create a music that was both of the American folk scene and universal. And we must not forget Deems Taylor, virtually unknown in Britain (except, much later, as the 'voice-over' in Disney's *Fantasia*). This busy man gave much to the Twenties. His music has been best described as 'unproblematic', and as such it was popular. Critic and mainly self-taught composer, he wrote for *The New York Tribune*, *The New York World* and *Colliers*, and edited *Musical America*. He wrote one of the few new American operas of the decade, *The King's Henchman*, commissioned by the Metropolitan in 1926, with a libretto by Edna St Vincent Millay, and had the courage to compose an orchestral tone-poem, for Walter Damrosch and the New York Symphony Orchestra, based on Cabell's *Jurgen*.

Who was doing something for new music? Elizabeth Sprague Coolidge was. In 1918 she had started the Berkshire Festival of chamber music, and seven years later she created a Foundation in the Library of Congress for festivals, concerts, prizes for new compositions. But in general America seemed concerned to build up city orchestras, whose conductors generally had to be European, with names like Stokowski and Toscanini – and they tended to play European music. Until Damrosch discovered Gershwin . . .

On neither side of the Atlantic could it be said that a major new composer was emerging. Delius, whose best work was already done but was not well known until Sir Thomas Beecham organized a Delius festival in 1929, was already ill and blind,

and in 1928 young Eric Fenby had joined him in Grez-sur-Loing as amanuensis. Ever since his orange-planting days in Florida Delius had loved the cadences of Negro music. In his last days, his favourite tune was Kern's 'Ol' Man River'. Now, unwittingly, he gave something back to the Negroes; for popular arrangers – Ellington in particular – used his luscious chromatic harmonies in orchestrated dance music.

One English opera stands out because it had an almost popular success. In an age of jazz and superficial cynicism and war-weariness it was possible to escape into a fairy story. Rutland Boughton's *The Immortal Hour*, brought from Birmingham by Barry Jackson, and produced at London's Regent Theatre in October 1922, was revived three times in the next four years. Its famous Fairy Song 'How beautiful they are, the lordly ones,' entered the repertoire of every soprano, tenor and café orchestra. There was a great season of opera at Covent Garden in 1927 – Melchior, Lotte Lehmann, Elisabeth Schumann and Pertile – but in general London was not well off for opera, and it was fashionable to go to Bayreuth and Salzburg.

Gwen Ffrangcon-Davies in 'The Immortal Hour', 1922

Gustav Holst, music master at St Paul's Girls School, never repeated the relatively popular success of *The Planets*, but produced a parody-opera *The Perfect Fool* (1923) and a choral symphony full of new experiments in harmony. He began to be more widely known in America after his visit to the University of Michigan at Ann Arbor in 1923. His friend Ralph Vaughan Williams, sharing his love of folk music, but much more English, was teaching at the Royal College of Music and conducting the Bach choir, and during the decade wrote his *Pastoral Symphony*, a mass, a cantata and two operas. He had not yet struck out into the starker, doom-laden mode of his *Fourth Symphony* in which, by hindsight, it is possible to see the coming of the Second World War.

There were other regional composers seeking the pastoral, but it was not yet fashionable: 'Old Vaughan Williams,' said a master at my school, 'he's rather like a cow looking over a gate, isn't he?' (This of the composer of 'The Lark Ascending'!) And there was one strange figure who went right back to Elizabethan music. Philip Heseltine ('Peter Warlock'), old Etonian, bearded, beer-swilling man-about-Chelsea, good critic and writer, the *petit-maître* who adapted Delius harmonies to sixteenth-century tunes, at the age of thirty-six suddenly lost faith in his talent and put his head in a gas oven.

Sir Edward Elgar, Master of the King's Musick

Sir Edward Elgar, 1927, by Percival Hedley

after the death of Sir Walter Parratt in 1924, had, in his own words, 'gone off the boil'. Since the death of his wife in 1920 he had moved restlessly from house to house, finally settling at Marl Bank, Worcester, his home town, in 1929, there to die five years later. He took a perverse pleasure in pretending not to be a musician, talking about racing and money and things proper for a bushy-moustached country gentleman to talk about. Younger composers (except Walton) regarded him as an Edwardian, and the nobility and emotion of his great works were out of fashion. (The only recorded meeting between Elgar and Walton took place in the lavatory at Hereford Cathedral during a Three Choirs Festival). Elgar was the man who had written, in 1924, *The Pageant of Empire*, seven songs to words by the flag-flapping Alfred Noyes; a carol for the King's recovery from his illness; an Empire march for the Wembley Exhibition; and a nursery suite for the little Princesses Elizabeth and Margaret Rose. There were constant rumours of a third oratorio, a third symphony – but they never materialized.

'Of course I've finished with music' Elgar told Compton Mackenzie (then editing *The Gramophone* with his brother-in-law Christopher Stone, Britain's first classical disc-jockey) as they went together to a Promenade Concert to hear Berlioz's *March to the Scaffold*. 'I've been forgotten.' Yet he lived to conduct a perfect recording of his *Violin Concerto* with a boy named Yehudi Menuhin, who in 1929 at the age of twelve had rocked London by a performance of Brahms's *Violin Concerto* at the Royal Albert Hall. It was as if the boy understood him as nobody else then did.

I am eleven. I am lying awake, listening to a musical evening in our sitting room downstairs. In the first years of the decade, at least in the provinces, we still had musical evenings. Friends were invited after dinner for coffee and sweet biscuits – 'and do please bring your music'. Miss Goodwin has brought *Rustle of Spring*, Mr Tucker *La Cathédrale Engloutie*: his unrelieved use of the 'loud' pedal sustains those ghostly bells more than Debussy intended. My pretty cousin Marjorie plays and sings Coleridge-Taylor's 'Onaway, Awake Beloved' in her hard little choirboy voice, my father sings 'Eleanore' and – most unsuitably for his teetotal Methodist upbringing – a drinking song by Sullivan called 'Ho, Jolly Jenkin'. My father and mother together sing old pre-war songs from Pélissier's Follies, 'There's a Sun Still Shining in the Sky' and 'My Moon'. All this slowly changed when we had our first gramophone, and our first wireless.

From the viewpoint of Tin Pan Alley, sheet-music was still the main source of profit: Lawrence Wright (otherwise known as Horatio Nicholls) used to launch new songs on Blackpool Front by singing them to holiday crowds, reinforcing this point-of-sale promotion by front-page advertisements in newspapers (printing a few bars of words and music to tantalize the prospective buyer). Thus were launched 'Shepherd of the Hills', a waltz called 'Babette', 'Among My Souvenirs' and 'When the Guards Are on Parade'. Sometimes the words of current song hits were printed on a large unfolding sheet of paper and sold separately to people who could remember tunes but could not read music. Our maid bought these regularly.

There were silly songs, doll songs, mammy songs, girl songs, baby songs, bird songs, topical songs, stammering songs, regional songs, telephone songs and, in an enduring class of their own, musical comedy songs, many of which are with us yet.

A harassed Italian fruit-vendor, on a hot day in New York, ran out of bananas and was heard to say 'Yes, we have no bananas.' A cartoonist named Ted Dorgan used the phrase as a gag line, and two song writers got together and produced the silly song of the decade, a world hit whose tune was singularly easy to remember because most of it was stolen from the Hallelujah Chorus and an aria from *The Bohemian Girl* – 'I Dreamt That I Dwelt in Marble Halls'. In Britain it sold 700,000 copies.

'Where Do Flies Go in the Wintertime? Do They Go to Gay Paree?' a pantomime song had been asking since 1919; to be answered with another song, 'I Know Where Flies Go', the flies themselves reporting that they

Lay their eggs and fly away,
Come back on the First of May,
Hatch their eggs and oh! what joy!
First a girl and then a boy!

and that they have in the meantime 'travelled far and eaten all the peaches down in George-i-ah'.

The craze for pogo sticks somehow became trans-

149

formed into an animal called 'The Jolly Little Ogo-Pogo', whose mother was an earwig and whose father was a whale. A film cartoon about Felix the Cat inspired 'Felix Kept on Walking'.

One famous comedian, who began on the halls and in concert party and sang many silly songs with Jack Hylton's band, was (and, happily, still is) Leslie Sarony, begetter of 'Don't Do That to the Poor Puss-Cat' and 'I Lift Up My Finger and I Say Tweet-Tweet' and more than a hundred others. Of 'Horsey! Keep Your Tail Up – Keep the Sun out of My Eyes' I can offer no explanation. Of 'It Ain't Gonna Rain No Mo' it might be said that it did almost as much for the 1924 General Election in Britain as the Zinoviev letter had done: it was one of the many cheer-up songs – 'Give Yourself a Pat on the Back', 'Happy Days Are Here Again' – which turn up in slumps after booms.

All through the Twenties dolls were used in songs as symbols – of what? Of the fluffy girl, the dumb blonde that business men yearned for; the paper-

Crinolined ladies were sometimes used to 'tidy away' the telephone

doll substitute for a girl who had broken one's heart; the pleasure-seeking broken butterfly, 'Poor Little Rich Girl', 'Dance, Little Lady', taken so seriously as a moral tract that Coward received letters of praise from clergymen all over the country.

The doll song coincided with the 'novelty dance', a piano solo in the then accepted jazz style of consecutive fourths (and rolled tenths in the left hand, as taught by Billy Mayerl's correspondence school) played at a speed which could only be managed by pianists who got their fingering right. So we had *Kitten on the Keys* in the early 1920s, *Doll Dance* and *Flapperette* (1926–7), both played by Nat Shilkret's Orchestra, *The Dicky Bird Hop* (written and whistled by a blind entertainer named Ronald Gourlay), *Fairy on the Clock* (by Montague Ewing, a concert-party figure of pre-1914 times who now wrote songs under the name of Sherman Myers) and, when talkies came, 'The Wedding of the Painted Doll', one of the several hit tunes of *Broadway Melody*.

The word 'baby' as an endearment ('Yes, Sir, That's My Baby') never caught on in Britain, so that unsophisticated British listeners, confronted with a song title like 'I Wonder Where My Baby Is Tonight?' tended to imagine a wayward infant in diapers knocking back cocktails.

Hair fashions called for frequent decision-making, and so Gwen Farrar and Norah Blaney sang 'Shall I Have It Bobbed or Shingled?' Every time anyone flew a long distance, every time any much-loved personality died, or when radio arrived, there was a song about it. 'Airman, Airman, Don't Put the Wind Up Me' – 'I'm an Airman, and I Fly-Fly-Fly-Fly-FLY! Up in the Sky, Ever So High!' When Caruso died in 1921, someone saw fit to publish a song, 'They Needed a Songbird in Heaven, So God Took Caruso Away'; and five years later 'There's a New Star in Heaven Tonight' mourned the death of Rudolph Valentino.

There were several telephone songs, beginning with Irving Berlin's 'All Alone', most movingly sung by Alice Delysia in a Cochran revue, and going on to the relative sophistication of Melville Gideon, the honey-voiced tenor of *The Co-Optimists*, whose 'I've Fallen In Love with a Voice' imagined a young and beautiful switchboard operator.

Many girls fell in love with Gideon's voice: he was the first of many 'crooners', and his only rival for some years was Jack Smith, 'the Whispering Baritone', a now largely forgotten singer who made 'Miss Annabelle Lee' and 'My Blue Heaven' peculiarly his own. There were two 'Spanish' songs, 'Valencia' (by Padilla, imported from Paris), and a clownish British imitation, 'Barcelona' ('I'm one of the nuts from Barcelona, I plinka de plonk, I Casa-bionck') which was the theme song of the General Strike.

Solemn sociologists have attributed the large number of regional songs to the homesickness, in big cities, of people who had come from faraway states and provinces. Was this in anyone's mind when in 1919 Irving Caesar and George Gershwin wrote 'Swanee'? Or when the Gershwin brothers wrote 'I'm just a lonely babe in the wood . . . I'm all alone in this big city . . . Lady, Be Good – to me'? Or when Irving Berlin wrote songs about Michigan, Dixie, and Alabama, where the Midnight Choo-Choo came from? No matter: as long as there were plenty of States there were plenty of songs – 'Every-

thing is Peaches Down in Georgia' (as the flies had discovered), 'Georgia on My Mind', 'Carolina in the Morning', 'Pasadena', 'Omaha' and 'Nebraska' (which, I seem to remember, was rhymed with 'if anyone should ask ya', and was sung in England by G.H. Elliott, the Original Chocolate-coloured Coon).

Girl songs – well, there have always been girl songs; and in the Twenties we had 'Sweet Sue', 'Tondelayo' (a half-caste girl, inspired by a play, *White Cargo*, about lonely men drinking themselves to death in the tropics), 'Ramona', 'Margie', 'Don't Bring Lulu', 'Chili-bom-bom', and – a perfect period piece now totally forgotten – 'Magnolia':

Clara Bow – ain't she delish!
Season her with Lillian Gish,
And what have you got? You've got Magnolia!

And when you were disillusioned with girls, there was always Mom – notably 'Coal Black Mammy', to whom the prodigal son returned in a song, not by a New Yorker, but by Ivy St Helier, who was one day to play Manon la Crevette in *Bitter Sweet*.

With 'Side by Side' and 'All By Yourself in the Moonlight' (1927–8) came a more durable kind of song, accepting the fact that man and woman need each other. Can the party spirit be dying down already? Back in 1921, it was 'Ain't We Got Fun?' the song usually accepted as the credo of the decade.

Not much money, oh but honey,
Ain't we got fun? . . .
There's nothing surer,
The rich get richer and the poor get poorer.

(or 'get children' in the alternative version). But now there is a new cosiness, or perhaps a yearning for security:

Just Molly and me
And Baby makes three –
We're happy in My Blue Heaven.

So Melville Gideon, with his 'I'm Tickled to Death I'm Single', is wrong! Good heavens, someone is saying that marriage is a good thing! 'My Blue Heaven', incongruously, swept along the Riviera in 1928 among renegade writers and artists who were living in sin with each other anyway. Students of Scott Fitzgerald will recall the significance of the 'neat, sad little waltz', 'Three O'Clock in the

Morning', the background to Gatsby's parties, the time before which nobody ever went to bed.

The word 'blue' had a new meaning. The Blues was a statement in song about one's troubles, and singing the Blues meant getting rid of those troubles. But just after Florence Mills and the all-Negro cast of *Blackbirds* stormed London, a song arrived called 'Bye, Bye, Blackbird'. 'Black' was now the sad word, and 'blue', because of an answering song, 'Hallo, Bluebird!' began to have cheerful associations.

Even so, there is a new sadness creeping into song lyrics, as the skirt-length falls and a satiety with pleasure combines with a suspicion that the boom cannot last for ever. Note the change of mood from 1925 – 'I want to be happy, But I won't be happy, Till I've made you happy too' (*No, No, Nanette*). And loneliness, always loneliness. It would be possible to write a composite lyric of those years (as in fact Sandy Wilson did in *The Boy Friend*), and it would be about a little boy who's looking for a little girl to love in a room with a view in a cottage for two where Baby makes three – and then 'Day will break and you'll awake And start to bake a sugar cake For me to take for all the boys to see'. (Vincent Youmans's 'Tea for Two', if you're in any doubt.)

The gentle, middle-class cosiness, the absence of passion, of many of these songs ('You're the Cream in my Coffee, You're the Salt in my Stew'), the decent tenderness, the soothing limitation of ideas, the mindless charm, the suburban small-worldliness (only Coward and Porter, waiting in the wings with jars of acid, ruffled the calm) pervaded the musical comedies that launched them. True, there had been a song in *Mercenary Mary*, sung by a randy old man, Lew Hearn, who ogled the girls' chorus with 'All I Can Do Is Look At 'Em!', which many people, including my father, thought objectionable; but these were very few.

Musical comedy and revue gave us 'My Heart Stood Still' (by Richard Rodgers and Lorenz Hart, before Rodgers teamed up with Hammerstein), first sung in London by Jessie Matthews and Richard Dolman in Cochran's *One Dam' Thing After Another*, and incorporated in the American production of *A Connecticut Yankee*. There was a swift and continuous invasion of London's West End by the brothers Gershwin, in a series of musical comedies which yielded 'Fascinating Rhythm', 'So Do I', 'Lady, Be Good', ''S Wonderful', all exhibiting the Gershwin trick of making a two- or three-note phrase do all the work against changing harmonies, with a fairly commonplace eight-bar 'middle', the whole adding up, magically, to a tune you never forget. Occasionally, as he approached the depths of *Porgy and Bess* (which would not be heard until 1935), he would produce something deeply felt, such as 'The Man I Love', which Beverley Nichols found 'not inferior to the organ music of César Franck'. But this was not the musical comedy Gershwin, who told Sam Behrman that he wrote 'for young girls sitting on fire-escapes on hot summer nights in New York and dreaming of love'.

We had no Gershwin in England, but we had Vivian Ellis, as European as Gershwin was American, with a consummate musicianship which no other light composer, with the exception of Coward, has ever touched. Two songs of theirs meet half way across the Atlantic – you would have said, if you didn't know, that they were by the same composer. 'Someone to Watch Over Me' happens to be Gershwin; and 'Spread a Little Happiness' (to Clifford Grey's lyric) –

Even when the darkest clouds are in the sky,
You mustn't sigh, and you mustn't cry:
Spread a little happiness as you go by –

is Ellis. These were the songs of the shows that people who dressed up in tails and long dresses used to see after a good dinner; these were the songs those libertine Bright Young People used to put on the gramophone after stooping to folly.

The big American musicals – *Rose Marie*, *The Student Prince*, *Show Boat* – all yielded great, surviving tunes, with almost invariably a big romantic waltz such as 'The Desert Song' from *The Desert Song*.

So did the very first talkies, whose possibilities were seen in the broadest terms: so was born the slogan 'All-talking, All-singing, All-dancing'. Maurice Chevalier in *Innocents in Paris* introduced a more European, more sophisticated romantic type of song, and Chevalier's *The Love Parade*, with Jeanette MacDonald, took it a stage further. So we heard 'Louise', and 'Dream Lover' and the other Victor Schertzinger tunes. But first came Al Jolson with 'Sonny Boy' in *The Singing Fool*, that historic tear-jerker whose impact was quite unspoilt by the subsequent rumour that 'Sonny Boy' was originally written, tongue-in-cheek, as a send-up of the traditional momma-poppa-baby song.

It is probably true to say that in the Twenties, for the first time, the successful song-writer achieved recognition, partly because he had made a lot of money, but also as a personality in his own right. Thus when Irving Berlin, whose fame in this decade rested largely on his waltzes (the polish and sophistication of the Astaire films belong to the Thirties) – 'What'll I Do?', 'The Song is Ended', 'You Forgot to Remember' – married Ellin Mackay, a founding contributor to *The New Yorker*, it was almost a society wedding. If Gershwin had ever married, they would probably have given him a ticker-tape ovation.

Cole Porter had a different kind of fame, as an international socialite; and England did not know him until 1929, when Cochran staged *Wake Up and Dream*, which contained a mournful but haunting tune, 'What Is This Thing Called Love?' and a raving hit, 'Let's Do It', with the most brilliantly contrived rhymes anyone had ever heard, which however was sung only diffidently before guests as it was considered rather risky.

All this popular music was played on the gramophone, not yet called a record-player because there was still some audience participation. You had to wind the damn thing up, until electric automatic record-changers (known at first as panatropes) came in 1928; you also had to change the steel needles (very thin for soft, thicker for loud) for every record but (for very good classical records) there were also fibre needles which could be sharpened with a special gadget, and long-lasting tungsten needles. The surface hiss was like escaping gas. The soundbox, with its mica diaphragm, pressed heavily on the waxed grooves of the 10- and 12-inch records, which were played at 78 or 80 revolutions per minute. The runaway hit record of 1927 in Britain was not 'Hallelujah' or any popular song, but Mendelssohn's 'O For the Wings of a Dove', sung by Master Ernest Lough with the Temple Church Choir, which has been a steady seller ever since.

There was live music in cafés, in theatre pits before and during any play, and in cinemas. Some cinemas had, in addition to first and second features, travelogue, cartoon and newsreel, a stage orchestra *and* a Mighty Wurlitzer organ: you certainly got your money's worth. While silent films lasted, there was the strange art of the cinema pianist, supplying and often improvising suitable emotional music to support the subtitles: the great standby was the diminished seventh chord, played *tremolo* and *crescendo* at moments of tension.

The era of Big Bands was approaching, and some of the band leaders, like Jack Payne, had been cinema pianists. So had a number of women, such as the De Jong sisters, Celeste and Florence. Celeste, resident pianist at Cinema House, Tottenham Court Road, London, also played at Daly's Theatre, and one evening, being pressed for time, allowed her thirteen-year-old sister Florence to deputize for her. Florence knew five tunes and earned fifteen shillings a week. A third sister, Ena Baga, took up the same career: all the sisters played both piano and organ, never having been taught (though they must have learnt something from their father, who ran one of the first cinema orchestras).

Because the first big bands played on stage they were expected to do more than just play music. Some began in London's West End restaurants, hotels or night clubs and then went on tour. Jack Hylton was the first to produce a complete band show, in which the musicians became, individually, comedians. In 1927 this was utterly new, especially on the end of the pier at our family watering place, and I shall never forget my father's account of it afterwards. 'In the middle of a tune,' he gasped, convulsed with mirth, 'one of the chaps playing saxophones got up and kicked the conductor up the backside!' (I think it must have been Chappie d'Amato.) There was a number called 'Forty-seven Ginger-headed Sailors' in which the scenery moved about like a rolling ship, and a brass-player named Freddie Bamberger went through the motions of vomiting into his trombone.

But it is the tunes that remain. Proust took fifteen volumes of his mighty masterpiece to summon up remembrance of things past; but it can be done in a few seconds with music either by the 'little phrase' of Vinteuil or – much more easily – by what Noël Coward, in *Private Lives*, just beyond the decade but very much of the Twenties, called the 'potency of cheap music'.

CHAPTER 14

The Literary Life

THOMAS MANN
EX·LIBRIS

I am eleven. I have read *The First Men in the Moon* and *Stalky & Co.*, and *The Greyfriars Holiday Annual* and *David Copperfield* and *Sherlock Holmes*, and one day I find a book with a funny title, *Babbitt*. It is about America, of which I know nothing except the Keystone Cops and Charlie Chaplin. It is so outlandishly American that Mr Hugh Walpole has written an apologetic introduction, explaining that life in America is not so 'ugly in speech, in background, in thought' as it seems. It is because there is so much of Babbitt in ourselves that we should persevere, for in Babbitt a friend is tenderly revealed. He is brother to Mr Polly, Uncle Ponderevo and Denry of the Five Towns. And Mr Walpole has added a glossary explaining that a dime is a coin worth ten cents, that 'doggone' is 'a puritanical euphemism for damn', that an ice-cream soda is 'a ghastly hot-weather temperance drink', that 'jeans' means trousers and 'kike' means Jew.

But to me *Babbitt* is a story about a family – a funny family, too, with Father slipping on the bath-mat and cutting himself while shaving, and those awful children, and Virgil Gunch with his verses, and all that swearing when Babbitt goes fishing with Paul Riesling. Even the Boosters are rather like my father's Rotary Club friends. It's almost as funny as *Three Men in a Boat*. I read this book once a year, understanding more and more, and when I am older go on to *Main Street, Dodsworth, Elmer Gantry*.

I cannot yet know what is happening to American literature. America is full of clever young men and women who go to New York and combine a hatred of provincialism with a secret nostalgia for back home. Like all the new writers in Britain, they are rebels. Why? 'Because of Prohibition' Donald Ogden Stewart tells me. 'Because of the War – we'd all wanted to die for Uncle Sam and make the world safe for democracy – we were mad – we didn't know what the hell about.'

Whatever the reason, all the enduring writing, American and British, of the post-war years was labelled Disillusioned, Dissenting and Destructive. In *Main Street* Lewis selectively reported the Middle West, its narrowness, its striving for culture. In *Babbitt* Lewis, himself pretty canny at business (especially as talent scout for Harcourt, Brace), attacked the average businessman, and himself coined the word that soon found its way into dictionaries: 'Two years from now,' he wrote to Alfred Harcourt in 1919, having changed his hero's name from Fitch to Babbitt, 'we'll have them talking of Babbittry.' Dodsworthery is much the same, but more vulnerable: when Sam Dodsworth, retired automobile manufacturer, takes his silly wife Fran to Europe, and is irritated by the (to him) false European sophistication about art and wine and food ('Harry orders the best meal in Paris'), he has in him something of Red Lewis, formerly of Sauk Center, Minn., who was never really happy abroad. While Fran flirts with the gigolo-idlers of impoverished Europe, Sam yearns for his noisy old friend back home, whom Fran thinks uncultured, because he calls Sam an old horse-thief. In the Twenties Lewis produced his best writing: all after *Dodsworth* is muddle-headedness.

Wells went a similar way: his optimism had been

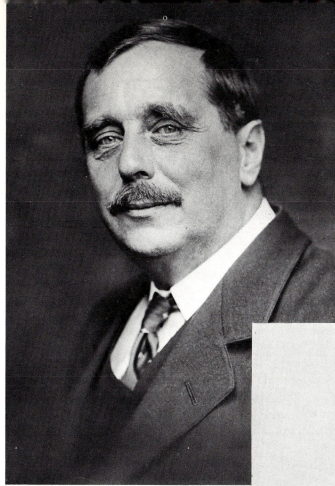

H. G. Wells

Arnold Bennett, by David Low

punctured by the War, and he now put his faith in education: novels such as *The World of William Clissold* and *Christina Alberta's Father* were vehicles for ideas rather than fiction, though there is plenty of satirical life in *Mr Blettsworthy on Rampole Island*. Like Shaw and many other British intellectuals, he went to Russia and met Lenin, whom he called 'the dreamer in the Kremlin'. Lenin's opinion of Wells was 'What a little bourgeois!' In 1920 Wells had astonished the English-speaking world with his enormous *Outline of History*, which came out first in weekly parts. Nobody had attempted anything like this before. It was the sort of thing academics hate ('I ceased to think about Wells when he became a Thinker' whinnied Lytton Strachey), but for ordinary people, bored by conventionally taught 1066-and-all-that history, it was a revelation. It was, says one of his biographers, Lovat Dickson, 'pure Wells, prejudices and brilliant insights, superficial judgments and intellectual depths all mixed up by no hand other than his'.

Arnold Bennett's best work was also done; but in 1923 he produced *Riceyman Steps*, the only one of his major novels set outside the Potteries, the tale of a miser in dingiest Clerkenwell. Wells was heard to say of certain younger writers, 'a flimsy crew, these moderns'; but Bennett was more generous and perceptive, being in fact the truer artist, in spite of his love affair with the Savoy Hotel.

Compton Mackenzie was never again to scale the heights of *Sinister Street* and *Carnival* – he took to living on islands and turning out satirical comedies. *The Four Winds of Love* was yet to come. On the way, his earlier books had infected the young Scott Fitzgerald with a romantic view of life and love and style.

We are in a decade when young writers are actually living the life they write about, drawing on autobiography for material, and putting each other in books like mad. It is almost true to say, of writers of the Twenties, that we are now, half a century later, more interested in how they lived than what they actually wrote.

Nothing was ever quite the same again after F. Scott Fitzgerald published, in 1920, *This Side of Paradise*. Whether he wanted to be or not, he was 'the spokesman of the Jazz Age', and the Fitzgerald cult was on. He was, long afterwards, to write to his publisher, Max Perkins at Scribner's (who had

made him rewrite it before publication) and accuse this first novel of 'utter spuriousness'. But it said something that young America wanted to hear; it justified and glamorized their way of life. He was twenty-three, the youngest novelist Scribner's had ever published, and he was making the same brash mistakes Noël Coward made, such as giving press interviews in which he said things like '*This Side of Paradise* . . . is a novel about Flappers written for Philosophers'. And he was already borrowing money from his publishers.

The 'message to youth' went on in *The Beautiful and the Damned*, a wonderful publicity title but a less effective novel than its predecessor. What Scott was trying to write, if we may believe the blurb (which he is thought to have written himself), was 'a devastating satire' on 'a section of American society which has never been recognized as an entity – that wealthy, floating population which throngs the restaurants, cabarets, theatres and hotels of our great cities'. And some vague fashionable philosophizing about the meaninglessness of life; and a convenient phrase, 'emotional bankruptcy'.

Let us hurry on to 1925, for this is the year of *The Great Gatsby*, Scott's only book that really deserves the word 'genius'. In it he raises envy of wealth to a kind of poetry. Here is a new view of the American dream, in the age of Prohibition and Coolidge. Jay Gatsby, a tycoon modelled partly on a Long Island bootlegger named Max Fleischman, believes – 'old sport' – that the good life has to be bought, and that the end justifies the means. 'Who was Gatsby?' people wonder. An ex-German spy? a scion of an European royal family? Had he really been at Oxford, been decorated in the War? Was it all lies? No, it wasn't – some part of him was genuine, but only a few people discovered it. He gave enormous, endless, much gate-crashed parties where many guests never recognized their host. All to impress Daisy Buchanan, the girl he had lost but never forgotten, now married to rich, useless Tom, who reads books about Nordic race superiority.

I once tried to count the magic, Twenties-ish but eternal, moments in *Gatsby*. They include, of course, the narrator's first sight, after a long time, of Daisy and Miss Baker, sitting on an enormous couch with their white skirts rippling in the breeze from the window; Daisy crying over Gatsby's beautiful shirts, so many that he never can wear them all;

Ernest Hemingway in Mexico

Klipspringer playing 'Love Nest' and 'Ain't We Got Fun?'; Daisy's hypnotic voice, whose quality Gatsby defines as 'full of money', and the bit that follows about 'high in a white palace the king's daughter, the golden girl'. It is almost impossible to imagine, fifty years after, the idea of a girl being unattainable because of money. But Tom and Daisy survive in our society – 'they smashed up things and creatures and then retreated back into their money or their vast carelessness, or whatever it was that kept them together, and let other people clean up the mess.'

Gatsby did not sell as well as *This Side*, but most critics knew that it would endure. 'It seems to me', wrote T.S. Eliot, 'the first step that American fiction has taken since Henry James.' (Hadn't he read *Main Street*?)

The life style of Scott and Zelda still fascinates today's younger generation. In 1972 a novel called *The Great Dethriffe* appeared whose characters believe that the American Twenties were 'the last years of Style', and they try to live life that way. It all goes wrong, but the fact that anyone tries to drop out in that particular fashion shows how the Fitzgerald legend is in danger of obscuring the writer.

For, while not everyone can remember whether Amory Blaine was the hero of *This Side of Paradise* or

of *Tender is the Night*, certainly everyone knows about Scott and Zelda romping in the Plaza Hotel fountain, and surviving memoir-writers of the Twenties still ask each other 'Were you there that day at Juan-les-Pins Casino when Zelda took off her pants and danced on the table?' I am of the school that believes Zelda ruined Scott: nothing I have read about her endears her to me, and while I would like to have known Scott in the pre-*Paradise* days, I would have hated to have them as guests. Eliot and Amanda, in *Private Lives*, at least knew when to go.

There are inexcusable vanities in which Scott fell below the gentlemanly standards he believed in (*Gatsby*, page 1), such as calling Michael Arlen, a man who had no illusions about his own work, 'a finished second-rater who's jealous of a coming first-rater'. And I hope he didn't mean it when he wrote to Edmund Wilson, with whom he had been at Princeton, 'God damn the Continent of Europe. It is of merely antiquarian interest.' And I am delighted by the squelch he received from Edith Wharton, whom he had accused of knowing nothing about life, and tried to shock by telling her that he and Zelda had lodged 'in a bordello'. 'But Mr Fitzgerald,' she said, 'you haven't told us what they *did* in the bordello.' Boring old Zelda, whom Scott described to a friend as 'a girl who gets stewed in public, who frankly enjoys and tells shocking stories, who smokes constantly and who makes the remark that she has "kissed thousands of men"'.

Fitzgerald had his greatest cult fame in the first half of the decade; Hemingway only really arrived in the second. He had served five hard years in Europe as foreign correspondent of the *Toronto Star*, and was known as a powerful short-story writer before he published, in 1926, *The Sun Also Rises*. Would Scott have benefited from having to cable a news story every day? Or would it have bruised that talent he was always talking about? *The Sun Also Rises* is set among 'lost generation' expatriates at a fiesta in Pamplona, Northern Spain. Here we meet the familiar Hemingway symbols – the potent bull, the impotent war-wounded man, the coolly sensual British Lady Brett Ashley. (Examination question: Compare Brett Ashley and Iris Storm, discussing their significance in the post-War world. 'I'd just *tromper* you with everybody' says Brett; 'I am a house of men' declares Iris.)

Hemingway and his then wife Hadley went several years in succession to the annual running of the bulls at Pamplona, and Donald Ogden Stewart describes a fiesta party consisting of the Hemingways, John Dos Passos, himself and other friends from Paris, at which Hemingway dared all the men of the party to run through the streets ahead of the young bulls and enter the ring with them. This they did, and were, to the delight of the Spaniards, tossed but not gored. 'Ernest clapped me on the back, and I felt as though I had scored a winning touchdown. . . . It had been a memorable week, a male festival, a glorified college reunion.'

'That hair on Ernest's chest,' said Negley Farson, 'was a goddam *toupee*.' Maybe, but does it matter? Any more than it matters that, in the American Twenties, drinking was regarded as a positive, constructive thing, an act of defiance? 'I'm Ernest's favourite drunk,' said Scott, 'as Ring Lardner is mine.'

Hemingway's literary reputation was clinched in 1929 by *A Farewell to Arms*, the story of a love affair – indeed 'a great love' – between an American officer and a British nurse in wartime Italy and in neutral Switzerland. This was the time of war novels, and while war is immoral to Hemingway, it is also important in a man's life. What he was by implication attacking was not war itself, but the hypocritical idealism which it engendered. Scott Fitzgerald never could get over the fact that Hemingway had been on active service and he

hadn't. If Gertrude Stein's expression 'lost generation' has any real meaning, then it enables us to differentiate between those who stayed lost (like Fitzgerald) and those who (like Hemingway) later found themselves with a real cause to fight for in the Spanish Civil War and then the Second World War.

But suddenly, at a sufficient distance from the War to make them acceptable to circulating libraries, the main stream of war books arrived. From Germany, Remarque's *All Quiet on the Western Front*, a deeply shocking and shocked book, violently anti-war. From England, Richard Aldington's *Death of a Hero*, attacking not only war but the values the hero had died for; and Robert Graves's autobiographical *Goodbye to All That*; Blunden's *Undertones of War*; and so many others. At last, too, Jonathan Cape took a big risk, and published e. e. cummings's *The Enormous Room*, which America had had since 1922. It described that most demoralizing of all war experiences, life in a prison camp, but in such a way (the obscenities were all in French) that the book stands on its own as a monument to the human spirit's ability to survive.

Now we knew what war was really like, and in the 1930s these books were to lead to anti-war exhibitions, a terror of the gas warfare which everyone imagined was to be unleashed on civilians, and the Oxford Union 'King and Country' debate.

From an age in which, it was said, many people would 'die rather than think', it is not easy to select the writers who were stirring things up; of whom it could be said that once you had read them, your mind had been altered. We could begin with *Jurgen*, the only one of Cabell's fifty-odd books still read, a learned and cynical (and often Freudian) attack on American values which was for some time suppressed as immoral. All the rebels read him, and Mencken called him 'the most acidulous of our anti-romantics'. John Dos Passos had published *Three Soldiers*, an anti-war novel, in 1921, and four years later *Manhatten Transfer* gave a foretaste of the whole-sale criticism of the social and economic system which was to come in the next decade with the mighty *U.S.A.* trilogy.

Theodore Dreiser, whom Mencken called 'the Hindenburg of the novel', had in 1925 his first real success after twenty-five years' novel-writing with *An American Tragedy*. It belongs to the Twenties, I suppose, and you would have been left out of the

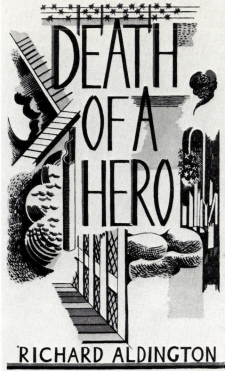

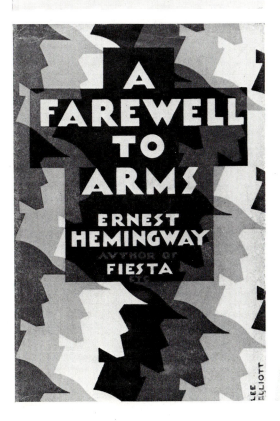

party conversation if you hadn't read it, but for me it remains unreadable. But the reader of 1929 would have pounced more hopefully on William Faulkner, whose war book *Soldier's Pay* he might have read in 1926. This writer had invented an unpronounceable place called Yoknapatawpha County, Miss., and in *The Sound and the Fury* there seemed to be a new kind of power. He went on a bit about the South, but he was readable, once you got used to this fashionable stream-of-consciousness technique which had come to America from James Joyce and Virginia Woolf.

New British authors, too, were stirring things up, but fewer of them were as direct-hitting and earthy as their American contemporaries. There was a good deal of tired satire, from a different kind of 'lost generation' which clung to the pre-1914 years for its standards while affecting to despise them. For such, 'witty and cynical' were the almost invariable epithets.

They were applied to Aldous Huxley when in 1923 he published *Antic Hay*. Drugs, lesbianism, birth control, fornication, devil-worship, nympho-

Aldous Huxley, 1928, by Alfred Wolmark

mania, people quoting Latin and Italian and French at each other (it must be indecent, or they'd say it in English) – people who said things like 'O all ye Beasts and Cattle, curse ye the Lord: curse him and vilify him for ever', and 'the real charm about debauchery is its total pointlessness . . . no better than going to church or studying the higher mathematics.' And Brian Opps, at a plebian coffee stall, says of 'the lower classes' 'I loathe them . . . I hate everyone poor, or ill, or old. Can't abide them: they make me positively sick.' Well, really! If this was how intellectuals behaved and talked, thank heaven for the rest of us. Cecil Beaton thought it 'open and frank and cleanly dirty . . . I especially like the part where the two people go to bed, stroke one another all over and fall asleep.'

No wonder Mr James Douglas of the *Sunday Express*, who attacked almost every heterodox book published during the decade, ranked *Antic Hay* with Aleister Crowley's *Diary of a Drug Fiend* and ensured its sales by condemning its 'ordure and blasphemy'. I have just re-read it for the first time since I was an undergraduate, and found it extremely irritating to be talked down to by this absurdly well-read pedant, parading his learning before me, making me feel inferior. I was not surprised to learn, years afterwards, that when Huxley went on a world cruise in 1926 he took with him the whole of the *Encyclopaedia Britannica*. In *Point Counter Point* (1928) he seemed to throw off the donnishness and tell a more direct satirical story, with characters (such as the Tantamounts) whom the initiated could recognize.

Much wickeder, much deadlier, forever fresh and young and observant, is Evelyn Waugh, whom I can re-read over and over. He went, like a woman, straight to the point and reported what he saw with a wonderful economy of words. A master of the short paragraph and the still shorter sentence. Either Alex Woollcott or Edmund Wilson, or possibly both, hailed him as 'the only first-rate comic genius since Shaw'. You can play happily for hours fitting real-life models to the characters of *Decline and Fall* (1928) and *Vile Bodies* (1930); and yet many of those characters are recognizable in Britain today – some of them poorer, working for their livings, but fundamentally unchanged.

Too bad for Beverley Nichols that his fame in the Twenties should rest upon his impudence in publishing his autobiography at the age of twenty-five,

instead of his mannered but elegant satire *Crazy Pavements*, published a year before *Decline and Fall* and set in the same mad world.

There were not many working-class authors in the Twenties. What is a working-class author, anyway? An author whose father is a worker usually writes himself out of the working-class. I mean, of course, Lawrence – the one English novelist-poet of international stature writing in the Twenties. He was, we know, already established, with *Sons and Lovers* and *The Rainbow* behind him. But only now did he exert his full influence on the world around him, and become a symbol of subversion.

'Working class' was – at least theoretically – fashionable. The Countess of Warwick professed herself a Socialist. Lawrence's books enjoyed a certain vogue among uppercrust people who might own shares in mines but had never been down one.

He had begun to travel, since the War; and to study psycho-analysis. *Women In Love*, privately printed in New York in 1920, and in London the next year, was quickly followed by *Aaron's Rod, Kangaroo, The Ladybird, St Mawr, The Plumed Serpent* – travel, criticism, psycho-analysis, poetry, plays – it was as if he knew he had only a few years left. Then came his most famous, notorious, last, worst novel, the only book that really made money (£1,615 in the first year of publication) in his lifetime – *Lady Chatterley's Lover*. Sex was always a 'problem', a 'question', something to worry about in the Twenties, and Lawrence's obsession with it as a mystical experience here reached its – I do not know whether to say height or depth.

Lady Chatterley was written three times, and what is Twenties-ish about it is the ways in which the third version (the one most people know) differs from the first two. In the first, the gamekeeper is called Parkin, aggressively working-class and rather disgusted by sex. There are no detailed descriptions of love-making. The results of the affair are that Parkin takes a job in a Sheffield steelworks and becomes a Communist, while Connie is left trying to shake off her own class ties and get closer to the working class.

The second version attacks the acquisitive society. Parkin, much less class-conscious, seduces Connie; they meet and understand each other; Parkin becomes a farm labourer because he doesn't want to be anything 'dreary and political'. In the well-known third version, Parkin becomes Mellors, loses

D.H. Lawrence, 1923, by Edmund Kapp

James Joyce, 1921, by Percy Wyndham Lewis

his class, and extracts a kind of poetry from his dialect. Lawrence, too, is rejecting politics. It is said that Frieda Lawrence preferred the first version; and there are critics who prefer the second.

'The greatest master of the English language since Milton' said T.S. Eliot of James Joyce. 'Genius it has, I think,' wrote Virginia Woolf of *Ulysses*, 'but of the inferior water. The book is diffuse. It is brackish. It is pretentious. It is under-bred. . . . I'm reminded all the time of some callow board-schoolboy . . .' And Lawrence wrote: 'My God, what a clumsy *olla putrida* James Joyce is! Nothing but old fags and cabbage-stumps of quotations from the Bible and the rest, stewed in the juice of deliberate, journalistic dirty-mindedness . . .'

You couldn't blame Joyce for not having a wide readership at this time, because he had as yet been published only in Paris, and copies of *Ulysses* had to be smuggled into Britain and America in one's luggage, and would be seized by any customs officer who could read. At Folkestone 499 copies were seized by the Customs. In New York 500 copies were seized and *burned* by the Post Office authorities. And of those who had copies, how many had read the whole book, and not merely Molly Bloom's soliloquy? There were those who asked whether *Ulysses* was written in English at all: we find it easier going today largely because all writers in English since 1922 have been influenced by it – indeed, the last few years of the Twenties abounded with interior-monologue and stream-of-consciousness, including Christopher Isherwood's first novel, *All the Conspirators*. But *Ulysses*, like *Tristram Shandy*, led where no one could follow.

Most people had heard of Joyce, but not read him. The same could be said of Proust, whose *A la Recherche du Temps Perdu* began to appear in Scott-Moncrieff's translation in 1922. He wasn't banned or burned, but his homosexual world was not for the general reader, though there were many readers of the early volumes who did not realize that Albertine was a man – no enlightening body of Proust criticism had yet arisen, analysing the analyst, probing into the real-life figures of Paris society who made up de Charlus, the significance of Madame Greffulhe and Robert de Montesquiou, the world of Marcel that was to become almost more absorbing than the book itself, whose later volumes were not published in English until 1925 and 1926. In the Twenties you were one-up if you had read Proust in French, though there was a defensive fashion for saying that the translation was better than the original. If *Ulysses* had taken all the history of Western man for its province, then Proust had taken the whole experience of one man's life for his. It was not quite interior-monologue, but you could lose yourself happily in sentences of unprecedented length: one of them, in *Cities of the Plain*, contains 958 words. And it all fitted in nicely with the intense interest in psychology (Freud had also been heard of but read only by a few), and perhaps a feeling of pleasant wickedness: the central character of Noël Coward's *Easy Virtue* (1927), disdaining the frolics and fresh air of an English country 'house party', is regarded as extremely odd and possibly immoral because she prefers to 'read Proust with the blinds down'.

If you read either of the last two authors, you were a highbrow (the Twenties word for egghead). If you were a middlebrow, not ashamed of being seen reading an author whose books actually sold well, and who gave you a soundly constructed story about the sort of people you knew, you read Hugh Walpole, whose best book, *The Cathedral*, came out in 1922, and whose mastery of horror was shown, very differently, in *The Old Ladies* and *Portrait of a Man with Red Hair*. Or, if you were an armchair traveller, you might have preferred Somerset Maugham, now writing mostly short stories (his greatest achievement) about the South Seas and the Far East; in 1925 came *The Painted Veil*, and in 1928 the first of a whole new genre of fiction, the spy story *Ashenden*.

The decade was rich in women novelists – Edna Ferber, whose *So Big* (the best-seller of the winter of 1923) and *Show Boat* were in great demand at Boots' and Smith's libraries and the Times Book Club, which, in the days before paperbacks, were the mainstay of middle-class reading; Rose Macaulay, whose *Potterism* and *Keeping Up Appearances* and *Orphan Island* set a new standard of wit and good sense and unsentimental comedy couched in brittle, pellucid English; and two important newcomers – Elizabeth Bowen (*The Hotel*, 1927) and Rosamond Lehmann (*Dusty Answer*, perhaps the only novel about university life since *Sinister Street* that had really worked).

The Forsyte Saga, given to us as prizes at school, showed Victorian Soames-Galsworthy dazed by the post-war world, but somehow, in its strange, clumsy way, established a gallery of unforgettable characters,

and in the later volumes faithfully recorded the trends of the times: silly, self-centred Fleur re-decorating her house in the voguish Chinese style, Michael Mont dabbling in Fogartism – any solution to social distress rather than the one going on in Russia – and, with Fleur and Jon, even a fashionable bit of adultery in the open air.

As if the decade were having a last escapist fling, J. B. Priestley, known hitherto for a couple of slight but entertaining novels, *Adam in Moonshine* and *Benighted* (later filmed as *The Old Dark House*) and a handful of excellent light essays, sat down in a rented house by the sea at Deal and wrote a novel against all the fashionable trends, a novel to please himself, weaving several groups of characters into one story, set in a Yorkshire wool town, a typically appalling prep. school and all over the country in a concert party. All the characters of *The Good Companions* were 'nice'; all ended happily. It was the first venture into picaresque since Compton Mackenzie, and some critics murmured the same thing that had been murmured about Mackenzie – that 'the mantle of Dickens' had fallen upon Priestley. It was also very long, which made Heinemann nervous about publishing it. They need not have worried. It made the long novel fashionable again (even if it cost more than the 7s. 6d. which, in publishing dogma of the day, must never be exceeded). And for years afterwards the fundamentally serious and introspective J. B. Priestley had to endure after-dinner speeches welcoming him as a Good Companion.

He had come a long way since the time, seven years before, when he had been living in Walham Green on £5 a week reading books for John Lane the publisher, and he had had a hand in discovering both Graham Greene and C. S. Forester. Who better to be co-founder – with Hugh Walpole, the President of Magdalen College and others – of the Book Society in 1928? The scheme was not quite new: in April 1926 the American Book of the Month Club, started by Harry Scherman, had made Sylvia Townsend Warner's *Lolly Willowes* its first selection, and the Literary Guild started up a year later. The idea was that a committee of literary figures saved you the trouble of reading book reviews, and so you could buy the books 'everyone was talking about' and inflate the royalties of any author lucky enough to be so chosen.

Another helpful thing for authors was the Literary

J. B. Priestley, 1925, by Robert S. Austin

Hostess. Any young writer whose first book had sold 1,000 copies or so could expect to receive an invitation to dinner, tea or cocktails from a rich lady who patronized the arts and whom he had never met before. (He could also, and usually did, put her in his next novel.) If you were invited to Lady Cunard's you might expect to meet George Moore, who loved her hopelessly. Lady Cunard, an American, who changed her name from Maud to Emerald, specialized in George Moore, who was then in his seventies, with all his major works (except *Héloise and Abelard*) behind him. You might run into Sir Thomas Beecham, reported to be Emerald's lover, and cer-

tainly indebted to her for the money that made possible London's 1921 opera season; or Michael Arlen – 'This is Michael Arlen, the only Armenian who hasn't been massacred!' And of course her unforgettable daughter Nancy, with her 'scimitars of gold hair', with whom all the young men were in love, including the unmassacred Armenian. This extraordinary girl ('What is it now, Maud,' inquired Margot Oxford – 'whisky, opium or niggers?') was said by Harold Acton to have been the inspiration of 'half the poets and novelists of the Twenties'.

The Cunards lived at 4 Grosvenor Square, and also at Nevill Holt, a huge crenellated mansion in

Leicestershire which is now a boys' school. Nancy, we may be sure, was Iris Storm in *The Green Hat* (but 'pagan body and conventional mind' hardly fits her), and also Lucy Tantamount in *Point Counter Point*, where she is described as dripping with earrings and bracelets (well, so were all Twenties girls of fashion) and jealously possessive of people. The Sitwells quite liked the Cunards (Osbert's verse 'Mrs Kinfoot is a dear, and *so* artistic' may or may not refer to Lady Cunard), but the Bloomsbury group didn't get on with them; while many people spoke of Emerald's 'frail Dresden china' beauty, and Peter Quennell praised her 'bird-like charm', Virginia Woolf called her 'a ridiculous little parakeet-faced woman'.

In 1928 Nancy, whose relations with her mother were getting very strained, disappeared to France and set up the Hours Press at Chapelle-Réanville near Paris. Here she published work by Richard Aldington, Robert Graves, Harold Acton, Louis Aragon and Norman Douglas (for whom she also typed). The subservient role of Nancy and other patronesses, without whom some Twenties geniuses might have

Lady Cunard by Cecil Beaton

died, must be very unpleasing to Women's Lib., but there is no mistaking Nancy's gift for talent spotting. Thus she refused to print *Lady Chatterley's Lover*, but published Samuel Beckett's *Whoroscope*, his first printed work, and paid him royalties of 33 per cent (some of her authors got 50 per cent).

At Sybil Colefax's you were likely to meet Artur Rubinstein whenever he was in London, Lord Berners, the eccentric composer who had a piano built into his Rolls-Royce, and Noël Coward, who once attended a Colefax house party at a rented country house that went on for a whole week. Next door to Lady Colefax in King's Road, Chelsea, lived Syrie Maugham (her estranged husband had just, in 1928, bought, from a Roman Catholic bishop who spent most of his time in Algeria, the Villa Mauresque with twelve cypress-fringed acres, on Cap Ferrat), and great was the competition between them in lion-hunting. In New York there was Bessie Marbury and her friend Elsie de Wolfe, afterwards Lady Mendl, famous, among many things, for standing on her head. The backing of these women, whether you took photographs, wrote poetry, decorated houses or opened the kind of shop which would now be called a boutique, ensured success.

With Lady Ottoline Morrell, we are almost in the Bloomsbury group, for many of them gathered at her manor at Garsington, near Oxford, and sponged on her, and played charades and spoke in the high-pitched whinney made fashionable by Lytton Strachey, and put poor Ottoline into their books. 'Always, somewhere, I shall find *some* woman who'll give me bed and board. Thank God for the women!' wrote D.H. Lawrence in a letter; and the sister of the Duke of Portland did this for many an artist. The Lawrences, the Middleton Murrys (until Katharine Mansfield's death in 1922), Yeats, Diaghilev, Mark Gertler, Bertrand Russell, Aldous Huxley, Epstein – all of them had been to Garsington.

'One good turn deserves a bad one' and Ottoline, unkindly described as horse-faced, with unskilfully dyed hair, several Pekinese dogs on the end of ribbons, clothes that always flapped in the breeze, and a shepherd's crook, found herself portrayed as Priscilla Wimbush in Huxley's *Crome Yellow* and Hermione Roddice in *Women in Love*.

The Sitwells were hosts with a difference. They were great talent spotters, and they were writers and rebels themselves. You were not asked to the Sitwells

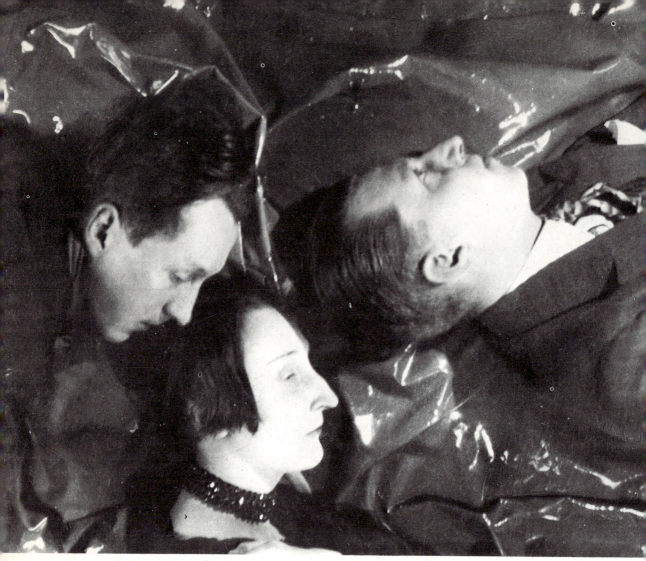

Sacheverell, Edith and Osbert Sitwell by Cecil Beaton

just because you had published or painted or composed something. You were asked because they thought you really had talent, and because of your entertainment value. In return, you had to put up with the storm of obloquy (largely from the *Daily Mail*) which they provoked, and of which you too became a target.

Façade is a blend of poetry by Edith Sitwell and music by William Walton, the poetry of which can be read separately, and the music of which has also a separate existence (and has been made into a ballet). The idea was so new in 1923 that it could be, and was, taken as a leg-pull. There had been a try-out at the Sitwells' house in Carlyle Square, Chelsea, and there was also a performance at Chelsea's Chenil Galleries; but the occasion everyone remembers was at the Aeolian Hall in Bond Street, a singularly depressing venue with bad acoustics which used to be hired by musicians seeking a wider public or any public. It afterwards became a B.B.C. studio. Edith Sitwell read her poems into a sort of loudspeaker called a Sengerphone, to Walton's music. As poems, they survive to illustrate the excellent principle 'Words are beautiful – never mind what they mean.' In Edith's own words, she wrote them 'at a time when a revivification of rhythmic patterns in English poetry had become necessary, owing to the verbal deadness then prevalent. The poems tell no story, convey no moral. Some have a violent exhilaration, great gaiety; others have sadness veiled by gaiety;

**Neil Porter and Edith Sitwell rehearsing
the latter's poems at the Chenil Galleries, 1926**

many are exercises in transcendental technique . . .'

Noël Coward, who was in the audience, didn't think so. Many of the spectators jeered all the way through, and the fireman of the Hall gave interviews to the press in which he said that he thought the Sitwells and Walton were 'barmy – they can't help it'; but Noël ostentatiously got up and stalked out. In his next show, a revue named *London Calling*, the Sitwells were impersonated as Hernia, Gob and Sago Whittlebot, rendering a skilful parody of Edith's verses. The Whittlebots for some weeks became more successful than the Sitwells, and Noël Coward contributed fictitious gossip paragraphs about the doings of Hernia, and himself read her poems from the new London radio station, 2LO.

We do not know whether, at that time, Mr Coward had read e. e. cummings, with whom he might have had a lot of fun, and who had somehow taken verse into a new dimension by leaving out both punctuation and capital letters; or Don Marquis, whose whimsical-satirical-philosophical fragments about *archy & mehitabel*, a cockroach and a cat recording their life-experience with extreme difficulty on a typewriter, had first appeared in his 'Sun Dial' column in the *New York Sun*.

'The verbal deadness' of contemporary poetry, Edith had said. Well, she might have meant Robert Frost and Edwin Arlington Robinson, Edna St Vincent Millay, even the Negro Langston Hughes, who were content, for the most part, with existing forms; Rupert Brooke and that bunch of poets, some recently dead in the war (Wilfred Owen and Edward Thomas – have any young men ever been angrier than they were?), others equally rebellious who were still alive, and all anthologized by Eddie Marsh and labelled 'Georgians'. She might even have meant Robert Bridges, who had rescued Gerard Manley Hopkins from twenty-nine years' oblivion, and whose *Testament of Beauty* was to appear in 1929 on his eighty-fifth birthday.

But surely she couldn't have meant T. S. Eliot, whose mighty *The Waste Land*, ruthlessly but skilfully cut and edited by Ezra Pound, another ex-patriate American, had been published in 1922. This is one of the world's poems of which it may be said that literature was never the same afterwards. A learned poet, too, containing Dante and Milton and the Metaphysicals, enough to keep scholars happy spotting the allusions; but also a messenger for his generation, breaking up his verse as the post-war world was broken up. Disenchantment, disillusion, disgust – it represented all the fashionable 'd's.

For a time, Edmund Wilson said, young poets now 'took to inhabiting exclusively barren beaches, cactus-grown deserts and dusty attics overrun with rats. . . . They had purged themselves of Masefield as of Shelley . . . and the sound of jazz, which had formerly seemed jolly, now only inspired horror and despair . . .'

Yet in 1920, in *The Sacred Wood*, Eliot had said 'Poetry is now perceived to have something to do with morals, and with religion, and even with politics . . .' He was *against* the trend, and also ahead of it. Auden and Isherwood were just going up to Oxford and Cambridge respectively, and in a few years' time all young poets would be Communists. But Mr Eliot – how nice to know him! – was received into the Anglican Church and British nationality. He also, thanks to the Bel Esprit fund started by Pound, Aldington and May Sinclair 'to raise £300 annually . . . in order that T. S. Eliot may leave his work in Lloyd's Bank and devote his whole time to literature', had done just that, and was on his way to becoming a director of Faber & Faber, publishers. Of *The Waste Land* Eliot himself afterwards said 'It was only the relief of a personal grouse against life; it is just a piece of rhythmical grumbling.'

T. S. Eliot was accepted by, but was not a founder member of, that curious gathering of English intellectuals that became known as the Bloomsbury Group. Were the 'Bloomsberries' really a group? They had no common style or subject; they were perhaps a cultural atmosphere; some, but not all, belonged to the Garsington set. They were all upper-middle-class, not at ease with anyone lower down the ladder; most were pacifists (but not Socialists) and atheists, and most of them had been at Cambridge or were related to Cambridge academics.

While conceding their great influence on the decade, and in spite of having been thrilled in adolescence by the naughtiness of *Eminent Victorians* (although published in 1917, it has been called 'the first Twenties book'), and having learnt from Virginia Woolf the true relation between poetry and prose, I must confess to not liking any of them much.

Lytton Strachey, 1928–30, by Stephen Tomlin

Virginia Woolf, 1928–30, by Stephen Tomlin

They seem to me to be Edwardians still revolting against the Victorians, instead of true Twenties-rebels reacting against everything.

Biographies, memoirs and letters of the Bloomsberries pour forth from the presses, why Virginia was frigid, who slept with who and how often, so that we now know more about their complicated lives than about the books they wrote or the pictures they painted. They snigger and sneer, they move in a leisurely roundabout of unrequited love for each other in various permutations, nervous breakdowns or even suicide just around the corner. 'They all backbite their supposed long and best friends' says Mark Gertler in a letter (how many hundreds of letters they all wrote, in an age when people who were on the telephone still did not use it for gossip!). 'Clive Bell has been at work again – mischief about Mary . . .' The jealousies, the mutual admirations, the charades, the daring each other to say dirty words – 'the word bugger was seldom far from our lips,' giggled Virginia.

If the Bloomsberries (to whom I know I have been unfair) did not truly belong to the Twenties, the Algonquin Set – in hardly any way comparable to them – certainly did. They could be bitchy too, but on the whole they loved each other a little more. Whether the Algonquin Round Table was inspired by the *Punch* Round Table does not matter. Around it, at various times, were gathered Alexander Woollcott, about 250 lb. of critic, essayist and broadcaster; Franklin P. Adams, who ran a column called 'The Conning Tower' in the *New York Tribune*; and Harold Ross, future editor of *The New Yorker*. These were the founder-members, who had all been on *Stars and Stripes*, the U.S. Army newspaper, during the War. It is said that Woollcott chose the Algonquin because he loved the pastries there. To them add Robert Benchley and Robert Sherwood, George Kaufman, Moss Hart, Donald Ogden Stewart, Deems Taylor, Marc Connelly, Heywood Broun, Charlie MacArthur, Harpo Marx, Douglas Fairbanks (Sr), Jascha Heifetz, Herbert Bayard Swope, and – well, practically anybody who could hold his own in invective and come out with a memorable wisecrack every half hour or so. If the Fitzgeralds were present, they might move on to drink home-made wine at Neysa McMein's studio, there to play charades and consequences. But if they stayed, there had to be wit.

Clive Bell and Family, 1924, by Vanessa Bell

That, it seems, was the trouble. 'I didn't like the Round Table' Donald Ogden Stewart says. 'You had to be so *brilliant* all the time.' I imagine them all thinking up wisecracks to drop into convenient holes in the conversation. Most of the witticisms associated

Alexander Woollcott

with the Algonquin are ascribed to Dorothy Parker; but it seems probable that some were invented by Benchley, a nice guy if ever there was one ('you felt better for being in the same room with him' says Donald Ogden Stewart). Benchley had a modest way of introducing one of his own cracks with 'As our Mrs Parker was saying . . .'

One of the really great contributions of the Algonquin Set, in the general iconoclasm of the times, was Crazy Humour. It probably originated in the universities to which nearly all of them had been (just as so much revue-type satire in England comes from the Cambridge Footlights); was developed by the Algonquins; and comes down to us via *The New Yorker*, *Vanity Fair*, *The Smart Set*, the Marx Brothers (scripted by Perelman), *Lilliput,* and all their imitators. It could be claimed, I suppose, that there is something of this anarchy in Saki and Stephen Leacock, whose enduring humour was published before 1914; but it needed the Algonquins and the Roaring Twenties to lift the lid off.

With Crazy Humour came Premeditated Rudeness, like Dorothy Parker saying her address was Bedpan Alley and calling *The House Beautiful* the play lousy, and if all the girls attending the Yale prom. were laid end to end she wouldn't be at all surprised.

The humour and the rudeness remained and grew, but the Algonquins did not long outlast the decade. They dispersed, when talkies and the Depression came, to Hollywood contracts, Marxism, Trotskyism, and the new world of the Thirties where 'applesauce' was an inadequate reaction to that world's problems.

But somewhere, let us hope, they are reunited, reminiscing, and wisecracking about – what? Perhaps Anita Loos, a bestselling lady I forgot to mention earlier in this chapter, anticipated my question. In *But Gentleman Marry Brunettes* (1927), sequel to *Gentlemen Prefer Blondes* (1925), the saga of blonde Lorelei Lee, who is 'engaged to a gentleman in the button business', and her 'very unrefined' brunette friend Dorothy, the two gold-digging girls meet some Algonquins. 'So they all started to tell about a famous trip they took to Europe. And they had a marvellous time, because everywhere they went, they would sit in the hotel, and play cute games and tell reminiscences about the Algonquin.'

CHAPTER 15

Best Sellers

Michael Arlen

It was a good time for writers who were content to consolidate, who did not wish to disrupt or probe too deep. Such novelists were beginning to make extra money by writing feature articles for the abounding popular magazines; and to set out on lecture tours of the United States, where, if they were British, they had to be pretty careful not to offend the daughters of America who composed the greater part of their audiences.

Sometimes these lectures would introduce one of the several books of the Twenties which defy classification except that they are 'seminal': their influence has reverberated ever since. Books difficult to explain to non-specialists, such as Keynes's *Economic Consequences of the Peace*, or Tawney's Christian Socialism in *Religion and the Rise of Capitalism*, or Oswald Spengler's *Decline of the West*, fatally easy to misunderstand (as it was deliberately misunderstood in Hitler's Germany). '*Decline of the West*', says a character in Susan Ertz's *Now East, Now West* (1927) who is (like the Dodsworths) in Europe for the culture – 'everybody seems to be reading that.'

But no; that was not at all what everybody was reading. The average lending-library subscriber was curling up with *The Green Hat*, which was *the* book of the Twenties on both sides of the Atlantic, and its heroine Iris Storm *the* heroine of the age. Iris has been in love with Napier Harpenden since they were both children, but his father, Sir Maurice, forbade the marriage because Iris, at eighteen, was too young, and also her family had no money and 'bad blood' (alcoholism). So he pushes her into

**The Film and Stage Ball at the Hyde Park Hotel,
1921 (centre Iris Tree)**

marriage with 'Boy' Fenwick. ('Boy' – notice how accurately the Armenian, but Malvern-educated, Mr Kouyoumdian, alias Michael Arlen, seizes on the upper-class pet-names of the time.) On their wedding-night 'Boy' commits suicide, and Iris puts it about that he 'died for purity' because he discovered that she was not a virgin. She continues to love Napier through her second marriage, which soon ends in separation, while drowning herself in passing affairs, of which she always seems to be ashamed (she speaks much of her 'Chiselhurst mind' in a 'pagan body', and the 'soiled loneliness of

desire'), and makes a final sacrifice by allowing Napier to make a clean marriage with a decent girl. Then she commits suicide by driving her Hispano-Suiza into a tree. (Is there any significance in the fact that Nancy Cunard had a friend named Iris Tree?) That Hispano-Suiza, which we meet on page 1, is a character in the story – 'a long, low, yellow car which shone like a battle chariot'.

But wait: the real reason why Napier threw himself out of that window was that he had confessed to Iris that he had had syphilis. The word leaps out of the page with an extraordinary effect of shock.

Nobody else, in 1925, had ever used the actual word in a novel. It was like a medicament after the disease of 'immorality' with which the book was charged. 'A Romance for a Few People' it was subtitled, which flattered the reader that she, too, lived in the glamorized Mayfair. There is much fearfully bad writing in *The Green Hat*, but much of it is very nearly good. All it needs is a ruthless editing, and the sort of advice that Maxwell Perkins gave to Scott Fitzgerald; indeed, Arlen sometimes has a genuine burst of poetic feeling which can stand comparison with – well, *Tender is the Night* if not *Gatsby*. But most of it is in the author's own reflections on contemporary England, which are all digressions. And do you know who advised Arlen to write about the things he did write about? D. H. Lawrence!

Lily Christine (1928 – about a girl who wore glasses at whom *everyone* made passes) is a more tightly-written and much better book; but it was *The Green Hat* that made half a million, and *Young Men in Love* that deserves to survive. In it, the three worlds of Serle the politician, Townleigh the newspaper magnate and Vardon the financier, as backgrounds to a love story, have the real scent of the Twenties. 'I was a flash in the pan in my twenties' Arlen told a *New Yorker* reporter in 1949. 'I had a hell of a lot of fun being flashy, and there was, by the grace of God, a good deal of gold dust in the pan.' Was it Rebecca West or Noël Coward who said he was 'every other inch a gentleman'?

Lower down the social scale there was Ethel M. Dell (inventor of the 'strong, silent man'), Ruby M. Ayres (good, clean love stories), and (quite different) E. M. Hull, who cashed in on the vogue for Arabs that persisted all through the Twenties. Her novel *The Sheik* had been published in 1919, but it was given a tremendous boost by Rudolph Valentino's film of the same name. E. M. Hull did not have to call spades spades: it was enough to write 'The shamed blood surged slowly into her cheeks. His dark passionate eyes burned into her like a hot flame . . . His touch was torture . . .'

Gilbert Frankau, G. B. Stern, Angela Thirkell – the names but not the books survive; *The Young Visiters*, the freak success of a story by a precocious child of eight whose innocent observations became catchphrases; the splendid unvarying world of P. G. Wodehouse, whose conversational slang –

'beans', 'fruits', 'crumpets' – partly absorbed and partly created speech; Lady Eleanor Smith and her gypsies, Sheila Kaye-Smith and her Sussex, Mary Webb and her Shropshire, soon to be slain by Stella Gibbons in her parody *Cold Comfort Farm*.

There was one kind of best-selling novelist who (and whose characters) had been stopped in their tracks by the War: they (and their characters) simply couldn't come to terms with the post-war world, and so they opted out of it; not into pacifism or any other 'ism', but back into the pre-War world. What remained after the holocaust was the officer class, with the only set of values worth having. So we have authors like Sapper and Dornford Yates, heroes like Bulldog Drummond and Berry Pleydell, the leisured, bored, private-incomed ex-officer for whom foreigners, crooks, lower classes, Reds and villains were practically synonymous.

Berry and his friends, happily cruising about France in their Rollses, are mourning the decline of the old landed aristocracy, with whom they are only indirectly connected. White Ladies, the Hampshire stately home, is the receding background, and nobody knows anybody who wasn't at Eton. This world is what the War was fought for, and they haven't got it any more. It is now in the hands of war profiteers like Dunkelsbaum (Jewish, of course), who has taken over Derry Bagot's house Merry Down. (Merry, Derry, Berry – pardon my confusion.)

Sapper at least gives us a rousing yarn, with certain wonderful unconscious absurdities (try *The Female of the Species*) which make them still readable today. Bulldog Drummond, his wife Phyllis (slim and loyal as a boy), the arch-villain Carl Peterson and his mistress Irma, the awful Lakington, the monocled Algy Longworth who, in the best upper-crust tradition, cannot pronounce his 'r's – well, if you're a serious mid-Thirties leftist you could call them Fascist beasts, though I prefer Alan Bennett's phrase 'snobbery with violence'.

Very different was the world of Tessa Sanger, fourteen-year-old heroine of Margaret Kennedy's *The Constant Nymph*, who falls in love with a composer, Lewis Dodd, who is twice her age. He is, we understand, a genius, and he has married Florence, a wealthy woman who virtually keeps him. Tessa's father, Albert Sanger, is also a genius, and lives with the children of both his dead wives in the Tyrol.

The enduring charm of Tessa is that she is completely uneducated, a circumstance which an English girls' school does nothing (thank God) to improve. She also has a weak heart, and in the dingy Brussels hotel to which she elopes with Lewis, the effort of trying to open a wedged window (uncouth Lewis wouldn't dream of doing it for her) is too much for her, and she dies.

Thus baldly summarized, the story is nothing; but it is so beautifully told that millions of middle-class readers were persuaded to accept the life of artists, the idea of 'free' love, and a situation akin to that of Lolita and Humbert Humbert, as romantic.

Mark Sabre also had a weak heart, which kept him out of the Army until things started getting desperate in 1916. Mark is the hero of A.S.M. Hutchinson's *If Winter Comes*, which was published in August 1921 and had gone through nineteen editions by the following March. If I tell you that it is about Mark's incompatible wife Mabel, his platonic affair with his old girlfriend Nora who has married a peer, his responsibility for his aged, ailing mother, a girl called Effie who has an illegitimate baby and poisons herself with oxalic acid . . . It's no good: the point about this novel is that Mark can be seen as a human saint, doing unappreciated good and being reviled for it, and somehow personifying the England which, since the War, serves 'a new God – Greed – Profit – Extortion' and needs 'the old God' but also 'Light, more Light! . . . Do you suppose an age that knows wireless and can fly is going to find spiritual sustenance in the food of an age that thought thunder was God speaking?'

Beau Geste, by P.C. Wren (for years I thought his initials meant he was a policeman), in 1924 took the average reader to an entirely believable Foreign Legion where the Geste brothers did unbelievable things in the fashionable desert where, however, the Arabs for once were the baddies. Warwick Deeping's *Sorrell & Son* was another best-selling weepie about the impoverished ex-officer bringing up a motherless little boy. Let us not judge these tales by the values of the 1970s; let us rather project ourselves back fifty years into a Britain that really believed in certain decencies.

And there were best-sellers that were not fiction at all. One of them used fictional characters to educate people in correct social behaviour: Mrs Emily Post's *Etiquette* which came out in 1922 and in the next twenty-five years sold nearly 750,000 copies. (This achievement was beaten by Lillian Eichler's *The Book of Etiquette*, published before Mrs Post's masterpiece: Miss Eichler sold over a million, possibly because her book was better publicized, using a series of 'What's Wrong With This Picture?' advertisements, written by Miss Eichler herself, who had been a copywriter.)

All Mrs Post's characters are 'in Society', and the villain of the story is 'the Guest No One Invites Again'. The cast includes the rich, snobbish Worldlys, who have a butler named Hastings and live at Great Estates; and the easy-going Gildings, who live in absurd luxury at Golden Hall, which has 'a guest annex' with 'perfectly equipped Turkish and Russian baths in charge of the best Swedish masseur and masseuse procurable', and 'a glass-roofed and enclosed riding-ring'. Lucy Gilding (*née* Wellborn) 'smokes like a furnace and is miserable unless she can play bridge for high stakes'. Among her friends are rich young marrieds like the Lovejoys and the Gailys, wealthy bachelors like Jim Smartlington and Clubwin Doe, and also Mr and Mrs Kindhart, who 'talk to everyone, everywhere and always' and cheer everyone up at a disastrous dinner where absolutely everything goes wrong.

The Littlehouses have less money, but nobody minds when you visit them and they 'press you into service as auxiliary nurse, gardener or chauffeur'. Definitely on the fringe are Grace Smalltalk (who however writes good bread-and-butter letters) and Mr Spendeasy Western. They are hardly fit to meet Mrs Oldname, *'une dame élégante'* who has 'an inimitable air of distinction', a tactful hostess who never forgets to say to a lady guest 'Mr Traveller, who is sitting next to you at the table, has just come back from two years alone with the cannibals.' She never swings her arms when she walks, never gesticulates when she talks. She does not know Mr and Mrs Upstart, Miss Nobackground or Mr Richan Vulgar, 'nor was there an article in the apparently simple living room that would be refused if it were offered to a museum'. English – or rather British – literature has no parallel to this sort of thing, because in Britain you betray yourself by speech rather than anything else. Besides, a gentleman knows when to be rude on purpose.

Britain, still divided broadly into Gentlemen and

Players, was at this time pioneering a literary genre which was beginning to cut across all class divisions, even if its heroes were mostly gentlefolk. I say 'pioneering' because although the detective story comes down to us from Poe's *Murders in the Rue Morgue*, through Gaboriau, Sherlock Holmes and *Trent's Last Case*, and Mary Roberts Rinehart's 'Fleming Stone' stories had started as early as 1908, we now have the strange phenomenon of *cosy* crime stories, often set at country-house parties, with no great moral disapproval of murder, very little blood, and no assault whatever on the reader's emotions. There were about 5,000 books of this kind between 1921 and 1930, and nearly 1,000 new authors (some with only one or two titles to their credit). Like doing a crossword puzzle in the comfortable knowledge that the solution is in the back of the book, the reader enjoys the conjuring trick by which the author conceals, until the very last page, who-dunnit. It goes with the connoisseurship of crime affected by Alexander Woollcott in some of his *While Rome Burns* pieces, and it belongs strictly to the armchair.

Thus President Wilson's favourite light reading was J. S. Fletcher's *The Middle Temple Murder*, and Stanley Baldwin was not ashamed to be seen reading Edgar Wallace, author of more than 150 books whose speed of production was so enormous that in 1928 *Punch* printed a cartoon of a newsvendor shouting to passers-by 'Seen the midday Wallace, Sir?' Wallace used to appear in advertisements for Parker fountain-pens, always with his long cigarette-holder (in reality he used typewriter and dictaphone). He had been a policeman himself, and knew his stuff, especially his underworld argot. His characterization and dialogue were often dreadful; probably *The Mind of Mr J. G. Reeder* (1926) has survived best.

There was a Chinese detective (Earl Derr Biggars's Charlie Chan), a blind detective (Ernest Bramah's Max Carrados); ponderous stories about jewel thefts on the Riviera – it didn't always have to be murder in those days – by William le Queux and E. Phillips Oppenheim; and two doctor-detectives, John Rhodes's Dr Priestley and R. Austin Freeman's Dr Thorndyke, whose first-person narrator tended to say 'I gave an emphatic affirmation' when he meant 'I said yes.' Freeman Wills Crofts, no stylist, wrote what would now be called 'carefully researched' novels featuring a solid policeman, Inspector French. In *The Benson Murder Case* (1926) we first meet Philo Vance, with an altogether more sophisticated bag of tricks: his creator, the art critic and dilettante Willard Huntington Wright under the pseudonym of S. S. Van Dine, was still in the English tradition.

In December of the same year Miss Agatha Christie suddenly disappeared, giving the press a 'nationwide woman-hunt', and was eventually found in an hotel in Harrogate. Whether it was loss of memory or a publicity stunt is not clear, but her famous story *The Murder of Roger Ackroyd* appeared almost immediately afterwards. It was probably the first detective story in which the murderer turned out to be the narrator. Miss Christie's Hercule Poirot had been well established for some years, and has been going on ever since.

Two more women who-dunniteers, of a most superior order, appeared shortly afterwards – Margery Allingham, whose private eye was Mr Campion, another mild, literate dilettante, and Dorothy L. Sayers, an advertising copywriter, whose Lord Peter Wimsey was a bibliophile and a connoisseur of wine, played Scarlatti on the piano, had won the D.S.O. in the War, belonged to the Bellona Club, bought rare books, and had a valet called Bunter. Miss Sayers wrote in aristocratic English prose, restful to re-read today, and her crime novels are full of recondite learning, especially about poisons.

In America, Ellery Queen gave the detective story a chromium-plated elegance in *The Roman Hat Mystery* (1929): his (or rather their – Frederic Dannay's and Manfred B. Lee's) new twist was that Ellery was both author and (in the third person) hero of the book; and suddenly we know the Twenties will soon be over, for Dashiell Hammett, ex-Pinkerton man, introduces the hard-boiled school in *Red Harvest* (1929). But meanwhile it seems that everybody is having a go at this whodunnit thing – Oxford dons such as G. D. H. Cole and his wife Margaret, Father Ronald Knox with his 'inquiry agent' Miles Bredon, even A. A. Milne, whose *Red House Mystery* (1924) came most unexpectedly from the man whose Christopher-Robin Pooh-Bear verses had made Dorothy Parker's Tonstant Weader Fwow Up.

CHAPTER 16

The Editor's Easy Chair

It was a great age for magazines, at all cultural levels. Perhaps the most sophisticated – well ahead of popular taste – was Frank Crowninshield's *Vanity Fair*, which employed a number of the Algonquins. It had, for a short while, Dorothy Parker as dramatic critic (she was standing in for P.G. Wodehouse, of all people), Robert Sherwood, and (as Managing Editor) Robert Benchley. When, in 1920, Mrs Parker was fired for excessive candour, the two Roberts resigned in sympathy. It was a good magazine to be on: it may have been slightly uppish, bootlicking the successful, but it was both American and international in outlook, classless and raceless, and recognized the leading Negro personalities of the day. It welcomed new arrivals in its 'Hall of Fame' feature; and people it didn't like were consigned to 'We Nominate for Oblivion'. It occasionally published an article in French for the 5 per cent of its readers who could translate it. As early as 1914 it had noticed 'an increased devotion to pleasure', as if the Twenties had already begun before the War.

It published the early work of Gertrude Stein, e.e. cummings, Edmund Wilson (afterwards Joint Editor with John Peale Bishop), Paul Gallico, Aldous Huxley; reached out to Hungary for Molnar, Paris for Colette; took a chance on Matisse and Gauguin for its colour plates; and printed avant-garde photographers like Steichen and Cecil Beaton. Never before had any magazine printed a headline like the title of Benchley's first article, 'No Matter from What Angle You Looked at It, Alice Brookhansen Was a Girl Whom You Would Hesitate to Invite into Your Own Home'.

To some extent *Vanity Fair* was doing – with commercial success – what the 'little magazines', underground and international, were doing on shoe-strings by way of publishing new writers. What it couldn't do was to print highly experimental writing or 'work in progress'. This was done by Eugene Jolas's *transition*, Ford Madox Ford's *Transatlantic Review*, and the *Little Review*, edited by Margaret Anderson and Jane Heap, who printed writing by Joyce, Eliot, Yeats, Pound and Hemingway, and pictures by Picasso, Matisse, Klee, Braque and Miró when they were relatively unknown. Not all the editors had much judgment – 'most of the stuff the *Little Review* prints is bad, I suppose,' said William Carlos Williams, 'but the *Little Review* is good.' In the last issue Jane Heap wrote: 'We have given space in the *Little Review* to twenty-three new systems of art (all now dead) representing nineteen countries. In all of this we have not brought forward anything approaching a masterpiece except the *Ulysees* of Mr Joyce . . . self-expression is not enough; experiment is not enough . . . Art today . . . is interesting only as a pronounced symptom of an ailing and aimless society.'

'Not for the old lady from Dubuque' was the slogan of the *New Yorker*, which began weekly publication in 1925 with Harold Ross as editor and Janet Flanner (Genêt) as Paris correspondent. It is not clear to an Englishman what is supposed to be wrong with the Iowan city, or for that matter with Podunk, about which H.L. Mencken once wrote a 3,000-word monograph; but the *New Yorker* picked up several writers from *Vanity Fair*, which it survives by nearly forty years.

There must have been considerable competition to find rebellious – but not too rebellious – writers. You couldn't, however, be too rebellious for the *American Mercury*, started by H.L. Mencken and George Jean Nathan in 1924. This 'lost generation's

Bible' was against religion, democracy, 'the bilge of idealism', and the stupidity of 'the gaping primates' who, in Mencken's view, constituted 95 per cent of the population. (To be fair, he was against Fascism too.) Mencken has been called 'America's Bernard Shaw', but in his scholarship and punditry he was more like Dr Johnson – Johnson without his Christian charity. For all his fury, Mencken didn't really understand the younger generation of artists: *The Great Gatsby* was without merit, Joyce was a crackpot and Hemingway a boob.

The *American Mercury* slogan was 'for a civilized minority' (as *The Green Hat* was 'for a few people'). It assumed that you knew roughly who Proust, Bertrand Russell, Martial, Eugene O'Neill, Einstein, Monteverdi and Jung were, and which of them were still alive. Was it left- or right-wing? You couldn't tell. Mencken and Nathan had come to it from the *Smart Set*, which had foundered after nine years, possibly because its title simply didn't fit into the post-War world.

Britain had nothing quite like these magazines. But, in an age when publications could survive on small circulations (20,000 to 60,000), there was a profusion of literary reviews. G. K. Chesterton had a weekly; so did T. P. O'Connor, who had founded the *Star* newspaper. The *Spectator*, two centuries old, had the *Nation*, the *New Statesman* and *Time and Tide* as weekly competitors, and a new, lighter *Saturday Review* edited by Gerald Barry. More solid fare was provided by *Life & Letters*, the *Adelphi*, the *Criterion* (edited by T.S. Eliot) and the *London Mercury*, edited by Sir John Squire the cricketing poet, the only member of the Athenaeum Club who ever wore a tweed jacket and flannel bags and jovially slapped bishops' backs when offering them a tankard of ale. Many of the reviews printed essays, still a respected literary form, and you could enjoy gently reflective-funny pieces by Robert Lynd, Gerald Gould and the young J. B. Priestley (whose *I For One* I was lucky enough to be given as a prize at school).

Popular magazines abounded in Britain, and there was a good living to be made by short-story specialists like Cutcliffe Hyne, Stacy Aumonier, and P.G. Wodehouse, who, although mainly concerned with writing musical comedies in New York, could earn £400 from the *Strand* for a Psmith or Wooster story. There were also the *Grand*, the *Argosy*, the *Passing Show*, *Pearson's Weekly*, *Britannia* (edited by Gilbert Frankau), *Nash's* (the English version of *Cosmopolitan*, whose fiction editor I was to become just before it crashed in 1937) and the *Happy Magazine*, all of whose stories had happy endings, and whose great claim to fame was that it published the earliest 'William' stories of Richmal Crompton, who was the childless wife of a retired general and modelled her eleven-year-old hero on a nephew. William has a secure place in English childhood reading: his Quixotic appeal is that he is only at peace when he is being naughty, and that any attempt to do good in the world (e.g. telling the truth) instantly lands him in trouble.

The world of the Browns, William's family, tells us much about suburban life in the Twenties. Mr Brown goes daily to the City, we are never told why; he has no car, which is the symbol, to William, of immense wealth, such as that of Mr Bott of Bott's Sauce, always depicted (in Thomas Henry's illustrations) as wearing striped trousers, top hat and spats, even in the country. Mr Bott's daughter Violet Elizabeth, aged six, is spoilt and lisps: whenever she fails to get her way, she threatens to 'thcream and thcream until I'm thick'. There is a certain class hatred of the Botts, who are *nouveaux riches* and have a lodgekeeper, a butler, a nurse, an odd-job boy known as Boots, at least one housemaid, and a full-time gardener.

The Browns, however, don't do too badly: they have a part-time gardener, a cook, and a maid who spends much time cleaning the silver and the knives (which are not stainless steel). William's amorous brother Robert (aged seventeen) has a bicycle but not a motorbike, and his sought-after sister Ethel (an auburn-haired Botticelli type aged nineteen) belongs to a tennis club but has no form of transport – why should she, with so many car-owning boyfriends? William's pocket money is 6d. a week (when he gets it, but it has usually been stopped for some destructive misdemeanour), which doesn't go very far, even though sweets are $\frac{1}{2}$d. an ounce.

Women's magazines, mostly rather thin and full of knitting patterns, received a nasty jolt when *Good Housekeeping*, big and glossy, arrived from America in 1924. But readers were reassured by the conservative line-up of authors on the cover – W.J. Locke, Marie Corelli and Robert Hichens, Lady Astor (who contributed an article on 'England

and the Dragon', the dragon being alcohol) and Clemence Dane, who was actually allowed to write on Divorce. Certain magazines were known as 'servant-girl papers'. Maids, often called 'skivvies', were watched carefully lest they should 'get into trouble', and publications like *Red Star Weekly* and *Red Magazine* (2d.) took this into account. Years afterwards I shared an office at Amalgamated Press with the editor of *Red Magazine*, a mild old man who was still printing stories that had been written before 1914, but brought up to date by substituting 'telephone message' for 'letter' and 'wireless' for 'pianola', and he told me that there was a strict code of conduct for heroines of 'servant girl' stories: 'Kisses on the forehead – all right; kisses on the cheek – only if they're married; kisses on the lips – *never*.'

At the Society level, the *Tatler*, the *Bystander* and the *Graphic* managed to coexist; at the schoolboy level, the *Magnet*, the *Gem* and the *Popular* continued to record the doings of Harry Wharton, Tom Merry and Jimmy Silver at Greyfriars, St Jim's and Rookwood Schools, the state-educated pupil's substitute for a public-school education, as they had done since before the War. For smaller fry there were *Chick's Own*, the *Rainbow* and *Tiger Tim's Weekly*. Science fiction appeared in the short-lived *Boys' Magazine*, which introduced a mad scientist with a German name, Dr Swarfschmidt, who had somehow flown to outer space and was returning to destroy the earth by means of a volatile metal called mallemite; and there were dozens of stories about schoolboy expeditions to Brazil to find the real-life explorer, Colonel Fawcett, who was missing, presumed eaten by cannibals. In the United States the *American Boy* featured the American counterpart of Billy Bunter, Marcus Aurelius Fortunatus Tidd, the stuttering fat boy created by Clarence Budington Kelland.

Magazines gave employment to illustrators, caricaturists and cartoonists. Britain had the Brock brothers, one of whom (H.M.) also drew regularly for *Punch*, Steven Spurrier, Heath Robinson and many others. But, with the notable exception of Lewis Baumer, few British illustrators could produce glamorous 'cover girls' like Bradshaw Crandall, and few of them became symbols of the age in the way that, for example, John Held did. Satirist and comedian, John Held virtually invented the 'flapper',

and his work was syndicated all over America. Girls with rolled stockings or garters reading books on psycho-analysis . . . John O'Hara used to amuse himself classifying people as Held types, Hugo Gellert types, Auerbach-Levy and Alajálov types (and he might have included Helen Hokinson, whose comfortable matrons first popped up in the *New Yorker* about five months after it started). 'The Scott-Fitzgerald people were drawn better by two artists named Lawrence Fellows and Williamson than by John Held. Held drew caricatures of the boys and girls who went to East Orange High School and the University of Illinois.'

But the inner heart of America was expressed by Norman Rockwell, whose life-work was one long documentary of people being decent and ordinary, in hundreds of *Saturday Evening Post* covers about childhood in the country, Mom's apple pie, Junior's first dance, Dad trying not to cry when Junior joins the Army, Auntie saying grace in a hamburger bar.

Wham! – Pow! – Zap! – *!?! – yes, the strip cartoons were coming into their own, which meant coast-to-coast syndication. In Britain they were mainly for children – Teddy Tail in the *Daily Mail*, the Arkubs (the Noah family of Ararat Avenue) in the London evening *Star* (J. F. Horrabin, artist of the

The Ace of Trumps for Automobile Salesmen – the Mention of Timken Bearings

'The Ace of Trumps for Automobile Salesmen', an advertisement design by John Held reproduced in 'Life', January, 1928

Teddy Tail for November 18, 1924

Arkubs also drew Dot and Carrie, a strip about two girls in an office with a bald-headed boss), and Pip, Squeak and Wilfred in the *Daily Mirror*. But from America British newspapers borrowed Mutt and Jeff (Arnold Bennett's favourite), Jiggs ('Bringing Up Father'), and a variety of characters in *Film Fun*, based on Ben Turpin, Harry Langdon and other Mack Sennett heroes.

Of all these, Pip, Squeak and Wilfred had the greatest impact on my young life. On holiday at Herne Bay, Kent, I could press my nose against the window of the Ship Inn and see A. B. Payne, their creator, actually creating them. Pip was a dog, Squeak a penguin and Wilfred a rabbit. They had various friends, such as Squeak's Auntie, and enemies, such as Popski, a literally dirty dog and an anarchist with a bomb in his pocket. Wilfred had a special language of his own, consisting of monosyllables such as 'gug', 'nunc', 'ick', 'pah' and 'boo'. What more natural, therefore, than that the *Daily Mirror* should use them in a circulation-building stunt called the Gugnunc Club, which readers' children could join, and which had the attraction of a blue enamel membership badge, and other still more exciting badges according to the number of new members you enrolled. You started as a plain Gugnunc, graduating masonically to Good, Great and Grand Gugnunc; and if you saw another child in the park wearing a Gugnunc badge, you rushed up and held the following dialogue with him or her:

'Gug?'
'Nunc!'
'Ick ick pah boo?'
'Goo goo pah nunc!'

Tom Webster, a London *Daily Mail* cartoonist who specialized in racing, made wonderful fun of a

famous horse of the day with exceptionally long legs called Tishy. Tishy's legs crossed and wound themselves round each other until he resembled Babe Ruth – 'twisted like a pretzel'. And the *Daily Express* had a political cartoonist called Strube – not a 'great' cartoonist in the Daumier tradition like David Low, who was just flexing his muscles on the *Star*, but the pioneer in England of the Little Man, in whose hatband the label 'Taxpayer' was usually stuck, and for whom all news was bad news.

Another Webster (Harold Tucker, no relation to Tom) had recently joined the *New York World*, there to create Caspar Milquetoast, 'the Timid Soul', the kind of man who apologizes to *you* if you stamp on *his* toe in the subway.

It was a time of Circulation Wars, for which two personalities, both mad in different ways, were responsible – Northcliffe, whose death in 1922 by no means extinguished his influence, and Hearst, who was to some extent his pupil. (Northcliffe, as Alfred Harmsworth, had designed the first experimental issue of the *New York World* as long ago as 1900, and had used the word 'tabloid' to describe it.) British newspapers were still pretty staid by American standards. *The Times*, the *Daily Telegraph* and the *Morning Post* still carried small advertisements on the front page, the *Daily Mail* carried much larger ones (£1,200 was the full-page rate), especially at sales time, when the first thing your breakfast-time eye lighted on was often cut-price woollen combinations (at 6s. 11d.) or the very latest cami-bockers from those down-to-earth Kensington stores, Barker's, Pettit's and Pontings, or it might be Arding & Hobbs at Clapham Junction or Gorringe's near Buckingham Palace.

But the *Daily Mail*, organizing stunts like mad, was progressing towards and beyond its slogan, 'Daily Mail – One Million Sale'. Like Hearst papers, it feared the Red Menace; but it did not attach the same importance that Hearst did to the Yellow Peril, whipped up by reports of the Japanese population explosion in 1928 and 1929. There was cutthroat competition between national dailies in the 'free gift' field, and the *Daily Herald* (which had started out after the War as a rallying point for leftist and angry young men like Siegfried Sassoon, Osbert Sitwell and Raymond Postgate) at one time was offering sixteen volumes of the works of Dickens for eleven shillings (about $2.60). In vain: what really sold the paper was Templegate's racing tips. But circulation was not everything: a new Liberal daily paper (more of a review, really) like the *Westminster Gazette*, first issued in October 1921, just before the beginning of the end of the Liberal Party, could stagger along on a very small circulation until 1928, when it was absorbed by the *Daily News*, which then absorbed the *Daily Chronicle*.

In America, by 1927, the Hearst and Scripps-Howard systems controlled 55 chains of 230 daily papers with more than 13,000,000 circulation. Syndicated features and cartoons were the order of the day – the only 'national' elements of a continent's press, very different from Britain, where there has always been a 'national' press circulating in every part of the compact British Isles.

But in the United States some of the stories became 'national'. Thus the Gray-Snyder trial got more space, coast-to-coast, than the *Titanic* disaster had done; and in 1924, the year of yellow journalism, an unfortunate young man named Floyd Collins, from Kentucky, dominated the world's news for eighteen days when he was imprisoned by a fall of rock in Mammoth Cave. He died, and his memorial is a film called *Ace In the Hole*. There were stories about marathon dancers, about the wretched Alvin Shipwreck Kelly who sat on a flagpole in Baltimore for twenty-three days; there was the emergence of the gossip writer (Valentine, Lord Castlerosse, in England, Louella Parsons in Hollywood) and the sob-sister.

Meanwhile, the 'war of the tabloids' was on – between Robert McCormick's *New York Daily News*, which had begun as a subsidiary of his *Chicago Tribune*, and Hearst's *American*. Hearst eventually, in 1924, replied with the tabloid *New York Daily Mirror*, and Bernarr Macfadden started his *Graphic*, three months later. We shall see in a moment how far in sensationalism a circulation war can go; but first a word about Mr Macfadden and his lasting contribution to Twenties and subsequent journalism.

His childhood in the 1870s had been one of brutal poverty dogged by tuberculosis, then generally known as 'consumption', and believed to be curable by chest and muscle development in a gymnasium. Soon he had set himself up as 'Bernarr Macfadden – Kinistherapist – Teacher of Higher Physical Culture'. It was a short step from this to special dieting, and in an age when the science of nutrition had barely

been born he lived for long periods on unbuttered baked potatoes and lemon squash. In 1899 he had started a magazine called *Physical Culture* whose slogan was 'Weakness is a Crime'. He published a novel called *The Athlete's Conquest*. His cult of the body beautiful caused his offices to be raided by Anthony Comstock, the anti-vice crusader, who, seeing a photograph of the Venus de Milo on the wall, tore it down crying 'Pornography!'

Physical Culture contained a heart-throb column for women. Suddenly, in 1919, Macfadden saw how this column could become a separate magazine. Thus was born *True Story*, a monthly magazine illustrated by photographs of living models, among whom were future film stars such as Norma Shearer and Fredric March. By 1926 *True Story* was selling more than 2,000,000 copies. There was no doubt that much of the confessional material was titillating, so Macfadden covered himself by appointing an inter-denominational advisory board of clergymen. *True Story* was followed by *True Romances*, *True Experiences*, and *True Detective Mysteries*, and Macfadden by 1929 was a multi-millionaire. He had also started *Photoplay*, one of many film-fan magazines that accompanied and promoted the growth of the movie industry.

The New York *Evening Graphic*, which he started in 1924, had as one of its aims 'fighting for the abolition of government censorship', and as another, 'dramatizing news and features'. He dramatized the famous annulment suit of a lady named Peaches Heenan Browning against her husband by running a faked picture of the plaintiff standing naked in the courtroom – Peaches' head and somebody else's body. Overnight the *Graphic* gained 250,000 new readers. After the Ruth Snyder–Judd Gray murder trial, Macfadden printed, in spite of New York's law against interviews with condemned persons, the alleged 'very last words – exclusive!' of Ruth Snyder. When Rudolph Valentino died, the *Graphic* printed 'spirit letters' from him. It also specialized in headlines of the kind which British readers associated with the *News of the World* – 'TWO WOMEN IN FIGHT, ONE STRIPPED, OTHER EATS BAD CHECK', and 'BEAT TWO NAKED GIRLS IN REFORM SCHOOL'. And there was an absolute ban on pictures of Marlene Dietrich: 'I don't want any more skinny-legged women in this paper' Macfadden instructed his editors. 'I want women with hips and breasts.'

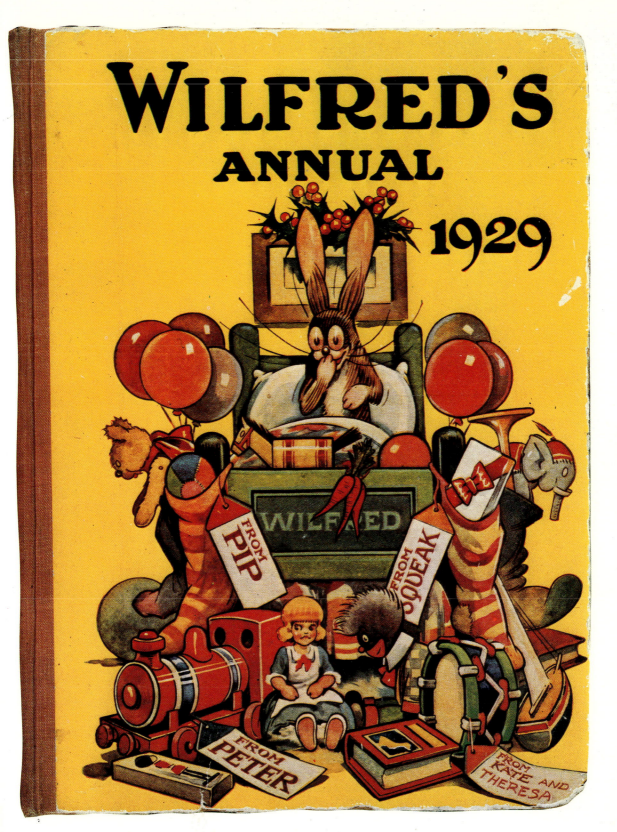

The cover of *Wilfred's Annual 1929*

Listening In.

CHAPTER 17

The Radio Music Box

I am fourteen. I am lying in bed, still awake at 11 p.m., listening with earphones to the Savoy Orpheans, or it may be Henry Hall's Band from the Gleneagles Hotel, playing 'Mean to Me' and 'Tiptoe Through the Tulips' and 'It Happened in Monterey'. Nobody knows I am doing this, because under my bed I have a crystal set (you could make one for 7s. 6d. – $1.40), and I am using the metal framework of the bed as an aerial, and the pipe of the gas fire as an earth. This is my first taste of the sweet life, for I can actually hear the customers at this night club or that restaurant, clapping between dances and talking to the conductor and sometimes drunkenly laughing into the microphone; the clink of glasses, the crash of dropped crockery. Night after night I fall asleep with the earphones on.

The Savoy Orpheans at the Savoy Hotel, London

(opposite) G. E. Studdy's popular cartoon dog Bonzo

Broadcasting variety from 2LO (London), 1929

Downstairs is my Ferranti Screened-Grid Three, a battery-operated valve set which I have made myself from foolproof instructions. I have had a row with my father about this. In order to buy the components (at wholesale prices from a friend who works at Brush Electric) I have drawn out all my Post Office savings (£9). How can I possibly be the only boy in the form at school who isn't building a valve set? Father said, rightly, that I know nothing about radio – or wireless, as you usually termed it in those days – and was terrified that it wouldn't work.

But it did work. The very first time I switched on, music came through loud and clear – from Bratislava, in Czechoslovakia, a station with a very pretty call-sign like a glockenspiel. That was the great thing in those days – to get foreign stations. There was a paper called *World Radio* which contained their wavelengths and programmes, and another called *Amateur Wireless* from which we learnt strange new terms like 'superheterodyne' and 'regenerative vacuum-tubes'. At school each morning we boasted that we had sat up all night listening to Duke Ellington from Schenectady or KDKA on short waves, or Hilversum or the Eiffel Tower on long waves. Nobody could prove we hadn't.

And in the course of time Father – who said we didn't need wireless, and what was wrong with the gramophone? – sat glued to my set every evening listening to Stainless Stephen, Leonard Henry, Mabel Constanduros and Flotsam and Jetsam.

The miracle of radio – I cannot tell you how wonderful it was, how it transformed our lives. Television was merely its logical consequence, and never had its me-to-you intimacy. Of course people had known about Senator Marconi and Poldhu for years, and how Dr Crippen and Miss Le Neve were trapped by wireless telegraphy, and what it had done for the Navy and the Army Signals Corps during the War. But here it was in our houses, if not with earphones, then with loudspeakers, little horns sometimes hidden under the crinoline of an eighteenth-century doll; then, when moving-coil loudspeakers with their enormous baffle-boards came in, they were part of the furniture.

In 1916 David Sarnoff, an engineer of the Marconi Company of America, had sketched out an idea for what he called a 'radio music box': There was a vague idea that it could be of enough educational value for serious-minded people – especially people who lacked the patience or know-how to build their own, as thousands of 'hams' were doing all over America and Britain. Marconi, Westinghouse and other electrical manufacturers figured that there could be profit in the sale of equipment and – who could tell? – it might even be used for advertising.

For some time Dr Frank Conrad, of Westinghouse, had been broadcasting records and sports results to amateur listeners from a barn studio. On November 2nd 1920 Station KDKA, installed at the Westinghouse plant in East Pittsburgh, went on the air with the news that Mr Harding had been elected President of the United States, building up to this result with the returns as they came in. The excitement was something like that of a World Cup link-up today. Radio, as entertainment, had arrived. Within a year there were eight more stations. Within two years there were 564. Already there was a shortage of wavelengths, and Station WEAF, set up in August 1922 by the American Telephone and Telegraph company, was offering air time for sale to advertisers. The expression 'sponsored program' was already in use. New York and Chicago stations had been connected by landline for the first broadcast of a football game.

Soon the Calvary Church in Pittsburgh was broadcasting services, and the Dixmoor Golf Club installed headphones so that the golfers could hear them. It is not clear why a Lieutenant Maynard broadcast an Easter sermon from an aircraft, except of course that somebody had to do it sometime. The first song about radio was in the *Ziegfeld Follies* of 1922, and in London André Charlot was quick off the mark in 1923 with a revue (starring Noël Coward, Gertrude Lawrence and other Bright Young People) called *London Calling!* (the call-sign of 2LO London).

In everybody's backyard stood an enormous pole with a thickish wire like a clothesline leading to a chimney or under the eaves, and the suburbs became a tangle of aerials. Millions of Americans made new friends in the persons of Roxy and his Gang, Rudy Vallee, and Graham McNamee the baseball commentator whose voice was better known than any President's. It was not thought strange that a classical concert should be introduced with a commercial about pyorrhœa for Forhan's Toothpaste. In 1922 $60 million of radio sets were sold in America; in 1929 $842 million.

In Britain, how different! – no boom, no commercial radio. For the British people broadcasting became a national institution, like the Church of England. But not before a delightfully long period of amateurism.

'Hallo, CQ! This is Two-Emma-Toc, Writtle, testing!' 'Hallo, CQ!' is the international hams' code-phrase for 'If anyone can hear this, please reply.' Writtle is a village just outside Chelmsford, Essex, and the jolly, jokey voice was that of Captain P. P. Eckersley, ex-Royal-Flying-Corps, and head

of Marconi's designs department, Britain's, if not the world's, first disc-jockey, speaking from an old Army hut. It was 1922. For three years Captain Round and Mr W. T. Ditcham, of the Marconi Company, had been broadcasting to a small band of fewer than 10,000 amateur listeners around Chelmsford itself ('This is the Marconi valve transmitter from the Marconi works at Chelmsford'), and in 1921 they had treated their audience to the voice of Dame Nellie Melba, then over sixty, singing songs of a certain patriotic content, which was entirely appropriate, since she came from Australia and the future task of radio, if it had one, would be to draw the Empire together. Melba's performance was subsidized, to the tune of £1,000, by Lord Northcliffe of the *Daily Mail*, who, fearing that radio would ultimately stop people from reading newspapers, had taken the precaution of renting a radio station in Holland. She had a little difficulty with the microphone, which somewhat resembled a cardboard ear-trumpet: like Melchior a year or two later, she thought that the louder she sang, the further away she would be heard. She need not have worried: she was heard in Paris, Berlin and The Hague. The first broadcast concert in Britain came from a garden fête in Hampstead in July 1922, when, said *The Times*, the programme consisted of 'unconsidered trifles of the lightest type'.

Station 2MT (Writtle) had a licence from the Postmaster General to broadcast 'vocal and gramophone selections and calibration signals for amateurs', most of whom belonged to the Radio Society of Great Britain. It was allowed to do this for fifteen minutes a week, and it had to shut down for fifteen minutes between each two items (this at a time when America had more than 1,000,000 receiving sets and anyone, in any State, could get a licence to open a radio station). 'We set about, rather light-heartedly,' Peter Eckersley afterwards said, 'putting together some valves, condensers and chokes on a board to produce the required low-power transmitter.' Outside, two masts 110 feet high supported the aerial. He recalled how one evening, after a particularly good dinner at his local pub in Witham, eight miles from 2MT, he started broadcasting and – did he run out of records, or had the dinner made him cheerful? Anyway, 'I failed to play the records . . . I went on talking and talking, convincing myself that I was being really funny.' Next morning he had

"MY DEAR BASIL, WHAT *ARE* YOU ROARING AT?"
"DUNNO—COULDN'T HEAR IT. BUT JUDGING FROM THE APPLAUSE IT MUST HAVE BEEN DEVILISH FUNNY."

'Punch' comment of 1924

'The Mullion Wireless', 1921, by Charles Ginner

**Dame Clara Butt and her husband
Kennerley Rumford recording in 1927**

**Evelyn Laye dressed as the 'Merry Widow'
enjoying a few moments 'listening-in', 1923**

a fan-mail of fifty postcards urging him to do it again. He did it again *and* again, and soon wasn't bothering to play records at all. One night he broadcast a spoof 'Night of Grand Opera', playing the piano himself and singing all the parts – even soprano – himself.

This was fun, therefore it must be stopped! The British Broadcasting Company was formed, with John Reith as General Manager, and Britain was in for sixteen years of righteousness. On January 17th 1922, 2MT broadcast for the last time, and Eckersley sang Tosti's *Goodbye*. Reith employed him for seven years, and then ordered him to resign because he had been involved (as the innocent party) in a divorce case, using these actual words: 'My son, you have strayed from the paths of righteousness.'

Without Eckersley, radio might have gone on broadcasting gramophone records for ever. He had shown what it could do by communicating a human personality. One year later, Britain had 500,000 receiving licences; by 1924 there were over 1,100,000 and by 1927 'wireless' was in 2,500,000 homes. Broadcasting became less local, more regional and national, in spite of the radio manufacturers, who had originally preferred low-power stations because they want to sell more valve sets, which were obviously more profitable than crystals and cat's-whiskers.

On November 14th 1922 the British Broadcasting Company (it did not become a Corporation until 1927) gave its first programme from Savoy Hill, London, with the call-sign '2LO calling'. It consisted of news, weather forecasts, and (as in America two years before) the first general election results. Soon there were eight regional stations, with names such as '5IT Birmingham' and '2ZY Manchester' (2ZY had been started by Metropolitan-Vickers). With the opening of 5XX (Daventry high-powered transmitter) a host of new personalities came flooding into British homes – Stainless Stephen, a Sheffield schoolmaster whose rich Yorkshire voice made fun of punctuation ('I was semi-conscious, semi-colon'); John Henry and 'Blossom', A.J. Alan, a brilliant short-story teller with a pleasant blend of humour and the macabre (he was a senior civil servant named Leslie Lambert, and the mystery of his identity added much to his publicity); Christopher Stone, our second and very classical disc-jockey; Tommy Handley, with his 'Disorderly Room' sketch,

carried over from the wartime Roosters concert party; Layton and Johnstone, the coloured duo who sang and recorded almost every song of those years, Wish Wynne, Norman Long, Clapham & Dwyer, Reginald Foort and other cinema-organists, J.H. Squire's Celeste Octet, and the Gershom Parkington Quintet, which always seemed on hand to play soothing 'light music' whenever anything went wrong.

In the warm summer of 1924 a nightingale was broadcast from the Oxted, Surrey, garden of Beatrice Harrison the cellist: she made it sing by playing to it. Waiting for the bird to perform required a great deal of patience on the part of both B.B.C. engineers and listeners, and attempts to repeat the occasion were not always successful, especially in bad weather, when the disgruntled commentator was heard to say things like 'I am lying on my stomach in the wet grass – we hope to hear the nightingale any minute now . . .' But the nightingale was heard all over the world, and King George V said to Miss Harrison 'You have done what I have not yet been able to do – encircled the Empire.' (He did, though, on Christmas Day 1932).

The B.B.C., having a mission to spread culture, gathered together some extremely clever young men. Tyrone Guthrie was among the first producers of drama at Radio Belfast. Lance Sieveking experimented with Pirandello and a new technique of speech-sound-music montage. In 1927 the first war play, just ahead of *Journey's End*, and equally realistic, healthily shocked 12,000,000 listeners: it was Reginald Berkeley's *The White Château*. There were a great many stunts, such as broadcasting from an aircraft; and what is believed to be the first radio play put out in Britain (*Danger*, by Richard Hughes, in 1924) was set claustrophobically in a coalmine. Director-General Reith's weary comment on all this was 'What was wonderful yesterday is mediocre today and futile tomorrow.' He himself had suffered a setback when, in 1923, he had wanted to broadcast the wedding of the Duke of York and Lady Elizabeth Bowes-Lyon, and the Palace had refused permission.

Sports broadcasting was hampered for several years by restrictions (like not revealing what horse had won a race), largely at the request of sports promoters who feared that the 'gate' would be killed. However, these were relaxed in 1927, when it became possible to follow H.B.T. Wakelam's commentary on a Rugger match with the aid of a diagram in the *Radio Times* – 'The ball is now in Square D.'

'Of course, broadcasting will kill concert-going, and probably gramophones too.' Not a bit of it. Radio and television never killed anything except possibly old-style Variety or Vaudeville and magazines such as the *Saturday Evening Post* and *Picture Post*; and they took nearly half a century to do that. The music halls and radio coexisted comfortably until television came along.

Never forget: the B.B.C. had a duty to educate, possibly born of the Director-General's regret that he had not been to a university. 'I do not pretend', said Reith, 'to give the public what it wants.' By 1924, 220 schools were listening to the B.B.C. schools programmes. So far from killing concerts, the B.B.C. saved them in 1927, when Henry Wood's Promenade Concerts would have petered out altogether without B.B.C. backing. Sir Walford Davies gave talks on musical appreciation. Concerts of 'chamber music' (a new term for millions of people to whom the word 'concert' meant a variety programme in the parish hall) brought letters of protest to the *Radio Times* and jokes about chamber-pots. The music-hating British of those days were summed up in a *Punch* joke showing a wife with headphones on and an expression of agony on her face. 'What is it, dear?' asks her husband. 'Bad news or Stravinsky?'

The bravest and least successful bid to educate the British public in music was the B.B.C.'s contemporary music competition. A prize of £300 was offered for a new symphony, £150 for a tone-poem or overture, £150 for a short piece for voice and orchestra, £100 for a work for military band, and £50 for a song cycle. There were 240 entries, to be judged by Sir Edward Elgar, Sir Hamilton Harty and Sir Landon Ronald. Incredibly – not even to save the B.B.C.'s face – the judges found none of them worthy of any sort of prize, and part of the money was given to the Musicians' Benevolent Fund.

The B.B.C.'s coat of arms, adopted in 1927, contained a lion holding in its paw what appeared to be a thunderbolt, and the motto 'Nation Shall Speak Peace unto Nation'. But nobody was speaking peace unto the B.B.C., which was criticized by everyone for different reasons. Why could comedians make jokes about mothers-in-law and beer on Saturday, but not on Sunday, which was all religion and that loathed thing, Good Music? And when, in 1925, a directive to comedians banned jokes about drink, illness, parsons, Scotsmen and Welshmen (but not Irishmen), what on earth was there left to be funny about? Why did all the announcers have Oxbridge accents? Why had there never, in B.B.C. News, been any reference to a murder case? Why couldn't anyone talk about politics or religion, as long as opposing viewpoints were fairly represented? Why had the B.B.C. never broadcast a programme about Soviet Russia? Or birth control?

Oh, but there had been a programme about birth control; very unfortunate; quite unsuitable. It was by Professor Julian Huxley and producer Cecil Lewis, who clumsily tried to excuse the controversial nature of the subject by having a bogus 'listener's voice' interrupt the talk with 'I protest! Here, I say, you can't do this!' When the stunt was exposed, the B.B.C. came in for more trouble. And whatever was Mr Reith doing that dreadful night in 1926, with the General Strike fresh in everyone's mind, when Father Ronald Knox was allowed to make a hoax broadcast (not unlike Orson Welles's *War of the Worlds* twelve years later) about a fictitious revolution in which there were eye-witness accounts of people being 'roasted alive in Trafalgar Square'?

The *Daily Mail* carried out a piece of market research among its readers and came up with the finding that the public wanted more light music and military bands and no chamber music or long plays. To his credit, Reith gave them exactly what they wanted for one week. The *Daily Express*'s Wireless League came to much the same conclusions.

And yet the B.B.C. had enormous authority. It had an advisory committee on spoken English which included such names as Bernard Shaw (whose voice was liltingly Irish), Logan Pearsall Smith (an American, but Anglicized by being Bertrand Russell's brother-in-law), and actor Sir Johnston Forbes-Robertson, all under the chairmanship of the Poet Laureate, Robert Bridges. If these gentlemen had anything in common, it was that they were all old. They were required to standardize English by deciding whether one should say 'cross' or 'crawss', 'golf' or 'goff', 'Paris' or 'Paree', 'Keltic' or 'Seltic', 'housewife' or 'huzzif'; and was the new B.B.C. high-powered 5XX station at 'Daventry' or 'Daintree'?

To know somebody in the B.B.C. was practically to be in Society. This feeling caught one young in the terribly cosy, well-bred Children's Hour, where all the announcers and their wives or girlfriends became Aunties and Uncles, and if your parents sent your name in early, they would wish you many happy returns on your birthday; especially if you were twins, and then you would be greeted by a special fanfare on the piano and the entire cast shouted 'Hallo, twins!'

To be an announcer (and their names were seldom known to the general public until the Second World War) was to be a kind of mysterious god, certainly superhuman. Somehow we knew the names of Stuart Hibberd, 'Uncle Rex' Palmer, John Snagge and the Hon. David Tennant, and we knew that they all wore dinner jackets every night. What we didn't know was anything about their private lives, such as the fact that David Tennant was married to Hermione Baddeley the actress and had helped to start the Gargoyle Club in Soho with his father Lord Glenconner, Lord Henry Cavendish-Bentinck and A. P. Herbert. I don't suppose the D. G. knew, either.

People never thought of announcers as being married. There was a song, written and sung by B. C. Hilliam and Malcolm MacEachern, better known as Flotsam & Jetsam, called 'Little Betty Bouncer' who

Loved an announcer
Down at the B.B.C.

She made more progress than most listeners, because when she wrote to her announcer she received a reply enclosing a photograph –

To Miss Betty Bouncer
From the wife *of the announcer*
Down at the B.B.C.

To be asked to broadcast (and there were over 700 people writing in for auditions every week) was such an honour that one did not mention money at all, but was agreeably surprised to receive the standard rate of a guinea a minute (often less). Only the 're-volting intellectuals' sneered at radio; as they joined the Won't-Go-To-Wembley movement, so they stood out against this vulgar toy, wireless.

Poor intellectuals: they were missing a lot; for example, the excitement, even the poetry, of George Allison's sports commentaries. Here he is describing the finish of the 1927 Derby, won by Call Boy: 'He leads, he leads! Come, gallant son of Hurry On! He nears the judge! Leap then, brave heart! Nothing can catch him now . . .' Cry God for Harry, England and St George!

In the United States broadcasting was closing its ranks, but differently. The listening audience had perforce to be regarded as the largest possible number of customers for advertised goods. The cost of net-work broadcasting had to be shared between pro-gramme sponsors and stations using the programme. In 1926 the Radio Corporation of America, which owned stations WJZ and WRC, with General Electric and Westinghouse together formed the National Broadcasting Company, and they took over WEAF; and next year United Independent Broadcasters and Columbia Phonograph begot the Columbia Broadcasting system.

On both sides of the Atlantic radio men were watching a new development which the radio public, still intoxicated by the wonder of words and music in the air, could barely imagine. Both C. F. Jenkins in America and J. L. Baird in England had shown, in 1923, that a black-and-white silhouette in motion could be transmitted electrically; and, in 1925, that a fuzzy moving picture in half-tone could be transmitted. A small advertisement had appeared in the London *Times*, typical of the un-wordly John Baird who had put it there: '*Seeing by Wireless.* Inventor of apparatus wishes to hear from someone who will assist (not financially) in making working model. Write Box S.686.' John L. Baird had only one thing in common with John Reith: they were both the sons of Scottish Presbyterian ministers. Baird's first experiments were carried out in his tiny laboratory over a shop at 8 Queen's Arcade, Hastings. The first human being whose face was televised was his business manager O. C. Hutchinson, in Frith Street, Soho. In 1926 Baird demonstrated his invention before the Royal Institution of Great Britain, and two years later came the great leap forward of transatlantic television: he actually transmitted pictures from England to the *Berengaria* in mid-ocean. But his method of 'scanning' never achieved high definition. The cathode-ray tube can be traced back to 1897, in principle, but he failed to rediscover it; and it was the E.M.I.–Marconi team, led by Sir Isaac Schoenberg, that perfected TV as we were to know it in Britain.

CHAPTER 18

Lively Arts

The precise opposite of the early Reith-B.B.C. mind was the mind of the American Gilbert Seldes. He was a complete man of the Twenties in that he welcomed what was new ('Make it new!' said Ezra Pound) and saw good in what many intellectuals (the Antic-Haymakers) saw as savagery. For Seldes the popular arts were full of vitality and imagination, and at their best were preferable to the established arts, which seemed to be receding too far from the life of the people. In 1924 he published *The Seven Lively Arts*, about films, revues, funny columnists, comic strips, jazz, vaudeville; about Charlie Chaplin, *Ziegfeld Follies*, Ring Lardner the sportswriter ('who has set down for posterity the accents of the American language'), circus clowns, W.C. Fields, Krazy Kat, Al Jolson and Irving Berlin. Seldes was making a good-humoured attack on genteel culture, and relating these lively arts to the jazz rhythms in Stravinsky and Edith Sitwell, Jean Cocteau's ballets and whatever it was that the Dadaists were trying to do.

In times when 'nobody is interested in politics', or even in times when people *are* interested, there need be no shame or guilt about escapist entertainment. 'The situation in Austria', people used to say in Vienna, 'is hopeless but not serious'. It is a legitimate viewpoint that the arts are here to enrich our lives, show us something better, and cheer us up. While waiting for Godot, we can do a great deal more than start pessimistic conversations: we can instead go on a trip of the imagination, needing no drugs to turn us on. All right, so it's all hokum, and we know it is hokum; so long live hokum!

The Twenties expressed themselves most happily in musical comedy and revue. People went to them in evening dress after a good dinner, and why not? Bring on the chorus at the beginning and end of each act, empty the stage instantly by crying 'Anyone for tennis?' or 'Let's all go swimming!', plant one big side-splitting drunk scene in Act Two, have the juvenile leading boy and girl break into a tap-dance or soft-shoe shuffle at the end of their love duet – Sandy Wilson caught it all beautifully in *The Boy Friend*. This is musical comedy, usually American, with books and lyrics adapted for London.

Revue meant different things in Britain and America. It could be intimate; it could be spectacular. In France it had meant a polished comment on the times, and this was grafted on to the traditional British seaside concert party, pierrots, Pelissier's Follies, with their 'songs and sketches', plus a bit of music hall, and played by a small group of rising young stars. In America revue tended to be bigger and brassier, built around one or two really big stars, as in the *Ziegfeld Follies* and *George White's Scandals*. You may or may not agree with Ronald Jeans, one of revue's most successful writers, that revue is 'a form of entertainment so designed that it doesn't matter how late you get there'.

Let us look through Mander and Mitchenson's book on *Musical Comedy*. 'Heather Thatcher as Lovey Toots and Leslie Henson as Odo Phillpotts in *The Beauty Prize* (1923), a musical comedy by George Grossmith and P.G. Wodehouse, music by Jerome Kern' (in which Heather and Leslie did a three-legged dance on the deck of a luxury liner, the

Two different aspects of the Ziegfeld Follies, 1923

Sidney Howard and Leslie Henson in the 'drunk' scene in 'Funny Face'

Majestania). Heather and Leslie turned up again in *Tell Me More!* (1925), with music by George Gershwin, in which, the *Daily Telegraph* sniffily reported, they indulged in 'numerous and fantastically applauded dances, most of them noted rather for agility and acrobatic ingenuity than for grace and elegance.' Adele and Fred Astaire came to London in *Stop Flirting* (1923), known in New York as *For Goodness' Sake*, and *Lady, Be Good!* by Guy Bolton and the Gershwins (1926). *Oh, Kay!* (Guy Bolton, P. G. Wodehouse and the Gershwins) presented Gertie Lawrence as Kay – the first British actress to create a star part on Broadway before it came to London.

The London Hippodrome was in luck. *Sunny* (Harbach-Hammerstein-Kern), with Jack Buchanan, Binnie Hale, Elsie Randolph, and an all-time hit tune, 'Who', was followed by *Hit the Deck*, with Ellen Pollock, Stanley Holloway, a coloured girl called Alice Morley and two more hits, 'Hallelujah!' (B.B.C. Reith's favourite tune and his only known concession to frivolity) and 'Sometimes I'm Happy' ('sometimes I'm blue, my disposition depends on you').

The Astaires were back again in 1928, in *Funny Face* (by the Gershwins again), singing 'I love your funny face, your sunny, funny face.' Fred, strangely anticipating his film *Top Hat* of seven years later, sang, with chorus, 'High hat, you've got to treat them high hat, Don't let them know that you care.' This was their last appearance in London together; four years later Adele became Lady Cavendish. *Funny Face* included one of the great 'drunk' scenes of all time, in which Leslie Henson was

partnered by the lugubrious Sidney Howard. It was also one of the last American musical comedies of its kind to come to London (the Cole Porter and Cochran shows-with-a-story-line of the 1930s were less intimate, more sophisticated), for by now the natives were beginning to hit back, and London had shows such as *The Five O'Clock Girl* (in whose chorus John Mills made his first stage appearance), *Mr Cinders* and others, usually with music by Vivian Ellis. *Mr Cinders* neatly reversed the Cinderella story with Binnie Hale, as a millionaire's daughter masquerading as a maid, sending Bobby Howes to a ball, having sung to him 'I'm a One-man Girl' ('who's looking for a one-girl man').

Charles B. Cochran

Revue, in London, was in the hands of two great producers, André Charlot and Charles B. Cochran. Charlot was the pioneer, but it was Cochran who brought revue to highly-polished perfection in a series of shows that became annual. He was always known as 'Mr', his chorus were known as 'Mr Cochran's Young Ladies', which gave them a tremendous prestige. Starting with *The League of Notions* (1921), Cochran gave London in 1925 *On With The Dance*, all of whose hit numbers – among them 'Poor Little Rich Girl', originally sung by Alice Delysia to Hermione Baddeley – were by

(above) **Lauri Devine and the masked chorus, designed by Oliver Messel, in 'Dance, Little Lady', 'This Year of Grace!'**

Noël Coward; *One Dam' Thing After Another* (a daring title at the time); *This Year of Grace!* (1928), in which book, lyrics and music were all by Coward, and the two big numbers were 'A Room With A View' and 'Dance, Little Lady'; and *Wake Up and Dream* (music mostly by Cole Porter).

Cochran introduced young designers such as Oliver Messel, then in his very early twenties, to do the décor of his shows. They always had two or three items which caused him to be accused of trying to raise the level of public taste. They were, however, usually shrewd showmanship in that C. B. had spotted a trend that was going to be, ultimately, a paying proposition. Ballet, for instance: in *This Year of Grace!* Tilly Losch danced to Bach – and danced *slowly*. Nobody for years had dared to

(above) **Richard Dolman and Jessie Matthews, singing 'My Heart Stood Still' in 'One Dam' Thing After Another'**

(left) **'Gothic; a Study in Arabesques' – Lauri Devine and Tilly Losch in 'This Year of Grace!'**

Maisie Gay in 'This Year of Grace!'

Ernest Thesiger and Douglas Byng in 'On with the Dance'

do anything slowly. The Russian ballet, under Diaghilev, had exerted, and was still exerting, a deep influence on contemporary taste and design, and its artists were regarded as refugees from a hated revolution, a nucleus of the old Russia which must be cherished. Cochran had noted how Diaghilev was commissioning work from the young, revolutionary talent of all Europe; that the names of Massine, Lifar, Lichine, Dolin, Danilova, Woizikovski, were becoming known, and that *The Sleeping Princess*, although a financial failure, had run at the Alhambra, hitherto the home of revue and music hall, for 105 nights. So *On With the Dance* contained two little ballets by Massine, expressing (as 'Poor Little Rich Girl' also did) the jazz-and-cocktail age in which Coward (for Britain) and Fitzgerald (for America) lived as participant-observers. It also contained one of the funniest sketches of all time, in which Ernest Thesiger and Douglas Byng, both renowned for their 'camp' performances, played two elderly ladies, sharing a boarding-house room, undressing for bed in an agony of prudish embarrassment.

Cochran-Coward shows were more 'daring' than other people's: there was always a risky sketch (risky for those days) near the beginning of the second half, such as the honeymoon scene in which the young husband, helping his bride to undress, says 'I always scratch myself on that damned hook!' (Black-out.) For simpler fare one went to shows like the Hulberts' *Clowns in Clover*, which had Cicely Courtneidge spoonerizing 'Two dozen double-damask dinner-napkins', Jack Hulbert's face-slapping routine, and a song, sung by June:

I've got those Little Boy Blues,
My heart's right down in my shoes . . .

The London and New York theatre scene in the Twenties is usually labelled 'escapist', trivial, dominated by Coward, Lonsdale and musicals; and Coward himself is on record as having attacked (in the *Evening News*) his older contemporaries for pandering to 'the desire of the British public to be amused and not enlightened . . . Is the theatre to be a medium of expression setting forth various aspects of reality, or merely a place of relaxation where weary business men and women can witness a pleasing spectacle . . . demanding no effort of concentration?'

**Noël Coward, photographed by Maurice Beck and
Helen Macgregor, as Nicky Lancaster in 'The Vortex'**

It was *The Vortex* that had caused all the fuss. Bernard Shaw had seen it and called it 'wonderful – damnable'. Arnold Bennett records in his journal that he 'dozed off in the last act'. James Agate praised it almost to the skies: 'Brains must ultimately come by their own, even in the theatre; and Mr Coward has brains to spare.' The problems of Nicky Lancaster, who was hooked on cocaine and whose mother had taken a lover (and the never-explicitly-expressed background of homosexuality) scandalized the actor-manager-matinée-idol, Sir Gerald du Maurier, who had written: 'The public are asking for filth . . . the younger generation are knocking at the door of the dustbin . . .'

So here was Noël Coward demanding the very sort of theatre he failed to live up to, and denigrating the kind of entertainment he was supremely good at providing, and which, thirty or forty years later, he was to defend against the new tide of dustbins.

It wasn't only *The Vortex*: there was *Fallen Angels*, in which two women got drunk while discussing their lovers. No wonder Noël's enemies – including the critic Hannen Swaffer, who once had his face slapped in the Savoy Grill by an actress he had panned – rejoiced at his downfall with the disastrous first night of *Sirocco* and the failure of *Home Chat*, both of which were rather lacking in what had come to be called 'Noëlisms' – shock-lines for which the audience waited, such as (in *Fallen Angels*) 'I shall come in naked on a tricycle if I choose,' or (in *Hay Fever*) 'She uses sex as a sort of shrimping-net.'

So the theatre of the Twenties was trivial and decadent, was it? Let us see exactly what it was doing: we may be forced to the conclusion that it was a cultural force for the middle-class audience which patronized it (there was no other audience) and that it had very little to be ashamed of. Take, for example, Broadway in 1928 and 1929. There were, somehow, 224 productions (which must have included some very short runs). A hundred and fifty of these were plays, and among them were *Journey's End* (from London); Elmer Rice's *Street Scene* (about New York's East Side, and what is escapist about that?); the first satirical revelation of life on a newspaper – a competitive Hearst-type, mass-newspaper of the Twenties – in Ben Hecht's and Charles MacArthur's *The Front Page*, a play (and soon afterwards a film) which set the pattern for all future scripts about newspapers on both sides of the Atlantic, and caused Fleet Street reporters to talk in a new way and subeditors to wear totally unnecessary eyeshades; a Philip Barry comedy at the Plymouth called *Holiday* which ran for 229 performances; and a classical array which included *Macbeth*, *The Cherry Orchard*, *The Seagull*, *Uncle Vanya* (all that Chekhov!), *Hedda Gabler*, *The Wild Duck* (all that Ibsen!) and *Major Barbara*. The revues were *This Year of Grace!* (with Bea Lillie and Noël Coward), *The Little Show* (Clifton Webb and Libby Holman, 321 performances at the Music Box), George Kaufman's *Animal Crackers* with the Marx Brothers, and Eddie Cantor in *Whoopee*. A livelier theatre you could hardly find.

In these allegedly decadent, superficial years it was possible in New York to offer the theatre-going public O'Neill's *Strange Interlude*, in which a wife whose husband's family was tainted with insanity has a child by another and healthier man; *The Captive*, a play about homosexuality; and *Strictly Dishonourable*, in which a 'nice' girl has an affair with an opera singer.

In London Miles Malleson's *The Fanatics* ran at the Ambassadors for 319 performances in 1927. You could call it the *Look Back in Anger* of the times. The way to get a West End production for a play with any controversy about it was to have it put on at a club theatre. This was what happened to John van Druten's *Young Woodley*, tried out by the Stage Society at the Arts Theatre before being passed for public performance at the Savoy Theatre in 1928: a

Ben Hecht's and Charles MacArthur's 'The Front Page'

The Marx Brothers in George Kaufman's 'Animal Crackers'

sensitive play about adolescence which was banned officially for some years because it might cause 'anxiety and grief to parents' by suggesting that public school boys did not spend all their time playing rugger and cricket, but might even fall in love with a housemaster's wife and sleep with a girl in the village out of frustrated curiosity. As so often in controversial plays of the Twenties, the unmentionable subject of homosexuality is lurking about in the background.

Stalls and dress circle 12s., pit 3s. 6d., trays of tea will be served in the interval, and ladies are requested to remove their hats. (*Punch* joke: girl takes off cloche hat to release a golliwog-shock of hair.)

From Czechoslovakia came Čapek's *R.U.R.* ('Rossum's Universal Robots') and *The Insect Play*,

Paul Gill, Ursula Jeans and Nicholas Hannen in 'The Fanatics'

both science fantasies with a strong anti-war, left-wing bias (the Beetle with his ball of dung is a capitalist, the robots show where our materialistic society may lead us). Playing the Poet Butterfly in *The Insect Play* was John Gielgud, in one of his first parts, looking very pretty in white flannels and wings. From Sutton Vane, an author who had been dead for ten years, came *Outward Bound*, a play about a number of people of all kinds and classes on a ship going no one knows where – and only one character knows that they are all dead. Produced at London's Garrick theatre in 1923, it ran for 227 performances, reached New York's Ritz Theatre the following year, and it has been revived several times since.

Upon this apparently hard-boiled age Barrie's *Mary Rose*, on the 'island that likes to be visited', with Fay Compton in the lead, could exert her tender fantasy, helped by Norman O'Neill's strange music; and the Bright Young People queued enthusiastically to see and hear Henry Ainley in the poetry of Flecker's *Hassan* (Basil Dean's gorgeous production at His Majesty's, with Delius's music), a story of lovers who suffer death by torture rather than separation. Homage to Bernard Shaw was beginning at the Malvern Festival, where *The Apple Cart* was first produced in 1929. Ruth Draper's famous monologues, which begat Cornelia Otis Skinner and Joyce Grenfell, first hit London at the gloomy Aeolian Hall in 1920, and became an institution at the Garrick in 1926 and at other theatres almost annually thereafter. Nigel Playfair filled the Lyric Theatre, Hammersmith, for 1,463 nights from June 1920 onwards with *The Beggar's Opera*, John Gay's ballad opera which had so delighted Dr Johnson at Drury Lane, full of traditional English tunes and revived four times before 1930.

Can we grumble at a theatrical decade which gave London *The Country Wife* (slightly bowdlerized), Edith Evans in *The Way of the World*, *The Beaux Stratagem*, *The Wild Duck*, *Rosmersholm*, *Ghosts*, Mrs Pat Campbell in *Hedda Gabler* ('Mrs Campbell's very magnificence makes nonsense of the play' wrote Agate), the whole of Chekhov; plays by Strindberg, Molnar, Pirandello, O'Casey and Elmer Rice, whose *The Adding Machine* added the word Expressionism to party conversation. What on

Henry Ainley and Cathleen Nesbitt in 'Hassan'

'At the Hippodrome', 1923, by William Patrick Roberts.
William Roberts was, with the writer Ezra Pound, Epstein, Gaudier-Brzeska, Percy Wyndham Lewis
(their leader), Edward Wadsworth and C. R. W. Nevinson, one of the participants of an English art
movement called Vorticism founded in 1912. They took their orientation from Cubism and, particularly
Futurism with its dedication to the rhythm and forms of the machine. The works of the movement show
flat, geometric lines and arcs radiating from one salient point, the vortex, giving the effect of rotary
and often vertiginous motion

SUNNY

Programme

6D

LONDON HIPPODROME

CHESNEY

Binnie Hale on the front of the programme for *Sunny*, 1926

**George Bernard Shaw, 1926,
by Prince Paul Troubetzkoy**

earth did it mean? In the play, a clerk murders his employer because he has been sacked and replaced by an adding machine. Agate thought this pessimistic view of the working class was wrong, and delivered himself of the surprising judgment that 'it would be nonsense to compare this minor play with any of the major Galsworthys.'

Oscar Wilde, strangely, was out of fashion, even in Dublin, where Micheál MacLiammóir produced *Salomé*, only to have his posters scrawled over with the word 'Degenerate!' Maugham's best comedy, *Our Betters*, came to the Globe in 1923. Two of Shaw's best, *Heartbreak House* and *Saint Joan*, the one containing Edith Evans, the other Sybil Thorndike, were given to a fairly grateful world. The last three plays had all been produced in New York first. And in 1929 came one of the great theatrical flukes of all time, the stunning success of *Journey's End*, revived with great success in London in 1972.

'How topping if we both get the M.C.' says a young lieutenant just out of school to a more seasoned officer as they prepare to go 'over the top' – and nobody laughed, for pathos and compassion were somehow made to overrule. Bob Sherriff (always known as R.C.) was a clerk with the Sun Insurance company in Trafalgar Square, where his father too had been a clerk for forty-five years. He was also captain of Kingston Rowing Club, for which he wrote plays to raise funds. The plays had to have a lot of parts for his fellow oarsmen, who were also encouraged to sell tickets by having parts written in for them. One such play was *Journey's End*, an all-male affair about a group of soldiers in a dugout. It is fact, not fiction: even the title was found by Sherriff chalked over the entrance to an actual dugout in Flanders. The commanding officer, Stanhope, is cracking under the strain, but is worshipped by the new young one-pipper. A middle-aged officer soothes his nerves by reading *Alice in Wonderland*. There is a Cockney called Trotter who thought he smelt phosgene gas but it was only 'a blinkin' may-tree' . . . I saw it when I was fourteen and began to ask my father questions about war.

Laurence Olivier, then unknown, played Stanhope at the trial performance by the Stage Society, but could not appear in the West End production because he had already signed on to play *Beau Geste*; and Colin Clive took the leading part through the play's two-year run. In New York it made Alex Woollcott weep. He called it 'the best play written for the English stage in this century and the finest work yet wrought by an Englishman out of his war experiences', and compared it to 'our own superb *What Price Glory?*' It was not, he insisted, a pacifist play, but 'a finger of accusation pointed steadily at the shambles of slack and selfish and silly living which we have the effrontery to call peace'. *Journey's End* was acceptable, at this latter end of the Twenties, because everyone (except possibly Wall Street) knew that the kissing was soon to stop.

In 1925 came the first to be seen in London of the big American romantic musicals, *Rose Marie*, which Arthur Hammerstein had staged in New York the year before. This was followed by others with Friml, Romberg and Kern as composers, and 'straight' books, notably those by Otto Harbach and Oscar Hammerstein II. *Rose Marie*, with Edith Day in London and Mary Ellis in New York, turned the fortunes of the Theatre Royal, Drury Lane, which had had many failures since its reconstruction in 1922. It had the 'Indian Love Call', the chorus of Mounties and, in the front row of the chorus of totem dancers, Marjorie Robertson, later to be known as Anna Neagle.

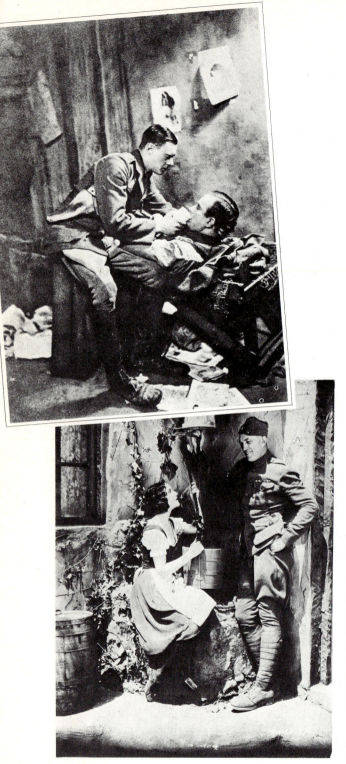

(top) R. C. Sherriff's 'Journey's End'

(above) Maxwell Anderson and Lawrence Stallings'
'What Price Glory?'

The Desert Song, with Harry Welchman as the Red Shadow and Edith Day as Margot; *Show Boat*; *The New Moon*; *The Student Prince* (His Majesty's, 1926), *The Vagabond King* (Winter Garden, 1927) – the music is still with us, and all are still performed by amateur operatic societies. *Show Boat*, in particular, had a basically tragic theme, dared to talk about miscegenation, and drew from Jerome Kern more serious music than anyone expected of his long musical-comedy background. From Hammerstein, too, it drew some tougher, deeper lyrics, of the kind that made him weep whenever he heard them sung, and caused *The New Yorker* to say 'His songs are distinguished by such lucid wording, such unabashed sentimentality, such a gentle, even noble, view of life, and such an attachment to love, home, small children, his native country, nature and dreams come true that he has been called the Bobby Burns of the American musical.'

Show Boat, first produced at Ziegfeld Theatre, New York, with Helen Morgan's legendary performance as Julie, reintroduced Paul Robeson, already known to Londoners for his performance in *The Emperor Jones*.

At the end of the line, already looking over the wall into the Thirties, came a native product, Noël Coward's *Bitter Sweet*, a terribly, terribly English Viennese operetta which cast a musical spell upon my young life which I hope will never be broken by its revival. Bits of it were written in the Algonquin hotel, while Noël was playing in *This Year of Grace!*, and at the Algonquin he found his leading lady, Peggy Wood. In *Bitter Sweet* Noël Coward took a terrific risk: the hero dies on stage, killed in a duel, and even though the tragic mood is softened by the jazzy, up-to-date last scene, the lump in the throat does not quite depart. The show was tried out, like all Cochran productions, in Manchester, brought to His Majesty's in London, and after a slow start ran for 697 performances in London, but only 159 at the Ziegfeld in New York, where it starred Evelyn Laye.

Provincial cities in Britain had few theatres. In the Midlands we had a oasis, Barry Jackson's Birmingham Repertory (all seats a 1s.) Theatre, which put on, among other things, the whole of *Back to Methuselah*; and the Shakespeare Memorial Theatre, rebuilt in 1928 after being gutted by fire, was only twenty-five miles away, so that if we were 'doing' *As You Like It* for School Certificate, the whole form could be taken in a motor coach (called, in those days, a charabanc) to see it. There were a few music halls, and an annual visit from either the Carl Rosa Opera Company or the D'Oyly Carte Gilbert and Sullivan.

You could say, in fact, that only about 7 per cent of the British population ever went to the theatre at all. Where *did* they go? Why, 'the Pictures', of course; at first to see Pearl White in a weekly serial, *The Perils of Pauline*, which left her in a predicament (such as being tied to the railway lines as the express train roared towards her) at the end of each instalment. Occasionally to British films, to see Chrissie White, Henry Edwards, Betty Balfour, Stewart Romè, and Alma Taylor in such slender products as the often-closed, impecunious British studios could offer (Cecil Hepworth, a pioneer producer, made *Comin' Thro' the Rye* in 1923 on a budget of £10,000), but overwhelmingly to Hollywood films, poured out from a booming town which, ten years ago, had been a village, and was now a community of new riches, vulgar display and soaring real estate values.

'Avast, my bullies!' Jiggling white letters on a speckly black screen. I am twelve, and I am seeing Julius Ulman, better known as Douglas Fairbanks, in *The Black Pirate*, fighting people and jumping improbably from rooftops. In *The Thief of Baghdad*

Harry Welchman and Edith Day in 'The Desert Song'

there was rather a lot of kissing, which was embarrassing. In *Robin Hood* – I *think* it was Robin Hood – someone was a leper and held his finger in a candle flame to show that he felt nothing. Fairbanks had founded United Artists with Mary Pickford

Anna May Wong and Douglas Fairbanks in 'The Thief of Baghdad'

Nº 1482.

6d EDITION

ISSUED IN CONJUNCTION WITH THE "FELIX THE CAT" CARTOONS
APPEARING EXCLUSIVELY IN Pathés "EVE & EVERYBODY'S
FILM REVIEW.

FELIX
KEPT
ON
WALKING

WORDS BY
ED. E. BRYANT
MUSIC BY
HUBERT · W · DAVID

Copyright.   Price 6d net

Lawrence
Wright

Mickey and Minnie Mouse

(Mrs Fairbanks, 'the World's Sweetheart', and they lived in a house called Pickfair), Charlie Chaplin and D. W. Griffith, all of whom made films just as they liked and had the full benefit of the profits they made. Fairbanks's films, his son has told us, 'epitomized . . . the whole American philosophy of energy and optimism . . . He used to say that the theatre was for the intellect but that the cinema dealt more simply with the emotions.' Mary Pickford, née Gladys Mary Smith, was apt to be seen in ringlet-curled little-girl parts, such as *Rebecca of Sunnybrook Farm* and *Daddy Long Legs*.

With the 'big picture' there was often a cartoon as well. Felix the Cat appeared in 1923, Mickey Mouse in 1928. Mickey arrived at about the same time as the 'Mighty Wurlitzer organ'. Disney's creation was obviously something entirely new and more ambitious in the cartoon sphere, and it soon became fashionable to say that 'the American cinema had produced only two men of genius, Chaplin and Disney.'

There were historical spectacles like *The Four Horsemen of the Apocalypse* and *Ben Hur*, to which I was allowed to go in a party organized by the school, our headmaster having first pointed out all the inaccuracies and anachronisms. There were cowboy films, with Tom Mix and W. S. Hart. There were dog films, starring two Alsatians called Rin-tin-tin and Strongheart. But the main impact, using the full knockabout potentialities of the medium, was laughter. Recent revivals, in the cinema and on TV, have shown how well the 'Golden Silents' wear. There was Chaplin in *Shoulder Arms*, *The Kid* (with Jackie Coogan), and *The Gold Rush*, in which the little man so wonderfully blends humour and pathos. Harold Lloyd, goggled and straw-hatted, in *Safety Last*, never used a stunt-man to do those incredible cliff-hanging feats. Nor did stone-faced Buster Keaton, hero of *The Navigator* and *The General*. Add to these great ones the by no means negligible talents of cross-eyed Ben Turpin, Fatty Arbuckle, Chester Conklin, bewildered Harry Langdon, Mack Sennett's Keystone Cops and, in 1927, brought together by producer Hal Roach, the brilliant partnership of Stan Laurel and Oliver Hardy: their first film together was *Putting Pants on Philip*.

For weirder tastes there was Erich von Stroheim, the monocled 'man you love to hate', the villainous

Charlie Chaplin in 'The Gold Rush'

German officer, humourless sadist of *Foolish Wives*, the behaviour of whose characters contributed to a rising demand for censorship (of course they were mostly foreigners, whom decent British and Americans would never dream of imitating); and the baffling phenomenon of Rodolpho Alfonzo Raffaelo Pierre Filibert Guglielmi di Valentina d'Antonguolla, whose names, being as numerous as those of the Prince of Wales, had to be shortened to Rudolph Valentino. Eddie Marsh, meeting him at a dinner party, thought him 'just a dago waiter . . . the ugliest man at the table, without a particle of charm'. Never mind: he personified lust and violence, and he danced the fashionable tango as it had never been danced before, and that was what women filmgoers seemingly wanted. He also popularized sideburns as a male virility symbol.

Beverley Nichols and others, seeing this little man go 'through reel after reel, hurling women about as though they were sacks of potatoes and smacking their bottoms' (and chasing them with whips too), constructed a theory about the masochism of newly-emancipated women who wanted to be raped, and demanded 'he-men' to overpower them so that it wasn't their own fault if they had to lie back and enjoy it. The great moment in *The Sheik* was when Valentino, having carried the kicking, struggling Agnes Ayres to his desert tent, flings her on to a divan. She, apparently unable to guess what everyone in the audience knew full well, asked 'Why have you brought me here?'

Buster Keaton in 'The General'

Rudolph Valentino and Agnes Ayres in 'The Sheik'

Rudolph Valentino lying in state in the Campbell Funeral Parlour in Broadway, New York

Valentino was a former vaudeville dancer whose unrealized ambition was to play Cesare Borgia, whom he greatly admired. There were moments in *The Sheik* when he looked uncannily like Lawrence of Arabia. His death in 1926, at the early age of thirty-one, was accompanied by apparently spon-

taneous outbreaks of mass hysteria which are now known to have been organized by his manager and the press agent of the undertaker who arranged his funeral. Before burial his body lay in state and was inspected by a file of people eleven blocks long.

His two marriages had not been happy. But the general public knew nothing of this. They were fed glamorous stories about all the film stars by a new industry, press-agentry, a new kind of journalist, the Hollywood Correspondent, and the publicity departments of film companies. It was known that in 1926 Harold Lloyd and Tom Mix were both getting £4,000 a week; Chaplin and Fairbanks £3,000 a week; Colleen Moore only £1,380 a week. 'Harold Lloyd was born on April 1st,' ran the publicity for *The Kid Brother* (1927), 'and the stork who brought him could hardly fly for laughing.' A star was expected to show the world a happy marriage, and this went hand in hand with censorship under the Hays Code. Will H. Hays, who had been Warren Harding's Postmaster-General, venerated 'that clean virgin thing, the mind of a child', and this was the standard of incorruptibility he set for the movies. In England, the London County Council invented the U-certificate – 'suitable for showing to children'.

When talkies came a new breed of sophisticated producer was seen in Ernst Lubitsch, maker of many silent films, who invented the satirical musical and in particular exploited the charm of Maurice Chevalier. Before *The Love Parade* (1929), starring Chevalier and Jeanette MacDonald, there had been films with songs: now the camera roamed at will and the songs and the dialogue and the movement flowed from one into the other.

There was a small band of idealists who admired what came to be called 'documentaries'. Some were inspired by the great Russian propaganda films such as *Battleship Potemkin*, which were shown only at special cinemas, and at the Film Society, founded in 1926. In 1920 and 1921 Robert J. Flaherty, equipped with a generator, an outfit for processing film, a portable phonograph and two cameras, went to live among Eskimos. He spoke about a hundred words of Eskimo, enough to make them do what he wanted. The result was *Nanook of the North*, underwritten by Revillon Frères, the fur merchants, who were in competition with the Hudson's Bay Company.

Flaherty found that the Eskimos, who had never

seen a gramophone before, shrieked with laughter at two records in particular: Harry Lauder's 'Stop Your Tickling, Jock' and Caruso singing 'On with the Motley'. He lived on bear and seal for sixteen months, and brought back a film which looks as fresh today as it did half a century ago. It ran for a week or two at New York's Capitol cinema, but did six months' business at the New Gallery, London, and the Gaumont in Paris. Paramount offered him anything he wanted to make another film. When, two years later, Flaherty came back from Samoa with *Moana of the South Seas*, and showed it to Paramount's top brass, they asked blankly 'But where are the blizzards?' They had expected a 'Son of Nanook'. *Moana* never got a circuit showing, was billed as 'the Love Life of a South Sea Siren', and the negative is believed to have been destroyed.

Flaherty's achievement was that he had invented, by simply recording what he saw, a new kind of film; and in reviewing a Flaherty film, John Grierson, a Scottish film-maker, first used the word 'documentary' to describe it and other films of its kind which Grierson himself was making – such as *Drifters* (1929), about the North Sea herring fishing fleet. And in the year of *Drifters*, a young man of twenty-two, Paul Rotha, published the first serious book on the art of film – *The Film Till Now*. He analysed every kind of silent film, noted the technical innovations of Griffiths, Chaplin, Murnau, Fritz Lang, Eisenstein and Pudovkin, close-up, cross-cutting and montage, and concluded that the coming of sound was 'a degenerate and misguided attempt to destroy the real use of the film'. A. P. Herbert, with unusual lack of perceptiveness, agreed with him: the talkies, he wrote in *Punch*, were 'doomed to an early but expensive death'.

We can see what they meant. The first talkies were unspeakable (but not unsingable). The Warner Brothers, Jack, Harry, Albert and Sam, found them-

selves near to bankruptcy in 1926, and they decided to gamble with a gimmick – the Vitaphone disc system that had been rejected by all other film companies. In 1926 they presented swashbuckling John Barrymore in *Don Juan* with synchronized music played by the New York Philharmonic. A year later they offered Al Jolson in *The Jazz Singer*, the first successful feature film with part dialogue in sound. It started off quite normally with background music, Al singing 'Blue Skies' to visual subtitles until the moment that made history: Jolson actually *spoke* out of the screen to the audience. Before singing 'Toot Toot Tootsie' he said: 'You ain't heard nothin' yet!'

Lights of New York followed, a story about a country boy on Broadway of which nothing is now remembered beyond the fact that the dialogue was all audible. Then came *The Singing Fool*, again with Jolson, who rendered 'I'm Sitting On Top of the World', 'There's a Rainbow Round My Shoulder' and, of course, 'Sonny Boy', which he sang over his dying son while audiences all over the world wept. The word 'tear-jerker' dates from about this time.

Talkies could now go anywhere they liked. Some silent stars with tolerable voices, such as Gary Cooper, survived, even though, back in 1927, *Variety* had written 'Cooper is improving and serving his masters well in everything but his love-making.' Lillian Gish told Cecil Beaton 'With the talkies stars are treated with less artistic authority. During the making of *The Swan* I was considered a novice . . . I don't want to make another talkie. I shall become a little old maid, looking after my invalid mother, going through the linen and counting the glass.' But she didn't: she went on to several more talkies and stage plays, and at forty played Ophelia to Gielgud's Hamlet at the Empire, New York, in 1936. Others, like poor John Gilbert, who had been hailed ironically whenever he attended the Algonquin Round Table with 'Why, hallo, Glamorous Star of the Silver Screen!', just disappeared. Henceforth publicity headlines could say 'At last – Pictures that Talk like Living People!' and 'Garbo TALKS!' (Yet the writers who flocked to Hollywood to supply the dialogue heard it still referred to, by old movie moguls, as 'writing the titles'). And perhaps the most famous line to describe the kind of film, represented by *Broadway Melody*, *Rio Rita* and *Movietone Follies*, that we were in for during the next few years was: 'All-talking! All-singing! All dancing!'

Still from 'Nanook of the North'

CHAPTER 19

Where Was God?

Where was God? Well, according to Bruce Barton, he was heading up an advertising agency, or possibly General Motors. Barton, founder of Batten, Barton, Durstine & Osborn, one of the proliferating advertising agencies of the mid-Twenties that have survived to this day, wrote a Life of Christ entitled *The Man Nobody Knows* which became a best-seller of 1925. Jesus, he said, was 'the founder of modern business'. He didn't quite say 'the Ford is my shepherd', – that was Aldous Huxley in *Brave New World* – but he had no hesitation in saying that the Apostles were a great sales force, and the Gospels were 'the most powerful advertisements of all time'.

These sentiments were in harmony with the world of Calvin Coolidge, the American belief in 'piety with profit', and that great text in Deuteronomy, 'The Lord giveth the power to get wealth.' Hardly any major writer of the Twenties was religious: Chesterton and Belloc were Edwardians; Graham Greene, received into the Roman Catholic church in 1926, as yet exerted no influence. The intellectuals went on about all gods being dead, and all those bishops blessing guns and tanks during the War; and war itself had left ex-soldiers in a state of honest doubt if not flat disbelief. War and religion were all mixed up in the Twenties.

A war memorial appeared in every English village, often in the churchyard. Sometimes the memorial was called a cenotaph, like the one in Whitehall. On Armistice Day in 1920 the French destroyer *Verdun* had brought to Britain the body of an Unknown Warrior, to be buried in Westminster Abbey, escorted thither by five admirals, three field-marshals, two generals and one air-marshal, followed by the Royal Family. Gramophone records of the burial service were sold at 7s. 6d. ($1.80) each. During the next few days more than 1,000,000 people visited the grave. The idea had been thought of by the Rev. David Railton, Vicar of Margate, a former Army padre; it was a very Christian idea, and the Abbey was a Christian church; but it led to a bitter exchange of letters between the Dean of Westminster and the Rev. S. I. Levy, Principal of the Liverpool Hebrew Schools, who complained of the line 'In Christ shall all be made alive', inscribed on the tombstone.

In Britain fewer people went to church: and those who did tended to go less often; it was the thing to do, of course, part of the established way of life; but on a fine Sunday morning it was pleasanter to lie in bed or go for a spin in the car. Yet people on the whole went on living in a Christian way and, apart from certain splendid exceptions, the standard of morality in personal life and business remained high. If you had been divorced, you were excluded from the Royal Enclosure at Ascot and the Honours List. 'Atheism tempered by hymns' was Bernard Shaw's description of the religious atmosphere of Britain; and John Reith defended the B.B.C. religious broadcasts simply by saying that 'Christianity happens to be the stated and official religion of this country.'

However, faced with the behaviour of the younger generation and convinced that the saxophone was the voice of the Devil, the clergy spent much of their time denouncing things. Cardinal Bourne, Archbishop of Westminster, did more denouncing than Randall Davidson, Archbishop of Canterbury, especially about the General Strike. The divorce rate in England was five times as high as before the War. *Punch* published a joke in which a girl says of her friend's wedding 'It'll be pretty binding, I should think – the jolly old Bish himself officiated.' Bishops and parsons condemned birth control, short skirts and even dances to raise money for war memorials. They condemned, but offered nothing except a return to established pre-War ways. In desperation they welcomed the religiosity of best-sellers like *If Winter Comes*, and the fact that it was fashionable (and inexpensive) to go and see the Passion Play at Oberammergau. They deplored the music-hall comedian Vivian Foster, the 'Vicar of Mirth', who for a short while was allowed to mock the parsonic voice, the Oboe-Pelvey of *Antic Hay*, on radio and gramophone records.

Hellfire was seldom mentioned by name in Britain; not so in America, where the Rev. John Roach Straton, pastor of the Calvary Baptist Church in New York, went to meet sin more than half way. He examined speakeasies and lewd entertainment himself, including a play called *Aphrodite* which he described as 'a nightmare of nude men and women slobbering over each other, lolling on couches, and dancing together in feigned drunken revelry'. To many people, the Twenties *were* hell, and even the Scott Fitzgeralds sometimes appear to be soaking themselves in sin so as to have plenty to confess; and doesn't Arthur Mizener have something when he says, of Dick Diver, in *Tender Is The Night*, that he is a sort of spoiled priest?

The Church of England did not lack controversy, even if it did not produce memorable personalities. Somehow it produced William Inge, one of a long line of unorthodox Deans of St Paul's, whose re-actionary pessimism caused him to be known as 'the Gloomy Dean', and who, as both preacher and journalist, was apt to say things like 'It is time to stop educating the children of the poor.' The great row of the age was over the Prayer Book in 1927. For about twenty years the Church of England had been dis-cussing whether, and if so how, to revise it so as to provide more services for more occasions. A pains-taking revision, approved by most bishops, clergy and lay members of the Church Assembly was thrown out by both House of Parliament. It was a victory for

fear, fear of innovation, the equation of change with the Red Menace; but most of all it was a victory for Sir William Joynson-Hicks, Home Secretary, who attacked it so violently that for him the peril must have seemed, not only the Red Menace, but the possibility of Letting the Catholics In.

As if the Twenties cared! But they hungered for something, were willing to try almost anything. America, untrammelled by an established Church, was rich in alternatives. You could be a Holy Jumper, down in Florida, among ecstatic people who cried 'Jump for the glory of the Lord, brother!', or a Holy Roller, rolling on the floor shouting 'Jesus Saves!', or a Buchmanite. Frank Buchman, lecturer in personal evangelism at Hartford Seminary, Hart-ford, Connecticut, had appeared in Cambridge, England, in 1921, long before his identification with Oxford, and was already claiming the support of Lord Salisbury and other notables. He came to Oxford only after being asked to cease his work on the campus at Princeton.

Almost anyone with a new faith, the weirder the better, was welcome. 'Darling, I had a *splitting* headache, absolutely *cry*-making, and I hadn't a *cachet faivre* left, so I Coué-ed it away.' Coué? Wasn't that what Australians shouted to attract each other's attention? No, indeed.

On New Year's Eve, 1922, the White Star liner *Majestic* was approaching New York in a 100-miles-an-hour gale. On board, confined to their cabins in misery, were Stanley Baldwin, Chancellor of the Exchequer, and Montagu Norman, Governor of the Bank of England, who were on their way to Washington to discuss Britain's war debts with President Harding. There were many other cele-brities on board, but none to compare with Emile Coué, a sixty-six-year-old retired pharmacist from Nancy, France. During the crossing, the *New York World*, which had a reporter on all transatlantic luxury liners, carried the headline: 'ROUGH SEA SICKENS MANY, NOT COUÉ: MAGIC WORDS TRI-UMPH OVER WAVES.' The magic words were *Tous les jours, à tous points de vue je vais de mieux en mieux* – 'Day by day, in every way, I am getting better and better', and sometimes *ça passe, ça passe* ('it'll soon be over') repeated many times. The system was known as auto-suggestion. Those who used it were not seasick, and the *Majestic*'s orchestra played a fox-trot called 'I'm Getting Better and Better'.

For about two years Coué, who had visited London in 1921 and 1922 to hold meetings at the Wigmore Hall, had been famous. He was simple and clean – none of that Freudian nastiness. Lord Curzon, a martyr to insomnia, had Coué-ed it away. Lady Beatty, wife of the hero of Jutland, had overcome an illness and been 'enabled to resume her role as a prominent London hostess'. King Albert of the Belgians had been cured of rheumatism. Mary Garden had Coué-ed her voice so that she could now reach a top note in *Tosca* which had been eluding her for years. Dr Edgar Blake, Bishop of the Methodist Episcopal Church in Paris, had preached a sermon on Coué at the Chelsea Methodist Episcopal Church in New York.

Dr Coué (sometimes called Professor) had been visited in Nancy by Mrs William K. Vanderbilt, who returned to America and founded a National Coué Committee, whose members included some of the cream of New York society. Somebody discovered that Coué had learnt auto-suggestion by a correspondence course on hypnotism run by an American, La Motte Sage, of Rochester, New York, back in 1901, but nobody took much notice. His book, *Self-Mastery Through Conscious Auto-Suggestion*, was selling like mad, sometimes in unauthorized editions. It had been serialized by the New York *Evening Mail*, whose circulation rose so fast that they had to have a Coué Department for supplying reprints. The rival paper, the *Evening World*, started serializing a different translation, which they claimed as authentic and 'unabridged', implying that the *Mail*'s version had been pirated.

In both London and New York, it was noticed that Dr Coué's waxed moustaches were tobacco-stained, and that he smoked up to forty cigarettes a day while lecturing, rolling them all himself. No doubt he could have cured himself of smoking, but did not wish to do so. He always said modestly 'I am not a healer. I merely help people to help themselves.' Much was made of his non-profit-making. Will Rogers wrote: 'They say the Doc's trip here is to be gratis . . . That feature alone will make him the outstanding novelty of all European visitors.' By no means averse from profit was Wanamaker's store, which sold both Coué's book and an auto-suggestion kit consisting of a framed illuminated card of the 'magic words' and a rosary for counting off how many times you said them. Likewise the Columbia

Emile Coué and Lady Pearson talking to blind men, April 1922

Gramophone Company was only too delighted to issue an album of records of his voice saying *ça passe, ça passe*, so quickly that it sounded like a machine-gun.

Dr Coué was meanwhile making enemies of doctors and parsons. The former were ungrateful to him for taking away their more hypochondriacal patients, and the latter were perturbed because Coué was not using divine aid. Moreover, he was competing with a Bible-healing movement which was trying to wean people away from gin, jazz and bobbed hair. And the headlines grew more and more extravagant: 'COUÉ MAKES PALSIED MAN RUN' – 'TWO CRIPPLES WALK!' – 'COUÉ HEALS LOVE'S HEARTACHES'. At last Coué made a tactical mistake: in a meeting which included John Barrymore and Mrs Andrew Carnegie he remarked that Christ had certainly used auto-suggestion in some of the miracles. Next day, in the Broadway Tabernacle, a Dr Benson made a new kind of headline: 'The issue is now Christ or Coué, the Antichrist!' Later, Dr Benson suggested that the whole thing could be smoothed over if only Coué could say 'Every day, with God's blessing, I am improving . . .'

Dr Coué lived for four more years, and died, it is said, of overwork. *Ça*, unfortunately, didn't *passe*. He had done no harm, and he had helped a lot of people. Not so the Great Beast 666, the Master Therion, Aleister Crowley. His study of black magic was known in London long before the War, but now, helped by the Sunday newspapers, his activities at the Abbey of Thelema in Cefalù, Sicily, were attracting new recruits, some of them from the fringe of Bohemia, others from universities. We may never know their names, for nobody, after the Paul Loveday scandal, wanted to be connected with Crowley.

Loveday was an Oxford undergraduate who had married a model known as Betty May. He had long admired Crowley's poems and 'magickal' writings, and when at last they met, Crowley chose him as his pupil and took him and Betty to Cefalù. There were stories of the ritual sacrifices of animals, of fearful penances (cutting their arms with razors for using the pronoun 'I'), of sex-magic rites, all headlined by the London *Sunday Express*, and after some months it was learnt that Loveday had died. There were rumours of ritual murder, but it would seem that Loveday died of enteritis. Soon afterwards the Italian Government, having outlawed all secret societies under the new Mussolini régime, ordered Crowley to leave Cefalù.

Much more uplifting was the cult of George Gurdjieff, which I found to be still active in London, under the direction of Jane Heap (she of the *Little Review*) just before his death in 1949. He had a system of teaching which involved self-observation, and a system of dances which were supposed to use the body to its fullest powers by breaking up its usual rhythms and attitudes. He never wrote his teaching down until he began *All and Everything*, the first two of whose three parts have been published since his death. This was one reason for his

Aimée Semple McPherson

famous quarrel with his pupil Ouspensky, who *did* write things down and intellectualized everything. Gurdjieff's Institute for the Harmonious Development of Man, which maintained a disciplined community life in a former priory near Fontainebleau, had among its pupils Frank Lloyd Wright, Alfred Orage, Editor of the *New Age*, Clifford Sharp, first Editor of the *New Statesman*, and Lady Rothermere, wife of the newspaper baron. Gurdjieff, born near Tiflis in Georgia, Russia, claimed to have walked all the way from there to Tibet, where he studied in a monastery and learned the Oriental wisdom that informed his teaching.

One of his best-known pupils was Katherine Mansfield, who in October 1922 tried to cure her tuberculosis by taking deep breaths over a cow-manger at Fontainebleau, where she died.

'Now, all those who have found Jesus with me – put up your hands! . . . I want you to shake hands with your neighbour and say 'God bless you'!' We are in a somewhat different world, to be precise in London's Albert Hall in 1928, and the speaker, or shrieker, is Aimée Semple McPherson with her 'angels' of the Four-Square Gospel Alliance, founded in 1926. The publicity has been enormous, but the Hall is by no means full, though in the audience is Evelyn Waugh, taking notes for *Vile Bodies*, in which Mrs McPherson will become Mrs Ape – an understatement rather than a caricature, if other eyewitnesses are to be believed.

Aimée, thrice married and twice divorced, called herself Sister, from the time of her early missionary work in China. Her Angelus Temple in Los Angeles, holding about 3,000 people, had imitation stained-glass windows full of angels, a stage and a screen on which the words of hymns were projected while people sang. Mrs McPherson, sometimes dressed as an angel, sang, shouted and beat time with a tambourine. Newcomers were brought up on to the stage and introduced to each other and to the audience, naming the States they came from. The Wurlitzer organ played jazzed-up church music. Then came the baptisms, in a tank of water on the stage, up to 150 in one evening. And then the collection. Oh, there were rumours of misappropriated funds, but nothing was ever proved, even though one of the accusers was Aimée's mother; and as show business it was certainly a money's worth.

Aimée, if you analysed her doctrines, was a kind of

Fundamentalist. There were many such in the Twenties. Tennessee, in March 1925, had, by the overwhelming majority of public opinion, made it illegal throughout the State to teach the theory of evolution. In May, John T. Scopes, a biologist and teacher of science at Rhea High School, Dayton, was arrested, and in July he was tried. The relevant clause of the law said that it was 'unlawful for any teacher in any of the universities, normals and all other public schools of the state, to teach any theory that denies the story of the divine creation of man as taught in the Bible, and to teach instead that man has descended from a lower order of animals.'

This was a test case of the new law. In New York the American Civil Liberties Union was already on the warpath, and its director, Roger N. Baldwin, had announced to all newspapers in Tennessee that he would secure the defence of anyone who deliberately broke the law to test whether it was really constitutional or not. Soon Baldwin received a telephone call from George Rapplyea, owner of a drug store in Dayton, saying that his friend Scopes was willing to be a guinea-pig.

William Jennings Bryan, orator, politician and committed Fundamentalist, was called in to assist the prosecutor; and Clarence Darrow, 'attorney for the damned', appeared for the defence. They were the two most famous lawyers of the age, two larger-than-life figures of folklore whom only America could have produced. Darrow, as if he alone were not enough, was assisted by Dudley Field Malone, a liberal Catholic, and Arthur Garfield Hays, specialist in civil liberties.

The flood of oratory from these men has never been equalled in a court of law since those eleven tremendous days of the trial. Every day the newsmen telegraphed about 175,000 words of copy out of Dayton, and the entire world's newspaper readers lapped them up. But much of it proved irrelevant, for the judge ruled that the only issue was: had Scopes broken the law by teaching evolution? And the defence could only admit that he had. But Darrow and Bryan had not come all the way to Dayton to be muzzled. Bryan had brought with him a long speech in his wonderful, rhythmic, Biblical style – but he was never able to deliver it, because he suddenly found himself being cross-examined on his doctrines by a merciless, sarcastic Darrow who got him so tied up that he was near to mental and physical collapse. It was a kind of filibustering way of preventing Bryan from saying his piece on the creation of Man, but it was in vain. Scopes was convicted and fined $100. And poor Bryan, five days later, died.

About this time Sinclair Lewis was putting together some notes for a novel attacking certain grasping, and in his opinion, charlatan leaders of the Protestant Churches, to be called, after much mind-changing, *Elmer Gantry*. Lewis liked to have a technical adviser on each specialized novel, and as he had borrowed Paul de Kruif to help him about doctors in *Arrowsmith*, so he now combed the Bible Belt until he found the Unitarian Rev. Leon Milton Birkhead, of All Souls, Kansas City, an old friend of H. L. Mencken. There was no subject too hot for Birkhead to handle in the pulpit – legalized gambling, Freud, political corruption, sex, Sacco and Vanzetti, pole-squatting, Prohibition, euthanasia and whether it was proper to pray for rain. He had done some research for Darrow in the Scopes trial, and had himself preached a sermon in favour of evolution while being heckled from a back pew by a team, organized by the Rev. Gerald Winrod of Wichita, known as the Flying Fundamentalists, who toured the Middle West denouncing Darwin. Birkhead filled his church every Sunday and could get away, in sermons, with statements of faith like 'I suppose I do have a feeling that there is something. Certainly I am not an atheist. I do not know enough about the nature of ultimate reality to be one.' And his sermons always had newspaper-style titles: 'Is the Resurrection a Myth?' 'Can Psychology Save Us?' and 'Why I Do Not Commit Suicide.'

In November 1927 Birkhead, who had just been vilified everywhere for his aggressive defence of *Elmer Gantry*, was asked by a freethinking publisher, Emanuel Haldeman-Julius, to marry his daughter Josephine, eighteen, to her boyfriend Aubrey Roselle – and they wanted the words 'till death do us part' left out, because the couple were so young. Birkhead did better than that – he also omitted 'with all my worldly goods I thee endow' because, as he told reporters, the bridegroom didn't have any worldly goods. The wedding suffered coast-to-coast front-paging. A Congregationalist minister said 'Birkhead has shaken the very foundations of Christian civilization.' The Roselles stayed married. But twenty years later the *Chicago Tribune* was still calling Birkhead 'the free-love parson'.

CHAPTER 20

Mysterious Universes

Another kind of evolution, not quite so alarming for the Fundamentalists, was being studied: that of the solar system, and beyond that the nebulae and the stars. And some scientists, against all expectation, were talking about God. Sir Arthur Eddington, who had an idea that the mass and the luminosity of stars were related, and had done much to popularize

Einstein's theory of relativity (testing it by eclipses), was one of several thinkers who were asking themselves: is Nature mechanical, or is there a Mind behind it? Nature might be abstract mathematics, said Eddington in the *Nature of the Physical World* (1928), yet there was 'something in human experience that cannot be accounted for by scientific symbolism because it belongs to another world'. His colleague Sir James Jeans, another great popularizer of science, seemed to be tending the same way in *The Universe Around Us*; Einstein himself was on record as saying 'God is subtle but He is not malicious'; and A.N. Whitehead, Cambridge mathematician and philosopher who had moved over to Harvard in 1924, was saying that we cannot make sense of nature without some conception which transcends nature, such as the existence of God, a hypothesis which 'seems more reasonable than any other'.

Could the universe be both finite and unbounded? If so, time as well as space must be curved. 'Phwhat *is* the stars?' asks a character in a Sean O'Casey play, all unaware that he was posing one of the great questions of the age. And the smallest solar system of all, the atom, was being broken down into its particles, which appear to be made of electricity or wave-systems, and all this is somehow connected with radioactivity and with those mysterious 'cosmic rays', now believed to be coming from outer space and being studied by Robert Andrews Millikan at California Institute of Technology. The atom would not be actually 'split' until 1932, but meantime 'atom smashing' and bombardment were going on, under

Sir Arthur Eddington

the supervision of Sir Ernest Rutherford, without the faintest idea that it could ever produce anything which could have any commercial or military application. Rutherford's specialist in magnetic research was Peter Kapitza, now believed to be working on the Russian space programme. Rutherford's toast at the annual Cavendish Laboratory dinner was 'To the electron – may it never be of any use to anyone.'

In Germany a Professor Oberth was developing rockets which in twenty years' time would land on Britain as V2s, and forty years later would take astronauts to the Moon, propelled by liquid fuel pioneered by Robert H. Goddard, of Clark University, Worcester, Mass., somewhere in New Mexico. But even science fiction hadn't got that far, and if you had asked H. G. Wells how to get to the Moon he would have imagined nothing more advanced than a space-gun.

·Of course the 'next war' was unthinkable. The last one was still in everyone's mind, especially if a near relative or friend lay under one of those millions of plain white crosses in the huge graveyards of France and Flanders. Many people found consolation greater than the Church could give in trying to communicate with the dead. People played semi-seriously with ouija boards and table-turning parties. Mediums such as Rudi Schneider became famous. Sir Oliver Lodge claimed to have been in touch with his dead son Raymond. From America came Judge Rutherford, to fill the Albert Hall with his promise that 'Millions now living will never die.' Hannen Swaffer, the dramatic critic, was convinced that Lord Northcliffe had 'spoken' to him, and about deeper matters than the circulation of the *Daily Mail*. The trouble with so many spirit messages was that they told you no more than that the sender was well and happy. 'I always knew the living talked rot,' Margot Asquith said to Chips Channon, after listening to Sir Oliver Lodge, 'but it's nothing to the nonsense the dead talk.' She was on the whole sorry for ghosts: 'Their appearances are so against them.'

Sir Arthur Conan Doyle, physician and creator of Sherlock Holmes, held seances of his own and attended many of other people's, often to be imposed upon, often to be mocked by the *Daily Express*, whose editor, R. D. Blumenfeld, he accused of treating him 'either as a charlatan, a fool, a lunatic or a child'. Doyle specialized in 'spirit photographs', and in

1920 went to Yorkshire to investigate a claim by two girls that they had not only seen 'real fairies' but had photographed them. 'The two little girls are absolutely honest' he wrote to Blumenfeld. 'The episode will prove to be the start of a new era.' And he wrote a book on *The Coming of the Fairies*.

The dead may have been well and happy, but how about the living? You could still die of many diseases which are now regarded as treatable, if not curable, such as 'consumption' (TB was not a term in general use). People who could afford it lived abroad for the sake of their lungs. The term 'coronary' was hardly known, possibly because there were fewer than 200 deaths a year per 1,000,000 from this cause (compared with nearly 3,500 twenty years later). An age which craved rejuvenation looked hopefully towards Dr Serge Voronoff, of the Collège de Paris, who claimed to be able to 'prolong active life' by grafting 'monkey glands' (actually testicular tissue) into old men.

In some hospitals leeches were still used. The treatment for pernicious anaemia was to have all your teeth out. There were two main anaesthetics, chloroform and ether. Blood transfusion was in a primitive condition. Fashionable medical opinion seemed to blame adenoids and tonsils for everything that was wrong with a patient above the chest, and constipation for everything below it. The whipping out of adenoids and tonsils became part of a British middle-class child's life, like preparatory school, public school and confirmation; and the weekly dosing with Beecham's pills or syrup of figs rectified the almost total ignorance of nutrition then prevailing.

School food consisted largely of carbohydrate. Eat up your pudding, finish up your fat, you'll sit there till you've eaten it. Many people read the articles of Sir William Arbuthnot Lane, medical correspondent of the London *Daily Mail*, but the 'New Health' movement towards raw salads and roughage was regarded as cranky, and also expensive. In 1923 there was an 'Eat More Fruit' Campaign, conducted on behalf of various fruit importers by Mather & Crowther, the advertising agency, with the aid of a song which went –

As Eve said to Adam,
The saucy little madam,
'Oh, Adam, you should eat more fruit!'

Fruit was regarded as an expensive luxury, though orange juice was given to babies to supplement milk. The virtues of milk in schools were loudly proclaimed, but milk was not yet safe to drink, and there was a widespread suspicion that pasteurization 'took all the goodness out of it.' The children of the poor, and sometimes of the rich, were often rickety because calcium deficiencies were not yet understood.

Breakfast foods were heavily advertised:

High o'er the fence leaps Sunny Jim,
Force is the food that raises him.

(Old Father Kruschen, of salts fame, was also pictured leaping over things.) Invalid port was much recommended, especially in advertisements on the sides of buses, and old age pensioners supplied testimonials to the manufacturers of what was generally understood to be a 'nerve tonic' but which was actually casein extracted from milk, so that they would have done better to spend their money on cheese.

There were carbohydrate diets, iron diets, lemon-juice diets, lettuce diets, all of which were supposed to keep you 'slim and regular'. Kensitas cigarettes cashed in on the vogue with a slogan: 'Don't eat between meals. Smoke a Kensitas instead.' The favourite iron tonic for children was Parrish's Food, which tasted like sweet wine and turned your teeth black.

Yet at least two great things were happening in medicine. In 1922 Frederick Grant Banting and Charles H. Best, at Toronto University, succeeded in preparing insulin for the treatment of diabetes; among the first notable people to be so treated was the actress Constance Collier, who had just created the part of the Duchesse de Surennes in Maugham's *Our Betters*. And in 1928, by 'a triumph of accident and shrewd observation', Alexander Fleming, engaged in research on influenza, noticed a greenish mould on a staphylococcus culture plate which created a bacteria-free circle around it. He called it penicillin.

The Dr Spock of the age was Truby King, who made breast-feeding fashionable again but said that babies must not be picked up every time they cry. Private primary schools began to announce their adherence to the principles of Froebel or Montessori, and the word 'kindergarten' became generally used. A.S. Neill published *The Problem Child* in 1925,

having founded Summerhill, 'that dreadful school', in 1924. The British public schools, not always full, soldiered on through difficult times, and a new one, Stowe, was started in 1923 by a consortium of businessmen, in the former stately home of the Dukes of Buckingham which was adapted to its new use by Clough Williams-Ellis. Among its foundation pupils was David Niven. Yet another new school was Bryanston, founded in 1927 in the former seat of Lord Portman in Dorset, which had been rebuilt towards the end of the last century by the great Norman Shaw.

Faster than education or medicine grew technology. My father went on using his cut-throat razor well into the twenties, but the younger generation were using safety razors, which were at first thought rather effeminate and common. Schoolmasters, in the interests of legible copperplate handwriting, tried to prevent their pupils from using those new-fangled fountain pens, instead of thin scratchy nibs dipped in sludge-coloured school ink. Cigarette-lighters, at first large and cumbersome, were coming in. You could now buy a Lyons ice-cream brick, but you had to eat it up quickly because few people had a reliable ice-box. Imperial Chemical Industries were interested in a new kind of fastener which might eventually replace buttons, and it was the Chairman, Lord Melchett himself, who christened it 'zip'.

The first transatlantic telephone service was opened in 1926: it cost £5 a minute. By the end of the decade only one-third of all Britain's houses had electricity, but the Coliseum Theatre had had neon lights blazing out over Trafalgar Square since 1923. In 1925 H.M.V. issued Britain's first electrically-recorded record (of Jack Hylton's Band), and the following year saw the first all-electric radiogramophone, a Brunswick-Panatrope, and also the first all-mains radio. In Britain radiogramophones were confusingly abbreviated to 'radiograms', but in America they tended to be known by a brand name. So it happens that a girl in John O'Hara's *Appointment in Samarra* says 'put "Poor Butterfly" on the Vic' (Victrola).

Somewhere, everywhere, inventors were inventing. And yet the Inventor as National Hero was passing away. There was indeed only one of his kind left. Henceforth, nearly all great inventions would be discovered by teams of scientists financed by industry. Thomas Alva Edison, who fulfilled the

American requirement of a hero that he be self-educated, had invented improved telegraph systems, an electric vote-recorder, an electric pen or mimeograph, the 'phonograph or speaking machine', a dictaphone, an incandescent lamp (he had invented the wireless valve too, but didn't realize it), and had taken out 1,033 patents by the time of his death.

Edison was eighty-two when, in 1929, to celebrate the fiftieth anniversary of the invention of the electric light bulb, Henry Ford presented him, and the American people, with a complete model of his old Menlo Park laboratory, faithful to the last detail, where with his 'insomnia squad' of assistants he had established the world's first industrial research unit. For 'the modern Faust' had fulfilled another criterion dear to the hearts of men like Ford: there had never been any nonsense about disinterested scientific research: everything he had ever achieved had been commercially viable and for immediate use. And yet – in 1929 Edison was still making cylinders for the old type of phonograph, although disc records were used by almost everybody. Commercially viable he may have been, but built-in obsolescence was still in its infancy.

In Vienna lived a man, now suffering from cancer of the jaw, who could not have been more different. Edison had made people's material lives easier, and perhaps happier, and everything he did was immediately understood by millions of people. Sigmund Freud, if his work could be understood at all by the millions, was seized upon to justify sexual freedom, and there were those who saw in it a new kind of religion, for were not those couch-sessions a kind of confession?

With Freud's name were coupled those of Adler and Jung, and only a few initiates knew exactly who said what and which of them invented the Inferiority Complex, the easiest point with which average citizen could identify himself. Adler delivered numerous lectures in the United States and eventually settled there. By 1927 there were nine practising analysts in New York, charging anything from $50 to $500 a sitting. There psychiatry was already fashionable; but in London it was still considered 'too, too shy-making'.

In 1922 it was the subject of one of the last great university hoaxes. On March 15th, at 8 p.m., a most distinguished audience was assembled in the Grand Jury Room at Oxford Town Hall. It included the

Master of University College, the Provost of Worcester, and several other leading personalities of town and gown, and their wives. They had been invited by an organization called the Home Counties Psychological Federation, and they were to listen to a forty-five-minute lecture by a Dr Emil Busch of Tübingen University who, according to advance publicity, had been a friend and colleague of Freud. He would be introduced by a Dr James Heythrop.

Dr Busch and Dr Heythrop were in fact two Balliol College undergraduates named respectively George Edinger and Henry Scrymgeour-Wedderburn. Ten other students, one of them a girl, were in the secret, there being safety in numbers if the hoax were discovered and Dr Busch had to make a precipitate exit. The prearranged signal for flight would be a question from the floor beginning with the words, 'Dr Ludwig Koenigsberger . . .'

At this distance of time there can be no harm in mentioning that the conspirators included Hilary Belloc (Hilaire's son); Douglas Woodruff, afterwards Editor of the Roman Catholic weekly, *The Tablet*; and Christopher Hollis, author and for ten years M.P. for Devizes. Three others became barristers, Edinger became a journalist, and Scrymgeour-Wedderburn became Under-Secretary of State for Scotland.

The lecture, introduced by Scrymgeour-Wedderburn and delivered with a strong German accent by Edinger, both suitably made-up and frock-coated, was a masterpiece of deadpan burlesque. It was based on a phenomenon called Co-aesthesia. The audience was never clearly told what it was, only that Freud had overlooked it. It was exemplified by the case-histories of 'a Lutheran pastor at Würzburg who was so affected by the death of his daughter that he started sticking pins in bicycle tyres', and 'a young man at Stralsund who had a horror of the sea' and yet had found himself able to sail a boat three times round the island of Rügen; it had something to do with his mother. All in all, Co-aesthesia, not sex, was the real explanation of the subconscious. Freud was Dr Busch's very good friend, but 'Sometimes for the number of the trees the wood he does not see.'

After dodging a number of questions about hypnosis, the lecturer left to catch a train. *The Oxford Chronicle* solemnly reported the occasion and welcomed 'the first savant from a German University to address an Oxford audience since the War'.

(opposite) Plate from an Asprey Catalogue of 1921

**WHITE ONYX AND BLACK
DERBY STONE CLOCK**
By Longine
£28 10 0
Height 6¾ ins.

ATMOS CLOCK
Derives its Power from the
Atmosphere
No winding or attention required
£25 10 0   Height 9 ins.
Other Models in stock

**MALACHITE, WHITE ONYX
AND BLACK DERBY STONE
8 DAY CLOCK**
£19 15 0
Height 5¼ ins.

**8 DAY CLOCK WITH
JADE ORNAMENT**
£31 10 0
Height 6 ins.

**8 DAY CLOCK WITH
CARVED JADE ORNAMENT**
£75 0 0
Height 11¼ ins

**8 DAY CLOCK WITH
JADE ELEPHANT**
£32 10 0
Height 5 ins.

**MALACHITE 8 DAY CLOCK
ENAMEL DIAL**
£85 0 0
Height 9½ ins.

**ONYX AND PERSIAN
LAPIS 8 DAY CLOCK**
£23 0 0
Height 9 ins.

**PERSIAN LAPIS 8 DAY CLOCK
WITH JADE CIRCLE**
£87 10 0
Height 7¾ ins.

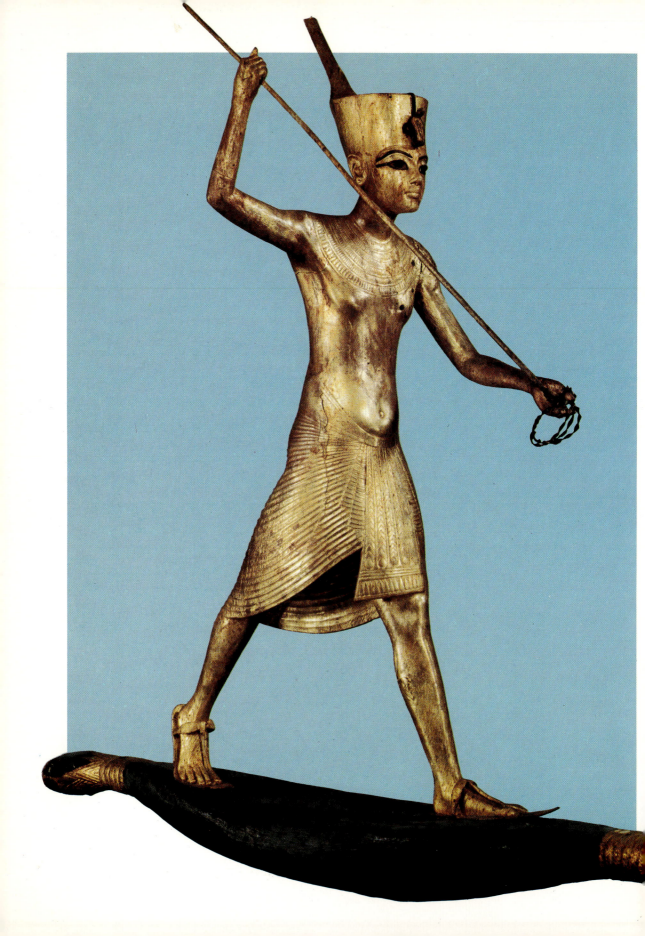

CHAPTER 21

Significant Form

'Wonderful things – I can see wonderful things!'

It was November 25th 1922, and the first stone had been removed from the wall which had sealed off the entrance of Tutankhamen's tomb, west of Thebes in Upper Egypt. Lord Carnarvon, his daughter Lady Evelyn Herbert, and Howard Carter took it in turns to peer through the hole at the jumbled personal effects of a boy king who had reigned for about six years more than 3,300 years ago. It was the greatest buried treasure the world had ever seen, and it had escaped the tomb-robbers largely because, by ancient Egyptian standards, it was so small, and the boy king so insignificant. It recreated a whole ancient world, with objects, it was thought, of unbelievable splendour.

Splendour, thought Roger Fry, the Bloomsbury art critic, but not really beauty. It all lacked 'the intense aesthetic sensibility' of the reign of his heretical father-in-law Akhenaton: it was 'official art', it was 'the most expensive rubbish that money could buy from the most fashionable furnishers.'

Lord Carnarvon's death, less than five months after the opening of the tomb, from a mosquito bite and pneumonia (his lungs had always been weak) seemed to prove the legend of 'the curse of the Pharaohs', a story which had been put about by the

Tutankhamen's Queen being brought from the Tomb

(opposite) Tutankhamen wearing the red crown of Lower Egypt and standing on a light papyrus boat

black-bearded, sinister Dr Joseph Mardrus, physician, orientalist, translator of *The Arabian Nights* and friend of Proust. The spell of Egypt was exercised in a different way on Alice Astor, Nancy's twenty-year-old cousin, who believed herself to be the reincarnation of an Egyptian princess, and pushed her way into the tomb in an attempt to claim a necklace of semi-precious stones and hundreds of ram's heads which she considered to be the symbol of her high birth. Perhaps it was this idea that influenced her marriage to Prince Serge Obolensky, the first of her four husbands.

Egyptianism instantly became a craze, beginning with fashions for women, and merging into what was later called Art Déco – sculpture, vases, ashtrays, cocktail-shakers, furniture and decoration. The Cambridge University Rag, Jacquetta Hawkes tells us, featured 'the disinterment of an undergraduate's mummiform body from the public lavatory in the Market Place.' Huntley & Palmer sold biscuits in tins shaped like Tutankhamen wine-jars. In Bond Street and the Burlington Arcade you could buy

Egyptian-style hat of February 1923

handbags covered with hieroglyphics. In Sale, Cheshire, there is a cinema (once the Pyramid, now the Odeon) modelled on the Temple of Karnak with a Pharaoh's head decorating the organ. This sort of thing had started in Hollywood with Sid Grauman's Egyptian Theatre, designed before the actual opening of Tutankhamen's tomb. It reached an aesthetic climax at the Astoria, Streatham, where the Ladies' Rest Room boasted 'a coloured relief mural decoration of an Egyptian female figure, bathing in a lotus-filled pool.'

In February 1972 Miss Sandie Shaw the pop singer told the *Daily Mail* that her husband had given her, for a Valentine present, 'a beautiful Art Déco bowl, the real thing'. Suddenly, after fifty years, Art Déco had become fashionable again; an ivory figurine, clothed in metal and poised on a marble plinth, would fetch several hundred pounds at Sotheby's; and in October 1972 the panels of the elevators at Selfridge's store, designed by Edgar Brandt in 1927, were acquired by the Victoria and Albert Museum and the London Museum. Brandt was the designer of the gateway to the 1925 Paris Exhibition, where Art Déco first established itself as an international style.

Was it ever a consistent style at all? Cubism, the Russian ballet, Aztec and Egyptian art, machinery, sunworship, nudity, jazz, nonconformism, streamlining, zigzag, chrome, the wonderful vulgarity of the Strand Palace Hotel – we can recognize Art Déco, but let us not attempt to define it. It includes most of the cinemas of the late Twenties and early Thirties, the work of the designer Chiparus, and the automobile which Al Jolson gave to Hollywood producer Joe Schenk as a birthday present. It was 'decorated with inlaid woodwork, engraved glass and tortoiseshell. The seats and carpet were woven with a design of paradise birds among futuristic globules.' It is not to be despised as trash, says Bevis Hillier, Art Déco's leading contemporary scholar, because trash is necessary. 'Art Déco is the ultimate test of tolerance thresholds.' Ho-hum.

We had better take a more general look at the trends. I am not competent to classify them, but at least one can separate the destruction from the creation. 'Come, then, good incendiaries!' F. T. Marinetti had called, before the War, 'Set fire to the shelves of the libraries! Deflect the courses of canals! Flood the cellars of the museums! For art can be

Percy Wyndham Lewis by himself, 1921

nothing but violence, cruelty and injustice.' This sort of thing was known as Futurism, and is thought to have been partly a by-product of Cubism: it came to Britain and merged with something called Vorticism, associated with the magazine *Blast* and Percy Wyndham Lewis, remembered for what Frank Rutter called a 'semi-Cubist, metallic-coloured portrait of Ezra Pound' and his vast satire *The Apes of God*. In Germany a somewhat similar movement was called Expressionism, and in pre-revolutionary Russia there was a trend known as Donkey's Tail.

It was but a short step from this to Dadaism, born, apparently, in Zurich, where it was supposed to shock the bourgeoisie, and taken to Berlin in 1918 by a man named Richard Huelsenbeck. 'The Dadaist loves life, because he can throw it away every day: for him death is a Dadaist affair . . .' Committed to action and anarchy, the Dadaists interrupted the inaugural assembly of the Weimar Republic with a manifesto of a Dada world government. Tzara, Grosz, Arp, Schwitters were associated with the Dadaist movement. Some of them, like Max Ernst, became Surrealists (the word begins to appear about 1917) and confined their action to their painting.

America, too, had her Cubists – Charles Demuth,

Stuart Davis and others; and a group called 'the Eight' who were laying the foundations of modern American painting: some of them – Robert Henri, John Sloan and George B. Luks – concentrated on the urban environment and became known as the 'Ash Can school'. Eyes had been opened by the famous Armory Show, held in New York in 1913, which introduced Picasso and Cézanne to 200,000 shocked visitors.

One of its organizers was Arthur B. Davies, who conspired with an art collector, Miss Lillie P. Bliss, to raise enough money to found a Museum of Modern Art. She, happening to spend the winter of 1928–9 in Egypt, met Mrs John D. Rockefeller Jr. Back in New York they formed a fund-raising committee which included Frank Crowninshield, editor of *Vanity Fair*, and had a wealthy collector, A. Conger Goodyear, as its chairman. They had already chosen a director for the Museum, a twenty-seven-year-old teacher of modern art named Alfred H. Barr, Jr.

On November 9th 1929, bravely in the middle of the Wall Street crash, the Museum of Modern Art opened its doors, on the twelfth floor of the Heckscher Building at 57th Street and 5th Avenue, with a superb display of Cézanne, Van Gogh, Gauguin and Seurat.

In Britain mainstream painting was in the safe hands of Walter Sickert, now living mostly in Dieppe and at last elected to the Royal Academy, and others of the London Group; Wilson Steer, like Sickert an Impressionist, and Augustus John, now fairly respectable, whose portrait of Mme Suggia the cellist was probably the best-known picture of 1925. Matthew Smith, in the Fauvist tradition, was to be seen in the Café des Deux Garçons in Aix-en-Provence and was painting landscapes and flower-pieces with liberal use of his favourite shade of red, not unlike strawberry jam. Mark Gertler, the Bloomsbury lover of Lytton Strachey's Carrington, was also fond of red, but his was that of a boiled lobster. The Nash brothers, Paul and John, were beginning to be known, and so were Duncan Grant, Edward Wadsworth and Gilbert and Stanley Spencer.

It was a great time for art criticism – Roger Fry's *Vision and Design* (he invented the term 'Post-Impressionism'), R. H. Wilenski's *Modern Art*, and *Since Cézanne* by Clive Bell, the Bloomsbery who

(above) 'The Hammock', 1921–23, by Duncan Grant   (below) 'Wood on the Downs', 1929, by Paul Nash

(above) 'A Seaport', 1923, by Edward Wadsworth (above) 'Christ's Entry into Jerusalem', about 1922, by Stanley Spence

(above) 'An Accident', 1926, by L.S. Lowry

'Mother and Child', 1925, by Henry Moore

'Metal Lady', 1923,
by Alexander Archipenko

'The Bath', 1922,
by David Bomberg

'The Birth of Venus', 1923,
by Charles Shannon.
The 'Punch' comment
when it was exhibited
at the Royal
Academy in 1924 was:
'Come on, Boys!
We'll get a Humane
Society's medal for this'

'East Wind' on the North Side, West Wing of 55 Broadway, London, by Eric Gill

'Night', by Jacob Epstein, 55 Broadway

Lighting of the Chairman's Room, 55 Broadway

coined the phrase 'significant form'. You were considered pretty advanced if you had heard of Matisse or had a print of Van Gogh's *Sunflowers* on your wall; and you could mingle with artists at the Café Royal in Regent Street, where Augustus John and Epstein were on show in person, or meet them later at night in 'Ma' Meyrick's 43 Club.

There was a general movement, which we see in Art Déco, towards the marriage of art and industry: it is in Archipenko's brass-and-copper *Metal Lady* and, much more familiarly, in posters of the time.

From the pioneer work of the 'Beggarstaff Brothers' (William Nicholson and James Pryde), the poster, linking up with growth of advertising, had very nearly become an art form. This was partly due to Frank Pick, general manager of the London Underground, who had commissioned Edward Johnston to design a new sans-serif type for the purpose, had also ordered sculptures for the new London Transport building by Henry Moore and Epstein, and recruited young artists such as McKnight Kauffer, now an 'Old Master' of poster design.

226

'Whitsuntide', 1925, by McKnight Kauffer

'Reclining Nude', about 1924, by Matthew Smith. Matthew Smith was one of the few British artists to have been thoroughly influenced by a group led by Matisse called the Fauves. Common qualities including strident colours, linear surface patterning, and a disregard for formal academic qualities of proportion and composition are individually interpreted

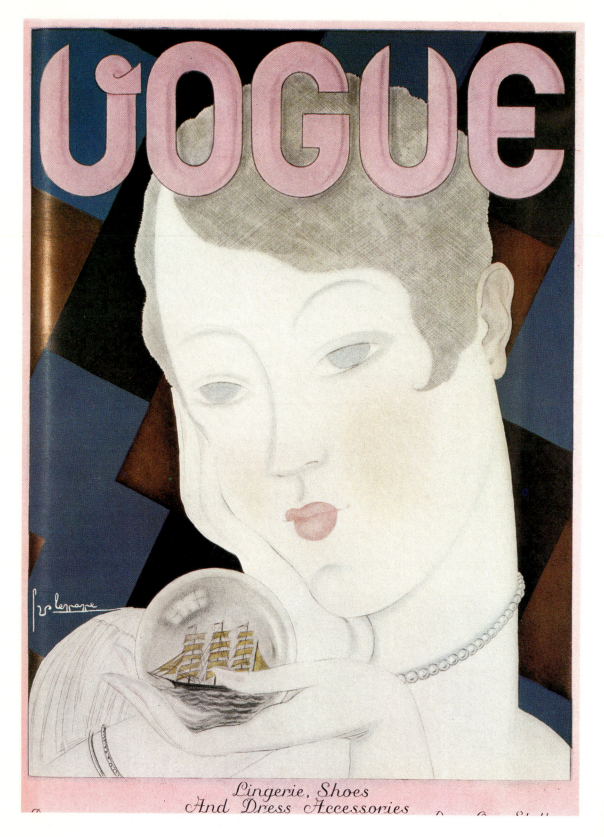

Vogue **cover for December 28th, 1928, by J. Lapage**

Both posters and photography developed with the spread of advertising and the new pictorial journalism. Helen Macgregor, working for *Vogue*, brought a new world of imagination into fashion photography: it wasn't just the girl and the clothes, it was a *picture*. Cecil Beaton, rushing about the world with his camera on semi-journalistic forays such as covering the Baroness d'Erlanger's pageant in Venice (its news value was ruined by the death of Rudolph Valentino) walked into the *Vanity Fair* offices in New York one day and was delighted to be told by Frank Crowninshield that Beaton, Steichen and de Meyer were 'the *only* photographers'.

Edward Steichen, a painter, changed to photography after the War, and produced clean-cut, precise photographic 'illustrations', often with a brilliant use of electric lighting: Carl Sandburg's book on him was perhaps the first book devoted to the work of one photographer. Charles Sheeler, also a painter by training, concentrated on the stark beauty of buildings, such as a Pennsylvania barn, and industrial structures. 'Soft-focus' was fashionable: you see it in Dorothy Wilding's portraits (often in sepia), and (in America) Edward Weston's romantic landscapes and figures. Weston later became interested in close-ups, shapes and enlarged details.

With Alfred Stieglitz we are in a world of experiment – the kind of thing Cecil Beaton had been playing with in photographs of his sisters reflected in a piano. Stieglitz pioneered the 'multi-photo' – a montage of different moods and expressions of the same person which he called 'equivalents'. Later he produced extraordinary pictures of skyscrapers and the brilliant, violent contrasts of city life. And in Paris Man Ray was experimenting with 'photography without a camera', placing objects on photosensitive paper and calling the result 'Rayographs'. Photography had established itself as an art. Any minute some fool would be shouting 'From Today Painting Is Dead.'

The Twenties were not much aware of sculpture, except in London's Hyde Park and Kensington Gardens, where stood Epstein's *Rima* (a memorial to W. H. Hudson) and *Peter Pan* (Sir George Frampton's tenderly pretty figure, which J. M. Barrie had put there at night so that children should think it had been brought there by fairies). Both of these were regularly tarred and feathered.

'Vogue' cover for Early May 1926

Mr and Mrs Sacheverell Sitwell by Maurice Beck and Helen Macgregor, 'Vogue' early and late June 1926

Of architecture one could hardly fail to be aware. London had allowed Nash's Regent Street Quadrant to disappear, almost without protest, in 1923. Architects were still busy erecting ready-made ancient monuments such as the Bank of England and other buildings inspired by Imperial pomp and Wembley, though perhaps Charles Holden's new Underground stations could be considered not ungraceful creations of the times, even if they clashed with the 'brewer's Tudor' springing up all over the new suburbs that were growing around them. It was fairly typical of the age that when Sir Giles Gilbert Scott was asked to design some scarlet telephone kiosks in 1926 some villages insisted on their being thatched.

Elsewhere, how different! Charles Edward Jeanneret, a Swiss who changed his name to Le Corbusier because he had a cousin called Lecorbesier and thought he had the face of a crow, had a friend named Amédée Ozenfant, a painter who eventually emigrated to New York. Together they produced an art magazine which asked questions like 'Should We Burn Down the Louvre?' and propounded the idea, then quite new, of functional architecture: 'A house is a machine for living in . . . we no longer have the money to erect historical souvenirs.' He had also founded a firm of architects, and had submitted a plan for the League of Nations Palace at Geneva which had been rejected. At once Le Corbusier was invited to lecture all over Europe and South America – and became fashionable and famous.

In 1921 Mies van der Rohe had conceived a skyscraper in steel and glass, with glass walls, which no underwriter in his senses would have insured. With Walter Gropius and Le Corbusier he had worked in the office of Peter Behrens, Germany's leading industrial architect, and he had developed radical ideas for tall office buildings which are only now, fifty years later, being realized. In a few years' time he would direct the Bauhaus before, like so many advanced designers, emigrating to America. Gropius had designed factories with glass curtain-walls, he could bring beauty into a school, indeed he himself founded one of the great design schools of all time, the much-attacked Staatliches Bauhaus at Weimar. Beauty and utility must be brought together – and so we find all modern theatre design owing something to Gropius's 1927 Totaltheater conception, in which part of the stalls were adaptable as a stage and part of the audience could if necessary be moved on wagons into the stage area.

There had been skyscrapers for more than a decade – the Singer, the Metropolitan and, in 1913, the Woolworth Building where Frank Woolworth, climbing to the rafters just below the roof of the Gothic tower, carved his name to show it was his. The man who made the skyscraper a thing of nobility was Frank Lloyd Wright, pupil of Louis H. Sullivan, champion of 'the Genius' versus 'the Mobocracy'. He built the first 'slab' skyscraper, a narrow block which used glass and steel. His Imperial Hotel in Tokyo was one of the few large buildings that proved safe in the 1923 earthquake; and in California he experimented successfully with reinforced concrete blocks. His 'organic architecture', making function and environment blend, left an indelible influence.

Interior decoration was much discussed, and in Britain the Society decorator emerged in Syrie Maugham. There was a vogue for orange and black, for the more conventional taste; and for the way-out of unlimited means, 'bedrooms of the palest lemon colour with furniture of white leather and little green tables on which nothing more substantial than a lipstick could ever rest . . . Staircases with glass ban-

Clapham South Station at the time of the opening of the new underground train line from Edgware to Morden – the world's longest tunnel, September 13th, 1926

Sir Philip Sassoon, 1923, by John Singer Sargent

nisters . . . bathrooms of glistening silver which caused agony to tired house-maids . . .' This comes from a novel, Beverley Nichols's *Crazy Pavements*, but it is good reporting. By way of contrast is Chips Channon's account of Sir Philip Sassoon's house at Lympne, Kent – 'a triumph of beautiful bad taste and Babylonian luxury, with terraces and flowery gardens and jade-green pools and swimming baths and rooms done up in silver and blue and orange'.

The American appetite for art was largely fed at this time by Joseph Duveen. As his biographer Sam Behrman has pointed out, the United States had plenty of money and Europe had plenty of art. It is believed to have been either Osbert Sitwell or Lytton Strachey who classified certain pictures as 'too, too Duveen'. Duveen, knighted, baroneted, and eventually raised to the peerage, was often thought by Americans to be British, which he was, and by British to be American, which he wasn't. He was in fact born of a family originally Dutch-Jewish, in Hull, Yorkshire.

He was the first art dealer ever to be on the Board of the National Gallery. He forced rich Americans of the day to buy good pictures, whether they liked them or not, by appealing to the Twenties spirit of monopolistic acquisitiveness, and to a particular kind of snobbery. 'When you pay high for the priceless, you're getting it cheap' – 'Mr Andrew Mellon is now ready for Duveen'. (Mr Mellon bought nudes, but would not hang them in his home; he bought religious pictures, but would not hang them in rooms 'where people might be smoking or drinking'.) And, of Edsel Ford, who had begun collecting pictures without Duveen's aid, 'Some day he'll be big enough for me.'

He sometimes bought back pictures from clients so as to keep the price up. He was reputed to have informers all over Europe who would tip him off when an impoverished nobleman might be about to sell his Old Masters. He made Mr and Mrs H. E. Huntington, of Pasadena, buy Gainsborough's *Blue Boy*, and Cole Porter wrote a song about it:

> *A silver dollar took me and my collar*
> *To show the slow cowboys*
> *Just how boys In England used to be dressed . . .*

He even persuaded Mrs Arabella Huntington to buy Sir Joshua Reynolds's *Sarah Siddons as the Tragic Muse*, despite her moral disapproval of having an actress on her wall.

Many are the stories of Duveen. One more will suffice. In 1920, a slump year for picture sales, Duveen and four other dealers got together to try to make Henry Ford start collecting. They made a list of 'the Hundred Greatest Paintings in the World', put prints of them, with learned captions, into three large beautifully bound albums, and called on Ford at Dearborn.

The great man, delighted, called to his wife, 'Mother, come in and see the lovely pictures these gentlemen have brought!' They must have cost an awful lot, he said; he couldn't really accept such beautiful books from people he didn't know. Gently, Duveen pointed out that these were pictures he could *buy*. Mr Ford seemed puzzled: 'But – what would I want with the original pictures when the ones right here in these books are so beautiful?'

CHAPTER 22

Away From It All

Edmund Kapp, the artist, and his wife about to set off on a walking honeymoon

In July 1926 the pound sterling was worth 244 francs, and the dollar just over 50 francs. An average meal, *table d'hôte*, *vin compris*, at a Paris sidewalk restaurant could thus be had for 15 cents, or 9d. This, indeed, was the lowest point to which the franc fell; but all through the Twenties the exchange rate was absurdly favourable to Americans and British. Even in 1938, when I first visited Paris, it was possible to get bed and breakfast for the equivalent of 2s. 6d., and a four-course meal for just over 1s. I was unemployed at the time, and I had gone there to *economize*.

This exchange rate was responsible for the swarm of Anglo-Saxons to Europe. Refugees from Prohibition came over ostensibly to taste culture, but also to get drunk. Among artists it was fashionable to say that one simply couldn't live and work in the stifling philistinism and puritanism of Britain and America. 'In Munich, in Budapest, in Vienna,' Donald Ogden Stewart remembers, 'we lived on fifty cents a day.' People wrote books datelined 'Ischia, 1926', 'Bucharest', 'Rapallo', 'Bandol'. The other reason for leaving one's homeland was unemployment: between 1921 and 1925, 635,000 people emigrated from Britain.

Escapism bore no stigma. There were dozens of ways of escaping. If you were a painter you could form a little colony in remote Cornwall, Brittany, the Channel Islands, Vieux Cagnes, Aix-en-Provence. You could drive around Europe in a car (the first trailer-caravans were appearing). You could walk (the new word was 'hiking') with a pack on your back, like the young Wandervögel, the hippies of their day, in Germany, playing guitars (yes, fifty years ago!) and singing for your supper. You could drink: 'It was understood and agreed,' says John O'Hara in *Butterfield 8*, 'that the big thing in life was liquor.'

People discovered the English countryside – hiking, biking, rambling – and in 1927 Robertson Scott launched a magazine about it called *The Countryman*. Youth Hostels began, and in 1930 acquired professor G. M. Trevelyan as their President. To fight the uncontrolled ravages of the speculative builder, the Council for the Preservation of Rural England was founded in 1926.

Travel agencies flourished. You could have a Lunn's tour of seventeen days in Lugano for £14. 2s. 6d., or a fourteen-day tour of the Holy Land for 49 guineas. People who had never had winter holidays before in their lives went skiing, a sport imported into Switzerland by the British, and villages like Grindelwald and Mürren became famous.

Sterner spirits did more perilous things. Colonel Fawcett went to Brazil and was never heard of again. There were several attempts to climb Mount Everest: a reconnaissance in 1921, an attempt in 1922 in which seven Sherpa porters were killed in an avalanche, and a brave assault in 1924, led by Brigadier-General the Hon. C. G. Bruce. Bedevilled by frostbite, a fatal case of pneumonia, and snow-blindness, the final attempt was made by A. C. Irvine and G. L. Mallory (the Charterhouse schoolmaster whose good looks were so admired by Lytton Strachey) equipped with oxygen apparatus. Last seen through a telescopic lens within a mile of the top, they disappeared into the mist and never returned. For several years afterwards it was believed that they had actually reached the summit. Captain Noël, the expedition's photographer, made a film of it, *Epic of Everest*, which was shown at cinemas all over Britain accompanied by the strange music of the Tibetan band which had been seen at Wembley Exhibition.

In 1922, British schoolboys were told that 'the greatest living man', who in that year won the Nobel Peace Prize, was Fridtjof Nansen, the Norwegian explorer, who had pioneered Arctic exploration in his ship *Fram*, but had not actually reached the North Pole. But it was now the age of the air, and in May 1926 Commander R. E. Byrd of the U.S. Navy flew from Spitzbergen to the Pole and

Cycling on Newquay Sands, August 1923

back in sixteen hours, just beating, by two days, the Norwegian Roald Amundsen. Amundsen had tried the same flight in an aircraft the year before, and now used an Italian airship, the *Norge*, accompanied by L. Ellsworth and the Italian General Nobile. They crossed the Pole and landed at Teller, Alaska, a distance of nearly 3,400 miles, in 71 hours. Nobile tried again in 1928, but crashed in North East Land on the way back. After six weeks on the ice Nobile and most of his crew were rescued by the intervention of a radio amateur in Soviet Russia who picked up their S.O.S. Nobile was heavily criticized for his conduct of the expedition.

One famous man of the age tried to get away from it all by burying himself in a crowd. In August 1922 Colonel T. E. Lawrence, C.B., D.S.O., Croix de Guerre, had eight copies of *The Seven Pillars of Wisdom* printed, at his own expense, by the *Oxford Times*, and then enlisted in the R.A.F. (a new service, developed from the old Royal Flying Corps) as 352087 Aircraftman J. H. Ross. His secret was betrayed by the *Daily Express*, and in the following year he tried the Tank Corps as a means of 'avoiding' publicity. Then back into the R.A.F., where he changed his name by deed poll to Shaw, which caused a rumour that he was G.B.S.'s illegitimate son.

Publicity? Well, it was partly the fault of a Princeton lecturer named Lowell Thomas, who, wittingly or not, had created the Lawrence Legend by a film-lecture, *With Lawrence In Arabia*, at the Century Theatre, New York, and afterwards at Madison Square Garden. This was followed by still more extravagant performances at Covent Garden and the Albert Hall in London. By 1929 there were wild reports that Lawrence 'the arch-spy' was being used by the Secret Service to do nobody knew what.

The other Lawrence, D.H., was travelling round the world, reaching the ranch of Mabel Dodge McLuhan in New Mexico, via Ceylon and Australia, in 1922. Not for him the Montparnasse set, and certainly not the show-business set of the Ritz Bar (Coco Chanel, Maxine Elliott, Mistinguett, Cole Porter and champagne cocktails at 1s. – 25 cents – each).

In Paris the Left Bank was said to be 'Europe's cultural centre'. (The tourists still went mainly to Montmartre.) Everyone who had ever written a book or a symphony or painted a picture or worked for a newspaper was, at some time or other, to be seen at the Dôme (or the more bourgeois Rotonde, but never both), or at the Deux Magots (Picasso on view daily), or at any of the cafés in the Rues Delambre and de Vaugirard or the Boulevard Montparnasse or within a sombrero's throw of the Métro Vavin. The Irish, James Joyce among them, gathered at the Café de Flore. The English painter Nina Hamnett lived in Modigliani's old studio with a Polish painter named Zawado. Russian intellectuals such as Ilya Ehrenburg were making up their minds whether to return to Soviet Moscow or Leningrad. A bartender called Jimmy Charters linked the English speakers – the original Jimmy of 'Jimmy's Bar'.

In Rue Jacob, with James Joyce as her neighbour, lived America's Natalie Clifford Barney, said to be the original of Valerie Seymour in *The Well of Loneliness*. At 'Mrs Barney's Fridays', Sylvia Beach said, 'one met the ladies with high collars and monocles.'

One of them, of course, was the authoress of *The Well of Loneliness*, Radclyffe Hall, whose sad novel about lesbians was reviled, and so publicized, by James Douglas, of the London *Sunday Express*. Douglas wrote that he 'would rather give a healthy boy or girl a phial of prussic acid than this novel'. It became the subject of an obscenity trial in London in 1928 at which the judge, refusing to hear any witnesses, condemned it outright. It had slightly better luck the following year in New York, where the judge's verdict was reversed by a higher court.

At Mrs Barney's you could also meet Ezra Pound and Dr Mardrus of 'the Pharaohs' curse'. Janet Flanner, correspondent of the *New Yorker*, you met everywhere. At Gertrude Stein's, 27 Rue de Fleurus, you met so many people, known, unknown, half-known, of so many languages and colours, that you felt famous even if your second novel had been rejected. 'Widely ridiculed and seldom enjoyed,' said Edmund Wilson of her, 'she has yet played an important role in connection with other writers who have become popular.'

In Paris, and indeed elsewhere in the world at this time, we had the spectacle of rich women (and also some relatively poor but devoted women) supporting geniuses. Sylvia Beach, daughter of a Presbyterian minister in Baltimore, was scrimping and saving while her protégé James Joyce was dining in state at the Versailles Restaurant and tipping the waiter 1,000 francs. Miss Beach, who had a bookshop called Shakespeare & Co., met Joyce at the house of the poet André Spire, and decided to publish *Ulysses* after the Hogarth Press had turned it down. In a contract which was the most unbusinesslike on record she promised Joyce 60 per cent of the profits. Robert McAlmon, who was married to 'Bryher', daughter of the shipping magnate Sir John Ellerman, paid Joyce $150 a month while *Ulysses* was being published, and Joyce

'The Day's End, 1927 by Ernest Procter

236

was also believed to enjoy the income of 5 per cent on £5,000 of War Loan given him by another benefactor, Miss Harriet Shaw Weaver. Meanwhile, it appears, McAlmon and Ernest Hemingway were rushing round Paris collecting subscriptions to finance the publication of *Ulysses*.

The book was printed in Dijon; about a third of it was rewritten on the proofs, which Miss Beach read until eyestrain gave her migraine. She didn't even have the satisfaction of being the first publisher of the book, because Joyce and Miss Weaver had arranged for John Rodker of the Egoist Press to bring it out before she could. Soon, a team of six linguists, led by Valéry Larbaud, were translating it into French, and editions were being pirated in America.

Strangely, Miss Beach refused to publish *Lady Chatterley's Lover*; but D.H. Lawrence belonged more to the Florence scene – not quite the Florence of Harold Acton, who was born there, but of the Orioli bookshop – the Florence of Norman Douglas, author of *South Wind*, multilingual, sometime Third Secretary of the British Embassy in St Petersburg, whose comfortable £2,000 a year came from cotton mills in the Vorarlberg; the Florence of Aldous Huxley and the Compton Mackenzies. Douglas and Lawrence disliked each other; Huxley and Lawrence liked each other, but not each other's books. Lawrence and Mackenzie unexpectedly liked each other and each other's books, and their days in Florence have been committed to a clerihew, believed to have been composed by Mackenzie himself:

D. H. Lawrence
Once lived in Florence;
If it had been Compton Mackenzie,
He'd have called it Firenze.

So different at Deauville; and yet not so far away from it all that you couldn't see the people you usually saw in London or Paris. In the early Twenties Deauville had two main hotels, a casino, a beach, a bar or two, a night club called Ciro's, souvenir shops, a post office. If you did not propose to stay at one of the two hotels, then you had to take a villa for the season. Those who did included the King of Sweden, King Alfonso of Spain (in his famous, Twenties-ish Hispano-Suiza), ex-King Manoel of Portugal, the Aga Khan – and Mr Noël

Coward. (You could hardly open a Society magazine without reading, either in the social gossip or in a caption under a photograph, 'and Mr Noël Coward.') The casino was run by a Mr Zographos, who was said to have made £5 million out of it. Deauville achieved a special musical comedy glamour for people who had never been there, and about one in three musical comedies was set in Deauville or a place with a name very like it. For one thing, it was an excuse to bring on the chorus in skimpy bathing dresses.

Deauville was one of the last of the north-coast French resorts to develop. Traditionally, Parisians and their families had gone north in the summer. The Riviera, for French and British alike, had been essentially a winter resort: one went there, as often as not, on doctor's orders. Only the French *petite bourgeoisie* ever went there in summer. But now people suddenly began to worship the sun: the ultra-violet rays gave one vitamins or something. The *ambre solaire* industry sprang up. You swam a little; you lay in the sun a lot. And the Bright Young People came. They had already followed Elsa Maxwell, the hostess with the weirdest, if not the mostest, to the Lido in Venice, and any minute she might turn up on the Riviera.

In between, there had been the fashion for Venetian Balls, given usually by the titled rich, but sometimes just by the rich. Cole Porter, pursuing the International Set round Europe ('the Prince of Wales is going, too, and it will be very gay'), rented the Palazzo Rezzonico for four summers, drawing strong criticism from an exiled Russian: 'The whole of Venice is up in arms against Cole Porter because of his jazz and his Negroes.'

One of the Negroes was 'Hutch', Leslie Hutchinson, who with his band played aboard a 'floating night club' organized by Cole Porter and moored on the Grand Canal. Singing, piano-playing Negroes were fashionable to sleep with among Bright Young Girls of Society.

Antibes, before the Twenties, was a sleepy little town with a few Roman remains and a pine-wooded Cap. A few years later Cole Porter was giving, as his reason for not working, 'Suppose I had to settle down on Broadway for three months just when I was planning to go to Antibes!' All along the Riviera Americans and British were gathering, drinking rather too much, not taking much interest in their less prosperous French hosts, often behaving like colonists, sometimes just behaving badly.

The stately Riviera hotels, how beautiful they stood! The Negresco in Nice, the Carlton in Cannes, and the Grand Hotel du Cap at Cap d'Antibes, on which Scott Fitzgerald is said to have modelled his Hotel des Etrangers in *Tender is the Night*: 'On the shore of the French Riviera, about halfway between Marseilles and the Italian border, stood a large, proud, rose-coloured hotel. Deferential palms cooled its blushing façade, and before it stretched a short dazzling beach . . .' Nearby was Eden Roc, where the *Tatler* photographer monotonously recorded the same people, year after year: Lady Ashley, Cecil Beaton (in his French matelot suit), a Rajah or two, Mr Ian Hay the novelist, the Marchioness of Milford Haven, Mrs Reginald Vanderbilt, Tallulah Bankhead, Bernard Shaw, Bea Lillie – and Mr Noël Coward.

Next door, a village called Juan-les-Pins overnight became a resort. A Monsieur Baudouin, who had seen a film about the Florida Boom which showed lots of girls in beach pyjamas, bought the casino, built a restaurant, invited Frank Jay Gould the hotel developer to join him, encouraged the Dolly Sisters, Mr Bentley the car manufacturer, and other celebrities to stay there, and behold, Juan was full of summer visitors.

As for Antibes, why, look who's here! *Vanity Fair* in 1927 notes Ina Claire, after a long run in *The Last of Mrs Cheyney*, beside the pool at Eden Roc in turquoise pyjamas. Marilyn Miller, New York's Queen of the Musical, and Clifton Webb. 'Grace Moore has been annoying the Antibes nightingales by practising scales all morning in her blue and pink villa.' Also in a nearby villa is Lady Mendl, the erstwhile Elsie de Wolfe. Actually *in* the pool is Robert Benchley and his two small sons. Any or all of these people, two years before, would have been seen in Deauville or Paris instead. By 1928 even D.H. Lawrence, having moved from Taos to Mallorca, was not far away, at Bandol.

It is usual to blame Gerald and Sara Murphy for the development of the Cap d'Antibes. They were part of the Paris American set, had discovered Antibes, and had persuaded the proprietor of the Hotel du Cap that he could create a summer season. Donald Ogden Stewart and John Dos Passos joined the Murphys there, and pretty soon it was Scott and Zelda and Woollcott and all the Algonquins and one helluva party. They swam and sunbathed at a small beach which would one day be developed, with chicken-on-the-spit and cocktail bar and E. Phillips Oppenheim (who drove over daily after golf at La Turbie), as the over-populated Plage de la Garoupe.

Cole Porter, Clifton Webb and Gilbert Miller

It is perhaps significant that Gerald Murphy had been at Yale with Cole Porter; for the Murphys played the piano and sang attractively, and among their favourite tunes were 'Runnin' Wild' and 'My Blue Heaven'. The parties – or maybe it was one long party – went on and on, and it might just as well have been Paris or New York. 'All over New York people telephoned. They telephoned from one hotel to another to people on other parties that they couldn't get there.' Thus Zelda Fitzgerald in *Save Me the Waltz*; and again in Paris – 'Nobody knew whose party it was. It had been going on for weeks. When you felt you couldn't survive another night you went home and slept.' Well, at Cap d'Antibes you at least knew whose party it was. For, as Cyril Connolly wrote:

We're back on the old Scott circuit
On a bender as big as the Ritz,
Where Gerald is shaking a Murphy,
And Zelda is throwing a Fitz . . .
All high on the old Scott Circuit,
While Ernest is boozing in Spain;
Shall we ever get back to Nantucket
And wear a tuxedo again?

Portrait sketch of T. E. Lawrence, 1929, by Augustus John.
Inscribed on the back are the words: 'Painted in the morning and afternoon
of an August day in 1929 at Freiern, Fordingbridge,
while I was going to Solent, for the Schneider Cup. TES.
John shows him as Aircraftman T. E. Shaw

L'Automne

Chapter 23

Crash!

If you look up 'Wall Street' in the *Encyclopaedia Britannica* you will find a cross-reference: '*See* PANIC.' If you then attempt to define 'Panic', you get nothing to do with economics at all. The market is going down *because* it is going down. What is happening is in the mob mind, which is suddenly changing from optimism to pessimism.

That optimism had been going on, on both sides of the Atlantic, for ten years. In Europe it was coupled with the idea of Peace. In America it was Optimism plus Prosperity, which were held to be mutually dependent.

President Hoover, who was listened to because he had 'fed Europe' and was always talking of 'the final triumph over poverty', was saying, according to a popular song, 'Now's the time to buy' ('. . . so let's have another cup of coffee, and let's have another piece of pie'). So was Calvin Coolidge, who as President had started it all, and who in retirement was writing 150-word syndicated articles containing such profundities as 'When a great number of people are unable to find work, unemployment results.' So was Andrew Mellon, Secretary of the Treasury, who was good at reducing income-tax; understandably, since his own income was the third largest in the United States.

What were the symptoms of prosperity, as understood by businessmen of the Twenties? Well, there were in 1929 11,000 millionaires in America, more than twice as many as there had been in 1914. There were also 26,500,000 cars, nearly four times as many as in 1919; and the two-car family was already a target of prosperity. Hire purchase was a

sign of confidence, surely – 'You furnish the girl,' said furniture shop advertising, 'we furnish the home.' Translated by morticians, this became 'You die; we do the rest.' And mail order – you could get almost anything by 'sending up' for it, assisted by huge catalogues from Sears Roebuck and Montgomery Ward. In Britain, by 1928, hire purchase accounted for half of all furniture and car sales, and so that your neighbour shouldn't know that you couldn't pay cash, Mr Drage delivered it 'in a plain van'.

Advertising – there was a boom symbol, surely. Not only 'Bovril Prevents That Sinking Feeling', and Colman's 'Mustard Club' (with Baron de Beef, Miss Di Gester, and other characters), and 'Monkey Brand Won't Wash Clothes', but (in America) the first embarrassing, fear-filling advertisements about hitherto unmentionable things like halitosis and B.O., Odorono and Kotex. And if your gums bled when you brushed your teeth, you certainly had pyorrhea, and the Forhan's toothpaste ads showed a pretty girl with a strip across her mouth.

'Advertising', wrote Wolcott Gibbs in the *New Yorker*, tracing the early life of John P. Marquand, the future novelist, 'was the new giant loudspeaker of American free enterprise, the full-throated, blaring horn telling millions what to eat, what to drink, and what to wear.' And in 1921, writing copy at the J. Walter Thompson Company for Yuban, Veedol and Lux, was young John P. Marquand, till one day the President, Stanley Resor, said 'John, I don't believe you have the business instinct', and John gratefully took 400 dollars to go away to New

(opposite) **'L'Automne', after a watercolour drawing by Georges Barbier,** reproduced in *Almanach des Modes*, **Paris, 1925**

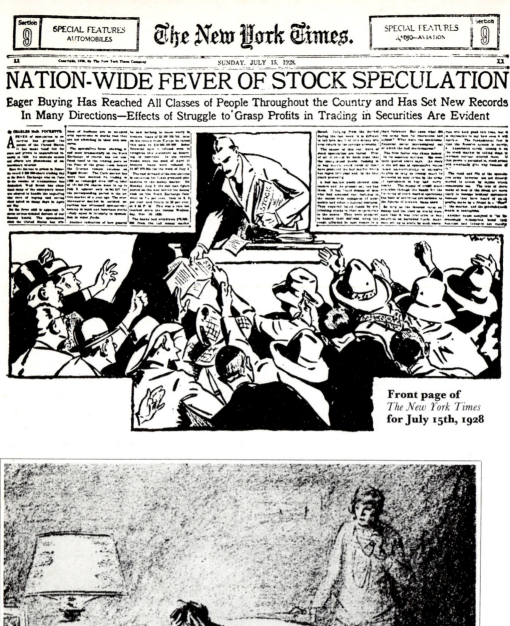

Front page of
The New York Times
for July 15th, 1928

The 'Crash'

England and write a novel called *The Unspeakable Gentleman*.

Britain didn't have a Great Bull Market going on and on: there was a series of little booms, and a few spectacular defaultings, and a continuing depression that differed only from that of the Thirties in that there was still some Hope and plenty of Escape. In the spring of 1922 the 144-year-old stockbroking firm of Ellis & Co. failed, and its senior partner Gerard Lee Bevan disappeared. He was arrested five months later with a French girl, brought back to London and sent to prison for publishing a false balance sheet. Bucket-shops proliferated, and so did unsound companies. The names of Hatry and Kreuger began to be heard, the former's always with a hint of risk, the latter's revered as a 'friend of Hoover' and as something akin to gilt-edged.

Speculation was the hobby of a small group in each British city. They were mainly financiers like Jimmy White, who had a telephone brought to his table at the Café de Paris so that he could deal on the New York Stock Exchange between dinner and dancing. But in America it was a national sport, like betting. People overheard tips in elevators or on subways, and made thousands of dollars overnight. Even the 'revolting intellectuals' were at it: 'Literary editors whose hopes were wrapped around American Cyanide B lunched with poets who swore by Cities Service.' It seemed to occur to nobody, not even to the President, that the whole stock market was being manipulated. And when the selling of speculative shares (such as Commercial Solvents and American Railway Express) began in March 1929, and went on intermittently through the summer, the *Wall Street Journal* tried to rally confidence by telling people that, although prosperity was a dream, it was patriotic to go on dreaming: 'Don't part with your illusions: when they are gone you . . . have ceased to live.' Or as Walter Bagehot put it in *Lombard Street*, 'All people are most credulous when they are most happy.'

On October 22nd 1929 more than 6,000,000 shares were sold, and the ticker-tape was an hour behind in recording the sales; on October 24th nearly 13,000,000 shares changed hands, and the famous skyscraper suicides began: 'You had to stand in line', cracked Will Rogers, 'to get a window to jump out of.'

On October 29th huge blocks of shares were being sold like a jumble sale, and the recorded number of sales was nearly 16,500,000. The ticker by now had had a nervous breakdown. Claud Cockburn, then a newspaper correspondent in New York, lunched at the Washington Square house of Edward Speyer, the Anglo-German-American banker. The meal was interrupted by the butler and the cook, who demanded Speyer's presence below stairs. 'My servants', Speyer explained to his guests, 'insist that I go to the kitchen to discuss the market situation. You see, they have a tape machine there and they are frightened about the fall in stocks. The cook has almost all her savings in Radio. The rest, I am sorry to say, have, against my advice, invested in Cities Service.'

They were, no doubt, among the 500,000 'margin accounts' on the books of New York stockbrokers. There may have been 1,500,000 more such investors who had paid only a percentage of the market value, and for the rest were being 'carried' by their brokers who had borrowed from banks to do it.

The London stock market reacted, and holders of American shares were badly hit. In New York Evelyn Laye, starring in Noël Coward's *Bitter Sweet*, heard that she had lost £10,000. 'The Wall Street Crash', she said in a radio interview thirty years later, 'meant more to America than two world wars.'

It was easy for London city editors to admonish New York for gambling; the extent of Hatry's mess was taking five months to sort out, and his forged securities were only a fraction of it. He went to jail for fourteen years.

In Germany there were 5,000,000 unemployed, and in the 1930 election the Nazis gained 107 seats. America was no longer going to save the world. Soon American assembly lines lay idle, businessmen lived in tar-paper shacks, farmers died of malnutrition. In the next three years 3,000 banks failed, 15,000,000 people were out of work, and one family in three had no money coming in.

One day in early 1930 Captain Joseph Patterson, Editor of the *New York Daily News*, walked into the office of his leader writer Reuben Maury and said 'We're off on the wrong foot. The people's major interest is no longer in the playboy, Broadway and divorces but in how they're going to eat, and from this time forward we'll pay attention to the struggle for existence.' Henceforth the *Daily News* attacked

Hoover and backed Roosevelt for President.

About a fortnight after the panic of October 29th 1929, somebody copyrighted a song called 'Happy Days Are Here Again'. In Britain it was sung by the coloured duo, Layton & Johnstone, and it became Roosevelt's campaign song. Happy Days were a long time coming. A new kind of escapism came in – the picaresque cheerfulness of *The Good Companions*, the spectacular musical films staged by Busby Berkeley, romantic fashions, longer skirts, sweeter music. A new kind of realism, too, in 'documentary' songs like 'Ten Cents a Dance', 'Buddy, Can You Spare a Dime?', and Cole Porter's 'Love for Sale'.

From Noël Coward, too, a touch of bitterness in Cochran's 1932 revue, with 'Children of the Ritz' (Bright Young People not quite knowing what to be bright about) and – was it a farewell to the Twenties? – 'The Party's Over Now'.

That was the Twenties. The Twenties *knew* they were the Twenties, a different decade, something which would never happen again. They were ripping, absolutely topping, weren't they, old thing, old sport? One of the theses I am never going to have time to write is on whether the speech of those years was invented by P. G. Wodehouse, or whether he simply reported it. Some of it still survived into university lingo of the Thirties. 'Bidding a fond farewell to Jackson' meant that you were going abroad and wouldn't be seen at the Embassy Club for some time (Jackson being the Embassy Club cat). There were all kinds of expressions for 'party': 'a do', 'an egregious caper', 'a monumental beat-up', 'a most imperial thrash'. Fortified with 'copious noggins', 'a libation' or a 'brief snort', you went for a drive with a girl in your 'cuddle truck'. Anyone over forty was an 'elderly fruit'. There were a few years when one called 'Coo-ee!' to attract someone's attention the other side of the street; and took one's leave by saying 'Toodle-oo' and even 'Toodle-pip'.

To the young upper and middle classes, not yet Marxist, the working classes were cute: one gaily helped them to dig holes in roads (this was done by London youths and maidens in eighteenth-century costume after the famous Mozart Party). One self-consciously used the Public Bar, and asked street violinists up to a party. And at all times, in this blessed plot without Prohibition, people solved every problem by waffling, tottering or oozing to the 'thirst clinic'.

The Twenties were full of writers who cursed the times as if they were hell, and then, in the Depression, looked back upon them with tearful nostalgia. And yet, and yet – Robert Benchley heaved a sigh of relief when the Twenties were over, swearing that he would never, as a dramatic critic, sit through another play about rebellious youth and little girls who got ruined.

It had been so wonderful to live without a social conscience, to escape without guilt. And yet, and yet – looking back from 1940, Scott Fitzgerald weakly protested, in *My Generation*, 'That old libel that we were cynical and skeptics was nonsense from the beginning. On the contrary, we were the great believers.'

To the British, the decade and the boom years were less clearly demarcated, and no British observer has left a really concise epitaph on them. I had almost settled for Heywood Broun: 'The Jazz Age was wicked and monstrous and silly,' he said; 'Unfortunately, I had a good time.' But even as I wrote that sentence, I heard that Noël Coward, born fifteen days before 1900 and always the same age as the century, for Britain the personification of the Twenties, was dead.

He had the usual quick obituaries, and one of them, by John Mortimer, described him as a boy who would not grow up. One of his first parts had been that of Slightly in *Peter Pan*, 'that much undervalued play'. Was this what the Twenties were doing – refusing to grow up? Was this the justification, before the guilt-ridden Thirties, for escapism? Do we *have* to be ashamed of being Peter Pan? May we not have, not only a talent to amuse, but a talent for *being* amused? And I remembered a paragraph from Coward's *Future Indefinite*:

> I knew, in my teens, that the world was full of hatred, envy, malice, cruelty, jealousy, unrequited love, murder, despair and destruction. I also knew, at the same time, that it was full of kindness, joy, pleasure, requited love, generosity, fun, excitement, laughter and friends.

ACKNOWLEDGMENTS

Among the many people whose brains and memories I have picked for this book, I should like to thank Mr Donald Ogden Stewart, for personal recollections of Fitzgerald and Hemingway and the Cap d'Antibes, and for allowing me to see excerpts from his autobiography-in-progress; Lady Lindsay and Mr Raymond Mortimer for putting me right about the original Bright Young People; Mr John Hadfield, his Saturday Book *and my publishers generally for many ideas; Mr Jeremy Hadfield for checking some details of jazz history; Mr Simon Nowell-Smith, for remembering silly songs; Mr G.N. Georgano for vetting my motoring history; Mr Raymond Mander and Mr Joe Mitchenson, those great archivists of the stage, for saving me from innumerable theatrical and musical solecisms; Mr Andrew Anspach, manager of the Algonquin Hotel, New York, for information; Mr John Foster White for a fantastically careful and sympathetic reading of the book in typescript; my wife, for her rich knowledge of Twenties fiction, and my daughter for help with research. For songs, I have sometimes had to rely on memory, and if one or two of the words are wrong, it is the spirit rather than the letter which counts. Finally, I want to acknowledge the great contribution to the book made by the picture researcher, Miss Mary Anne Norbury (Mrs Sanders).*

The following were among the books consulted, as distinct from books remembered:

Crazy Pavements (Beverley Nichols), Cape, 1927
Only Yesterday (Frederick Lewis Allen), Harper & Brothers, 1931
Arnold Bennett's Journals, 1932–3, Cassell
Present Indicative (Noël Coward), Heinemann, 1936
While Rome Burns (Alexander Woollcott), Penguin, 1937
Taste and Fashion (James Laver), Harrap, 1937
A Number of People (Sir Edward Marsh), Heinemann, 1939
Red Letter Nights (James Agate), Cape, 1944
The Nineteen Twenties (Douglas Goldring), Nicholson & Watson, 1945
Left Hand, Right Hand (Osbert Sitwell), Macmillan, 1945
Famous Trials (ed. James Hodge), Penguin, 1950
The Far Side of Paradise (Arthur Mizener), Eyre & Spottiswoode, 1951
The Great Beast (John Symonds), Rider, 1951
Hugh Walpole (Rupert Hart-Davis), Macmillan, 1952
The Palm Beach Architect (Alva Johnstone), New Yorker, 1952
A Pattern of Islands (Sir Arthur Grimble), Murray, 1952
King George V (Harold Nicolson), Constable, 1952
Duveen (S. N. Behrman), Hamish Hamilton, 1952
The Great Crash, 1929 (J. K. Galbraith), Hamish Hamilton, 1955
The Twenties (John Montgomery), Allen & Unwin, 1957
The General Strike (Julian Symons), Cresset Press, 1957
The Sweet and Twenties (Beverley Nichols), Weidenfeld & Nicolson, 1958
They Saw It Happen (Asa Briggs), Basil Blackwell, 1960
Vanity Fair (ed. Cleveland Amory and Frederic Bradlee), Viking Press, 1960
The Wandering Years, 1922–39 (Cecil Beaton), Weidenfeld & Nicolson, 1961
The Bootleggers (Kenneth Allsop), Hutchinson, 1961
A Picture of the Twenties (Richard Bennett), Vista Books, 1961
The Age of Illusion (Ronald Blythe), Hamish Hamilton, 1963
A History of the U.S.A. from Wilson to Kennedy (André Maurois), Weidenfeld & Nicolson, 1964
Encyclopedia of Murder (Colin Wilson and Pat Pitman), Pan Books, 1964
Jazz Masters of the Twenties (Richard Hadlock), Macmillan, 1965
The Queen Mother (Helen Cathcart), W. H. Allen, 1965
The Astors (Lucy Kavaler), Harrap, 1966

Ladies Bountiful (W. G. Rogers), Gollancz, 1968
Leslie Bailey's BBC Scrapbooks, Allen & Unwin, 1968
Talk About America (Alistair Cooke), Bodley Head, 1968
Cockie (Sam Heppner), Leslie Frewin, 1969
Musical Comedy (Raymond Mander & Joe Mitchenson), Peter Davies, 1969
The Literary Life (Robert Phelps & Peter Deane), Chatto & Windus, 1969
The Bright Twenties (Cecil Roberts), Hodder & Stoughton, 1970
Zelda Fitzgerald (Nancy Milford), The Bodley Head, 1970
Life in Britain between the Wars (L. C. B. Seaman), Batsford, 1970
We Danced All Night (Barbara Cartland), Hutchinson, 1971
You Might As Well Live, the Life and Times of Dorothy Parker (John Keats), Secker & Warburg, 1971
The Penguin Book of Comics (George Perry & Alan Aldridge), 1971
Young in the Twenties (Ethel Mannin), Hutchinson, 1971
Encyclopedia of American Automobiles (ed. G. N. Georgano), Dutton, 1971
When Luxury Went to Sea (Douglas Phillips-Birt), David & Charles, 1971
Ocean Liners of the Past: Aquitania, Patric Stephens, 1971
The World of Art Déco (Bevis Hillier), Studio Vista, 1971
Edward VIII – The Man We Lost (Robert Gray & Jane Olivier), Compton Press, 1972
The Most of John Held Jr., Stephen Greene Press, 1972
Tribulations and Laughter (S. N. Behrman), Hamish Hamilton, 1972
The Stock Exchange Story (Alan Jenkins), Heinemann, 1973

ILLUSTRATION ACKNOWLEDGEMENTS

8   Lunch at Eton, '4th June', 1921.
    Radio Times Hulton Picture Library, London

9   (left) A 'His Master's Voice' Gramophone with lumière pleated paper diaphragm of 1920.
    Mander and Mitchenson Theatre Collection, London

9   (right) Paul Robeson and Edith Day in Show Boat.
    Mander and Mitchenson Theatre Collection, London

10 (above left) Lux advertisement.
    Radio Times Hulton Picture Library, London

10 (below) Gala Day at the new Thames resort at Hampton Court.
    Radio Times Hulton Picture Library, London

11 Old Regent Street, 1924, by J. Kynnersley Kirby.
    City Art Gallery, Bradford

12 (above) Edith Thompson.
    Syndication International, London

12 (below) Frederick Bywaters.
    Syndication International, London

13 Front page of the Daily Mirror, October 5th, 1922.
    British Museum, Colindale, London

14 Binnie Hale and Seymour Beard singing 'Tea for Two' in No, No, Nanette, Palace Theatre, 1925.
    Mander and Mitchenson Theatre Collection, London

15 Zelda and Scott Fitzgerald.
    Mansell Collection, London

16 James P. Johnson.
    Bettmann Archive Inc., New York

17 (above left) Dorothy Dickson and her first husband Carl Hyson, 1921.
    Mander and Mitchenson Theatre Collection, London

17 (above right) Bee Jackson, 1925.
    Mander and Mitchenson Theatre Collection, London

17 (centre) Learning the Charleston.
    Radio Times Hulton Picture Library, London

18 The Black Bottom illustrated by Mr and Mrs Victor Silvester. The Dancing Times.
    Mander and Mitchenson Theatre Collection, London

19 (above) The Hambone Club, December 1928.
    Radio Times Hulton Picture Library, London

Victoria and Albert Museum, London (Photo S. Eost)

106 (below left) The 'Gold Coast' section.
Radio Times Hulton Picture Library, London

107 Cigarette cards recording the British Empire Exhibition.
Collection Mr Peter Scully

108 William Tatem Tilden II.
Radio Times Hulton Picture Library, London

109 (above) Jean Borotra, 1926.
Radio Times Hulton Picture Library, London

109 (below) Helen Wills.
Radio Times Hulton Picture Library, London

110 (above) Suzanne Lenglen playing at Wimbledon, 1925.
Radio Times Hulton Picture Library, London

110 (below) Punch, July 2nd, 1924.
Victoria and Albert Museum, London. (Photo S. Eost and
P. Macdonald)

111 Cigarette cards.
Collection Mr F. H. Pitts

112 'Steve Donoghue, June 4th, 1921', by Sir Alfred Munnings.
Reproduced by the kind permission of the Stewards of the
Jockey Club (Photo Messrs John Slater Ltd, Newmarket)

113 (above) The Jack Dempsey and Georges Carpentier fight at
Boyle's Thirty Acres, July 2nd, 1921.
United Press International Photo, New York

113 (below left) The reach of Jack Dempsey.
Radio Times Hulton Picture Library, London

113 (below right) Georges Carpentier.
Radio Times Hulton Picture Library, London

115 (below left) Jack Hobbs.
Radio Times Hulton Picture Library, London

115 (below right) Don Bradman.
Radio Times Hulton Picture Library, London

116 (left) Herman 'Babe' Ruth.
Bettmann Archive Inc., New York

116 (right) Ty Cobb.
Bettmann Archive Inc., New York

117 Gertrude Ederle is crowned Queen of the Waves after
swimming the Channel in 1926.
Radio Times Hulton Picture Library, London

118 and 119 'The Jockeys' Dressing Room at Ascot', 1923,
by Sir John Lavery.
Tate Gallery, London

120 Bobby Jones, 1927.
Radio Times Hulton Picture Library, London

121 Walter Hagen, 1924.
Radio Times Hulton Picture Library, London

123 Photograph showing the actual moment of death by
electric chair of Ruth Snyder.
New York Daily News Photo

125 The jury arriving at the Armstrong case, 1922.
Radio Times Hulton Picture Library, London

127 Starr Faithfull.
United Press International Photo, New York

129 (above) Federal agents Izzy (Einstein) and Moe the Peerless
(Smith) confiscating liquor.
Radio Times Hulton Picture Library, London

129 (below) Al Capone.
Radio Times Hulton Picture Library

131 (above) A speakeasy bar.
United Press International Photo, New York

131 (below) A speakeasy bar.
Bettmann Archive Inc., New York

133 The St Valentine's Day Massacre, 1929.
Radio Times Hulton Picture Library, London

135 Nicola Sacco and Bartolomeo Vanzetti.
Radio Times Hulton Picture Library, London

136 Jelly Roll Morton.
Historical Pictures Service, Chicago

137 Detail from 'Nightclub, Marseilles', 1928–29, by C. R. W.
Nevinson. Collection Mr and Mrs Peyton Skipwith

138 and 139 Design for the 'Rhapsody in Blue' set of George
White's Scandals, 1926, by Erté.
Collection Mr and Mrs Eric Estorick

140 Constant Lambert, 1926, by Christopher Wood.
National Portrait Gallery, London

141 'Louis Armstrong's Hot Five', 1926.
Historical Pictures Service, Chicago

142 Benny Goodman.
Bettmann Archive Inc., New York

143 Fats Waller.
Bettmann Archive Inc., New York

144 At rehearsal: (left to right) Jack Donahue, George
Gershwin, Sigmund Romberg, Marilyn Miller and Florenz
Ziegfeld.
United Press International Photo, New York

145 William Walton, 1925, by Christopher Wood.
Courtesy Magdalen Street Gallery, Cambridge

146 Nikitina and Lifar in the London production of La Chatte,
1927.
Mander and Mitchenson Theatre Collection, London

147 Gwen Ffrangcon-Davies in The Immortal Hour, 1922.
Mander and Mitchenson Theatre Collection, London

148 Sir Edward Elgar, 1927, by Percival Hedley.
National Portrait Gallery, London

149 (above) Music front of 'Where Do Flies Go in the
Wintertime?'.
Mander and Mitchenson Theatre Collection, London

149 (below) Music front of 'Horsey! Keep Your Tail Up'.
Mander and Mitchenson Theatre Collection, London

150 (below left) Music front of 'It Ain't Gonna Rain No Mo'.
Mander and Mitchenson Theatre Collection, London

150 (above right) Music front of 'All By Myself'.
Mander and Mitchenson Theatre Collection, London

155 (above left) H. G. Wells.
Radio Times Hulton Picture Library, London

155 (below right) Arnold Bennett, by David Low.
National Portrait Gallery, London

157 Ernest Hemingway in Mexico.
United Press International Photo, New York

159 (above left) Jacket for The Good Companions, 1929, by J. B.
Priestley.
Collection Mr and Mrs A. G. Sanders